Cambridge School Shakespeare

中文详注剑桥莎士比亚精选

悍妇降服记

原版创始主编：[英] 瑞克斯·吉布森（Rex Gibson）
原版主编：[英] 瑞查德·安褚斯（Richard Andrews）
　　　　　[英] 维姬·维南德（Vicki Wienand）
原版编注：[英] 琳孜·布雷迪（Linzy Brady）
总主编：陈国华
分册主编：程丽霞

社图号 20120

Cambridge School Shakespeare: The Taming of the Shrew [Third edition] [978-1-107-61689-9] was first published by Cambridge University Press in 2014. All rights reserved.
This Simplified Chinese edition for the People's Republic of China is published by arrangement with the Press Syndicate of the University of Cambridge, Cambridge, United Kingdom.
© Cambridge University Press & Beijing Language and Culture University Press 2020.
This book is in copyright. No reproduction of any part may take place without the written permission of Cambridge University Press or Beijing Language and Culture University Press.
本书版权由剑桥大学出版社和北京语言大学出版社共同所有。本书任何部分之文字及图片，如未获得出版者书面同意，不得用任何方式抄袭、节录或翻印。
This edition is for sale in the People's Republic of China (excluding Hong Kong SAR, Macao SAR and Taiwan Province) only.
此版本仅限在中华人民共和国国境内销售。

北京市版权局著作权合同登记图字：01-2020-4094 号

图书在版编目（CIP）数据

中文详注剑桥莎士比亚精选．悍妇降服记：英文／陈国华总主编；程丽霞分册主编．-- 北京：北京语言大学出版社，2020.9
书名原文：Cambridge School Shakespeare: The Taming of the Shrew
ISBN 978-7-5619-5727-1

Ⅰ.①中… Ⅱ.①陈… ②程… Ⅲ.①多幕剧－剧本－英国－中世纪－英文 Ⅳ.① I561.33

中国版本图书馆 CIP 数据核字（2020）第 152109 号

中文详注剑桥莎士比亚精选：悍妇降服记
ZHONGWEN XIANG ZHU JIANQIAO SHASHIBIYA JINGXUAN: HANFU XIANGFU JI

项目策划：李 亮	责任编辑：孙冠群
封面设计：乔 剑	排版制作：北京创艺涵文化发展有限公司
责任印制：武晓东	

出版发行：北京语言大学出版社
社　　址：北京市海淀区学院路 15 号，100083
网　　址：www.blcup.com
电子信箱：service@blcup.com
电　　话：编 辑 部 8610-82301019/0178
　　　　　　发 行 部 8610-82303650/3591/3648
　　　　　　北语书店 8610-82303653
　　　　　　网购咨询 8610-82303908
印　　刷：北京博海升彩色印刷有限公司
版　　次：2020 年 9 月第 1 版　　印　　次：2020 年 9 月第 1 次印刷
开　　本：787 毫米 × 1092 毫米 1/16　　印　　张：13.75
字　　数：396 千字
定　　价：69.00 元

PRINTED IN CHINA

序

由于观察角度不同，评判标准不同，关于哪个国家哪位诗人或小说家的成就最大，世人可能难以达成一致；可是说到剧作家，大家的共识是，莎士比亚不仅是英语国家有史以来最伟大的剧作家，也是全世界最伟大的剧作家，在知名度、影响力和传世作品的数量上，没有任何一位剧作家可以与之比肩。正是由于其公认的文学成就和人文精神，在过去400多年里，莎士比亚戏剧的演出在英语国家和许多非英语国家经久不衰，莎剧的阅读和鉴赏已成为这些国家英文教学的必选内容。

莎剧进入中国，已经有100多年历史，莎士比亚全集已经有了四个中文译本。不懂英文的人可以通过译本来欣赏莎士比亚剧作。然而文学作品的语言，尤其是诗歌的语言，具有相当程度的不可译性，而几乎所有莎剧的大部分台词都是素体诗（blank verse）。例如《哈慕雷》（Hamlet）里主人翁的名言"To be, or not to be, that is the question"，不论怎样译，都难以完全再现原文的深刻内涵和形式特点。要想真正欣赏莎士比亚的语言和戏剧艺术，还得阅读其英文原作。最早由剑桥大学出版社出版的这套莎剧精选，收录了最受读者和观众喜爱的14部剧目，涵盖莎剧的各个类别，以其独具匠心的设计和编排，成为所有英文原版莎剧中最适合英语学习者阅读、最适合戏剧爱好者排演的莎剧选集。

本选集的创始主编瑞克斯·吉布森（Rex Gibson）在本书引言（Introduction）里指出："不论做什么，都要记住，莎士比亚写下他的剧本是为了演出、观看和享受的。"秉承这一宗旨，这一新版莎剧选集有四个鲜明的区别性特点：

一、书的开本和页面的宽高比例特别适合学校的老师和学生以及剧团的导演和演员在排练莎剧时把书打开，拿在手里，随时参阅，而且左边页面上有许多有关排演活动的建议。

二、书中配有大量世界各国莎剧演出的彩色剧照，为莎剧爱好者和剧团排演莎剧提供了灵感。

三、书的正文部分打开后，右页是未经删减、原汁原味的剧本原文，左页是多种不同栏目，包括导演技巧（Stagecraft）、剧中语言（Language in the play）、人物分析（Characters）、主题分析（Themes）、写作练习（Write about it）及词语注释等。每幕之间（本幕回顾）和最后一幕后（本剧回顾）有与剧情相关的各种思考题。

四、在剧本之后有各种针对全剧的专题论述，以《哈慕雷》为例，包括视角与主题（Perspectives and themes）、人物分析（Characters）、《哈慕雷》的语言（The language of Hamlet）、《哈慕雷》的演出（Hamlet in performance）、笔论莎士比亚（Writing about Shakespeare）、笔论《哈慕雷》（Writing about Hamlet），还有一份莎翁年表（William Shakespeare 1564–1616）。

左页上的栏目对于解读和排演莎剧特别有帮助，剧本后面的专题论述对于撰写有关莎士比亚的文章特别有帮助，而参加莎剧排演，背诵台词，撰写论文，又是提高英语水平的极好途径。

为了方便更多的中国读者阅读、欣赏、排演莎士比亚原作，北京语言大学出版社携手剑桥大学出版社，将这套莎剧精选引入中国。我有幸应邀担任这套书的中文版总主编，组织起一个团队，对原版进行一定程度的改编和汉化，以适应中国读者的需求。我们不仅将原版提供的关键注释基本译成了中文，而且针对中国英语学习者和莎剧爱好者阅读理解上的难点，主要做了以下四件事：

一、参考 *The Oxford Dictionary of Original Shakespearean Pronunciation* (David Crystal 2016)、*Oxford Dictionary of Pronunciation for Current English* (Clive Upton 2003) 和 *Shakespeare's Names: A Pronouncing Dictionary* (Helge Kökeritz 1950)，给每个剧本前面人物表里的人名加上了国际音标。为了便于读者识别，我们将第一本发音词典里一般中国读者不认识的个别音标替换成了大家熟悉的近似音标。

二、为左页顶端的剧情简介添加中文译文。

三、左页中以及剧本后面论文部分里有一些具有挑战性的词和术语（如tableau），我们为其中的大部分添加了相应的中文释义。

四、适当增加了原版里没有的词语注释。

给剧中人物的名字加了国际音标之后，我们发现，现有莎剧中文译本里一些人名的中文译名与原文的读音差别较大且互不相同。根据定名不咎、译音循本、音义兼顾、音系对应的原则，我们给出了新译名。根据前两个原则，我们将剧本 *Julius Caesar* /ˈdʒuːlɪəs ˈsiːzə(r)/ 译成《儒略·恺撒》，而没有采用《尤利/力乌斯·恺撒》《裘利/力斯·凯撒》《居里厄斯·恺撒》等现成译名中的任何一个，因为从公元前1世纪到公元16世纪西方使用的儒略历（Julian calendar）就是以这位 Julius Caesar（拉丁文读音是 /ˈjuːlɪ.ʊs ˈkae̯sar/）命名的。根据音义兼顾的原则，我们将剧本 *Hamlet* /ˈ(h)amlət/ 译成《哈慕雷》而不是《哈姆莱特》或《哈姆雷特》，因为"慕雷"比"姆莱"或"姆雷"更适合用来给男子起名，结尾的辅音 /t/ 在实际说话中往往不发音。根据音系对应的原则，我们借鉴了曹禺的译法，将剧本 *Romeo and Juliet* 译成《柔密欧与茱丽叶》，没有将 Romeo 译成更常见的"罗密欧"，因为"柔 /rou/"比"罗 /luo/"更接近原名 Romeo /ˈroːmɪoː/ 的读音；同时我们将 Juliet /ˈdʒuːlɪət/ 译成"茱丽叶"而不是"朱丽叶"，因为这样做不容易让人误以为这个女孩姓"朱"。

这套经过改编并且带中文注释的《中文详注剑桥莎士比亚精选》不仅可以用作中国高中和大学的英文教材，而且适合中国所有具有较高英语能力的莎剧爱好者阅读和欣赏，将戏剧从书中提升到自己心中，将剧本从课堂搬演到戏台。

相信《中文详注剑桥莎士比亚精选》会带给中国广大英语爱好者一个惊喜。

陈国华

北京外国语大学

2020年5月于英国剑桥家中

Contents 目录

Introduction 引言	iv
Photo gallery 剧照精选	v

The Taming of the Shrew 《悍妇降服记》

List of characters 人物表	1
Induction 1 序幕1	3
Induction 2 序幕2	13
Act 1 第1幕	21
Act 2 第2幕	57
Act 3 第3幕	85
Act 4 第4幕	109
Act 5 第5幕	155
Perspectives and themes 视角与主题	178
The contexts of The Taming of the Shrew 《悍妇降服记》的创作背景	181
Characters 人物分析	182
The language of The Taming of the Shrew 《悍妇降服记》的语言	186
The Taming of the Shrew in performance 《悍妇降服记》的演出	191
Writing about Shakespeare 笔论莎士比亚	198
Writing about The Taming of the Shrew 笔论《悍妇降服记》	200
William Shakespeare 1564–1616 莎翁年表	202
Acknowledgements 鸣谢	203

Cambridge School Shakespeare

Introduction 引言

This *The Taming of the Shrew* is part of the **Cambridge School Shakespeare** series. Like every other play in the series, it has been specially prepared to help all students in schools and colleges.

The **Cambridge School Shakespeare** *The Taming of the Shrew* aims to be different. It invites you to lift the words from the page and to bring the play to life in your classroom, hall or drama studio. Through enjoyable and focused activities, you will increase your understanding of the play. Actors have created their different interpretations of the play over the centuries. Similarly, you are invited to make up your own mind about *The Taming of the Shrew*, rather than having someone else's interpretation handed down to you.

Cambridge School Shakespeare does not offer you a cut-down or simplified version of the play. This is Shakespeare's language, filled with imaginative possibilities. You will find on every left-hand page: a summary of the action, an explanation of unfamiliar words, and a choice of activities on Shakespeare's stagecraft, characters, themes and language.

Between each act and in the pages at the end of the play, you will find notes, illustrations and activities. These will help to encourage reflection after every act and give you insights into the background and context of the play as a whole.

This edition will be of value to you whether you are studying for an examination, reading for pleasure or thinking of putting on the play to entertain others. You can work on the activities on your own or in groups. Many of the activities suggest a particular group size, but don't be afraid to make up larger or smaller groups to suit your own purposes. Please don't think you have to do every activity: choose those that will help you most.

Although you are invited to treat *The Taming of the Shrew* as a play, you don't need special dramatic or theatrical skills to do the activities. By choosing your activities, and by exploring and experimenting, you can make your own interpretations of Shakespeare's language, characters and stories.

Whatever you do, remember that Shakespeare wrote his plays to be acted, watched and enjoyed.

Rex Gibson
Founding editor

This new edition contains more photographs, more diversity and more supporting material than previous editions, whilst remaining true to Rex's original vision. Specifically, it contains more activities and commentary on stagecraft and writing about Shakespeare, to reflect contemporary interest. The glossary has been enlarged too. Finally, this edition aims to reflect the best teaching and learning possible, and to represent not only Shakespeare through the ages, but also the relevance and excitement of Shakespeare today.

Richard Andrews and Vicki Wienand
Series editors

This edition of *The Taming of the Shrew* uses the text of the play established by Ann Thompson in **The New Cambridge Shakespeare**.

The Taming of the Shrew brings together two strong personalities: Petruchio, who is determined to marry a rich woman from Padua, and Katherina, who is feared by most of the men in the city because of her sharp tongue and violent temper.

Petruchio and Katherina find they have met their match in each other. Their first encounter is more like a fight than a courtship – a verbal skirmish (小冲突) that quickly gets physical. Neither of them is willing to lose face or back down. The story of their fiery 'engagement' always provokes a strong response in the audience.

◀ Baptista is desperate to be rid of Katherina and her violent temper, so he forbids anyone to court Bianca until her older sister is married. Petruchio has come to Padua in search of a rich wife, and decides to woo Katherina despite her shrewish reputation. Baptista makes arrangements with Petruchio and also with Bianca's suitors in order to settle the dowries (嫁妆) and secure the marriages of both his daughters.

▼ Lucentio, a young nobleman visiting Padua to further his education, falls in love at first sight with Bianca. Lucentio schemes with his manservant, Tranio, to come up with a plan to win Bianca's love behind her father's back.

The date for Petruchio and Katherina's wedding is settled quickly, despite the bride's very vocal protestations. Even though Petruchio had been so eager to marry Katherina, he causes a great scandal at the wedding by arriving late, keeping Katherina waiting at the altar, and wearing a ridiculous costume.

Petruchio hauls Katherina off to his house immediately after the wedding ceremony. It is cold and intimidating (令人胆怯), and his household is full of incompetent servants.

Left alone, Petruchio confides to the audience that his behaviour is part of a plan to curb his headstrong wife. He is determined to make Katherina change her shrewish temper by using the strategies of a falconer (驯鹰人).

Meanwhile, Lucentio disguises himself as a classics teacher called Cambio in an effort to get close to Bianca and win her favour.

Petruchio's plan does not progress smoothly, and there are further skirmishes and violent outbursts. However, he gradually wears down Katherina's resistance and eventually wins her trust and respect. Meanwhile, Lucentio confesses his true identity to Bianca and she agrees to marry him.

▶ Petruchio and Katherina's return journey to Padua marks a turning point in their relationship: they gain a new understanding about each other and the way they will view the world together.

◀ Katherina and Petruchio seal their own marriage contract with a very public kiss ('in the midst of the street') and work together to win a wager (赌注) at the end of the play.

List of characters 人物表

The Induction 序幕
(set in Warwickshire) (场景在沃里克郡)

CHRISTOPHER SLY /ˈkrɪstəfə(r) sləɪ/ (克瑞斯特夫·斯雷) a tinker
HOSTESS (老板娘) of an alehouse
LORD (爵爷)
BARTHOLOMEW /ˈbɑː(r)tlmjuː/ (巴特尔缪) the Lord's page (pretends to be Sly's wife)
Huntsmen and Servingmen attending the Lord
A Troupe of Actors visiting the Lord

who present 出演

The Taming of the Shrew 《悍妇降服记》
(set in Padua) (场景在帕多瓦)

The Minola family 米讷拉家
KATHERINA /katəˈriːnə/ (凯特芮娜) the Shrew
BIANCA /bɪˈaŋka/ (碧昂卡) her younger sister
BAPTISTA MINOLA /bapˈtiːsta ˈmɪnəla/ (巴普提斯塔·米讷拉) her father

The suitors 追求者
PETRUCHIO /pəˈtruːkɪoː/ (珀楚秋)
LUCENTIO /luˈsensɪoː/ (卢森修) (pretends to be Cambio /ˈkambɪoː/ [坎毕欧])
HORTENSIO /hɔ(r)ˈtensɪoː/ (郝坦修) (pretends to be Litio /ˈlɪsɪoː/ [理修])
GREMIO /ˈgremɪoː/ (葛莱缪) a rich old man

The servants 仆人
GRUMIO /ˈgruːmɪoː/ (葛儒缪) Petruchio's personal servant
TRANIO /ˈtranɪoː/ (川纽) Lucentio's personal servant (pretends to be Lucentio)
BIONDELLO /biːənˈdeloː/ (卞代娄) Lucentio's second servant
CURTIS /ˈkɜː(r)tɪs/ (柯提斯), NATHANIEL /nəˈtanɪəl/ (讷塔涅尔),
PHILIP /ˈfɪlɪp/ (菲利普), JOSEPH /ˈdʒɔːsəf/ (约瑟夫), } Petruchio's servants
NICHOLAS /ˈnɪkələs/ (尼科勒), PETER /ˈpiːtə(r)/ (彼得)
Servants attending on Baptista and Lucentio

Other characters 其他人物
VINCENTIO /vɪnˈsensɪoː/ (文森修) Lucentio's father
MERCHANT (商人) (pretends to be Vincentio)
WIDOW (寡妇) in love with Hortensio
HABERDASHER (帽子商)
TAILOR (裁缝)

Christopher Sly quarrels with the Hostess as she throws him out of her tavern. He falls into a drunken sleep. A nobleman returns from the hunt and talks about the day's sport.

 剧情简介：克瑞斯特夫·斯雷被酒馆老板娘赶出来，二人争吵。醉酒的斯雷昏睡过去。一位爵爷打猎回来，说起当天的狩猎。

Stagecraft 导演技巧

Staging the scene (by yourself)

Induction 1 opens in the middle of an aggressive argument between a man and a woman. Different productions have tried elaborate ways of grabbing the audience's attention. One was set in a modern wine bar, others in a working-men's club, in a pub outside Stratford-upon-Avon, in an Italian café and even on a cruise ship.

- How would you stage this first scene for greatest impact? Think about where you would set the scene and then consider how you would want the characters to be portrayed. What would they look like? What clothes would they wear? Would they have accents? How would you advise the actors to use the available stage space?
- Begin a Director's Journal in which you record your ideas about *The Taming of the Shrew* in performance. Add to your journal as you continue reading, exploring aspects of stagecraft, actors' perspectives and dramatic possibilities.

1 Christopher Sly (in small groups)

Christopher Sly is terribly drunk in lines 1–11.

- Read through these lines and then compile a list that highlights examples of his drunken behaviour. Talk together about other kinds of behaviour you might expect from stereotypical representations of people who are drunk, and add them to the list with your own ideas.
- Afterwards, write a stage direction for each of Sly's lines to emphasise how outrageous his behaviour is.

2 Two dramatic entrances (in pairs)

Compare the entrances of Christopher Sly and the Lord in the script opposite, and consider the two levels of society that Shakespeare presents at the start of the play.

- Sly does not say much, but his few lines suggest a great deal about his character. How would you choose to portray him: what appearance, costume and accent would suit him best?
- The Lord makes an equally dramatic entrance, with his hunting dogs and Servingmen. He uses a very different style of language from Sly. How would you choose to portray the Lord?

1 feeze 收拾
2 A pair of stocks 一副脚枷
3 rogue 流氓
4 baggage 贱女人
5 Chronicles 史书
6 Richard Conqueror （斯雷错把征服者威廉 [William the Conqueror] 说成理查）
7 *paucas pallabris* 少说废话
8 slide 过得去
9 Sessa! 闭嘴！（滚开！）
10 denier 一分钱
11 Saint Jeronimy （斯雷搞混了拉丁学者Saint Jerome和戏剧《西班牙悲剧》中的Hieronimo的名字）
12 thirdborough 巡警
13 by law 法庭上
14 and kindly 务必（嘲讽口吻）
15 Wind horns 吹起号角
16 Breathe Merriman 让迈瑞曼（猎犬名）喘口气
17 embossed 累得口吐白沫
18 couple 拴在一起
19 deep-mouthed 叫声响亮
20 brach 母狗
21 made it good 找到了失踪猎物的气味
22 in the coldest fault 就在猎物气味消失的那一刻

The Taming of the Shrew

Induction 1

Outside an Alehouse in Warwickshire

Enter CHRISTOPHER SLY *and the* HOSTESS.

SLY	I'll feeze[1] you, in faith.	
HOSTESS	A pair of stocks[2], you rogue[3]!	
SLY	Y'are a baggage[4], the Slys are no rogues. Look in the Chronicles[5]; we came in with Richard Conqueror[6]. Therefore *paucas pallabris*[7], let the world slide[8]. Sessa![9]	5
HOSTESS	You will not pay for the glasses you have burst?	
SLY	No, not a denier[10]. Go by, Saint Jeronimy[11], go to thy cold bed and warm thee.	

[*He lies down.*]

HOSTESS	I know my remedy; I must go fetch the thirdborough[12]. [*Exit*]	
SLY	Third, or fourth, or fifth borough, I'll answer him by law[13]. I'll not budge an inch, boy. Let him come, and kindly[14].	10

He falls asleep.

Wind horns[15]. *Enter a* LORD *from hunting, with his train* [*of* HUNTSMEN *and* SERVINGMEN].

LORD	Huntsman, I charge thee, tender well my hounds.	
	Breathe Merriman[16] – the poor cur is embossed[17] –	
	And couple[18] Clowder with the deep-mouthed[19] brach[20].	
	Saw'st thou not, boy, how Silver made it good[21]	15
	At the hedge corner, in the coldest fault[22]?	
	I would not lose the dog for twenty pound.	

3

The Lord challenges the Huntsman's assessment of his hounds. Seeing Sly asleep, he decides to play a trick on the drunkard. When the low-born Sly wakes, everyone will pretend he is really a nobleman.

 剧情简介：爵爷反驳猎人对他的猎犬的看法。看到昏睡的斯雷，爵爷决定拿这个醉鬼开个玩笑。当出身卑贱的斯雷醒来时，众人要假装他确实是一位贵族。

1 'dead, or drunk?' (in small groups)

At line 27, the Lord and his Servingmen discover the drunken Sly. In groups, form a tableau (戏台造型 [演员全部静止不动]) (a 'human sculpture', like a still photograph), featuring Sly, the Lord and the others on stage in the positions you imagine them to hold at this point. Your postures should project a sense of each character's status and personality. Before forming your tableaux, talk together about what you want to suggest by your choice of staging.

Themes

Transformation through trickery (in pairs)

The Lord decides to play an amusing trick on Sly. Deception is an important motif in the play, and this first example comes very early.

- Read lines 32–50 aloud together, taking alternate lines. Then compile a list of questions you want to ask the Lord about the details of his plan to trick Sly and what he hopes to achieve by this deception.
- Put the Lord in the hot-seat*. Take turns in role as the Lord and try to answer the questions you compiled above. List his reasons in order, from the most fun to potentially the most harmful.

1	cried … loss	闻到几乎消失的猎物气味并叫起来
2	fleet	快
3	sup	喂食
4	image	样子
5	practise	调戏；施计
6	brave	穿戴体面
7	wanton	情趣；淫秽
8	Balm	洗，浸泡
9	distillèd	有香味
10	sweet wood	香木（燃烧时散发香味的杜松木）
11	music	安神静心的美妙音乐
12	dulcet	优美动听
13	reverence	行礼

* hot-seat 热座位，一种课堂游戏，玩法是请一位同学坐到讲台上的一把椅子上，其他同学轮番给他/她出难题，哪个问题他/她回答不出就算输。

▼ The entrance of the huntsmen in this production is ominous (不吉利), with the Lord towering over Sly slumped on the floor, and large shadows looming above them. Is this how you imagine the entrance of the huntsmen?

The Taming of the Shrew Induction 1
悍妇降服记

1 HUNTSMAN   Why, Belman is as good as he, my lord;
             He cried upon it at the merest loss[1],
             And twice today picked out the dullest scent.   20
             Trust me, I take him for the better dog.
LORD   Thou art a fool. If Echo were as fleet[2]
             I would esteem him worth a dozen such.
             But sup[3] them well, and look unto them all:
             Tomorrow I intend to hunt again.   25
1 HUNTSMAN   I will, my lord.
LORD   What's here? One dead, or drunk? See, doth he breathe?
2 HUNTSMAN   He breathes, my lord. Were he not warmed with ale,
             This were a bed but cold to sleep so soundly.
LORD   O monstrous beast, how like a swine he lies!   30
             Grim death, how foul and loathsome is thine image[4]!
             Sirs, I will practise[5] on this drunken man.
             What think you, if he were conveyed to bed,
             Wrapped in sweet clothes, rings put upon his fingers,
             A most delicious banquet by his bed,   35
             And brave[6] attendants near him when he wakes –
             Would not the beggar then forget himself?
1 HUNTSMAN   Believe me, lord, I think he cannot choose.
2 HUNTSMAN   It would seem strange unto him when he waked –
LORD   Even as a flatt'ring dream or worthless fancy.   40
             Then take him up, and manage well the jest.
             Carry him gently to my fairest chamber
             And hang it round with all my wanton[7] pictures;
             Balm[8] his foul head in warm distillèd[9] waters
             And burn sweet wood[10] to make the lodging sweet;   45
             Procure me music[11] ready when he wakes
             To make a dulcet[12] and a heavenly sound;
             And if he chance to speak, be ready straight
             And with a low submissive reverence[13]
             Say, 'What is it your honour will command?'   50

The Lord gives detailed instructions for the execution of his plan, and Sly is carried off to the Lord's house. Trumpets sound, which herald the arrival of a company of actors.

剧情简介：爵爷为实施他的计谋做了详细的安排，斯雷被抬到爵爷府邸。喇叭声响起，预告一个戏班子的到来。

1 Luxury (in fours)

a One person reads aloud lines 42–64. The others 'echo' words associated with certain topics by whispering them back to the reader. One of the 'whisperers' should echo words that suggest wealth and luxury. Another should echo words that suggest a master-servant relationship. The third person should echo the verbs in the passage. Afterwards, swap roles, so that a different person is the reader, and repeat the exercise.

b Collect images from magazines or the Internet that reflect the sense of luxury and service that the Lord creates through his language. Assemble these into a collage (拼贴画) and annotate it with suitable quotations from this scene.

Stagecraft 导演技巧

Stage directions (by yourself)

There is a great deal of movement on stage during lines 68–76, and Shakespeare included several directions to the actors about sound effects, movement, entrances and exits.

- In role as a director, write more detailed stage directions that tell the cast exactly how you would like this part of the scene to end in your own production. Think about when and how you want Sly's exit to take place. Does he wake up as he is moved? What are the other characters doing on stage while this is happening?

Write about it 写作练习

'He is no less than what we say he is'

Through a series of deceptions, the Lord aims to persuade the low-born Sly that he is actually 'a mighty lord' too. The first Huntsman agrees that treating Sly as if he were a lord will make the drunkard believe he really is a member of the nobility. Do you agree?

a In pairs, discuss how treating someone differently might cause them to change their behaviour and assume a different identity.

b Write a paragraph in which you predict what will happen when Sly wakes up to find himself being treated like a lord.

---

1 bestrewed 洒满
2 ewer 大水罐
3 diaper 毛巾
4 apparel 衣服
5 disease 犯病
6 when he says he is 当他说自己一定是疯了的时候
7 kindly 自然（让对方相信）
8 passing 非常，极其
9 husbanded with modesty 做得恰到好处
10 warrant 保证
11 As = So that
12 to his office 各司其职
13 Sirrah 小子（用来称呼下人，复数为sirs，如上文第32行出现的，表示"小的们"）
14 Belike 也许
15 repose 歇息
16 An't = If it
17 players 一个戏班子

THE TAMING OF THE SHREW INDUCTION 1

悍妇降服记

               Let one attend him with a silver basin
               Full of rose-water and bestrewed[1] with flowers;
               Another bear the ewer[2], the third a diaper[3],
               And say, 'Will't please your lordship cool your hands?'
               Some one be ready with a costly suit   55
               And ask him what apparel[4] he will wear;
               Another tell him of his hounds and horse,
               And that his lady mourns at his disease[5].
               Persuade him that he hath been lunatic,
               And when he says he is[6], say that he dreams,   60
               For he is nothing but a mighty lord.
               This do, and do it kindly[7], gentle sirs.
               It will be pastime passing[8] excellent,
               If it be husbanded with modesty[9].

1 HUNTSMAN My lord, I warrant[10] you we will play our part   65
               As[11] he shall think by our true diligence
               He is no less than what we say he is.

LORD Take him up gently and to bed with him,
               And each one to his office[12] when he wakes.

[Sly is carried off]

Sound trumpets.

               Sirrah[13], go see what trumpet 'tis that sounds.   70

[Exit Servingman]

               Belike[14] some noble gentleman that means,
               Travelling some journey, to repose[15] him here.

Enter Servingman.

               How now? Who is it?

SERVINGMAN   An't[16] please your honour, players[17]
               That offer service to your lordship.

LORD Bid them come near.

The Lord welcomes the players and willingly agrees that they should stay at his house. He asks them to perform before a 'Lord' (Sly), but warns them that the 'Lord' is given to strange behaviour.

 剧情简介：爵爷欢迎戏班子的到来并同意他们住在他府上。他请戏班子为一位"爵爷"（斯雷）表演，但提醒他们这位"爵爷"行为乖张。

1 The players' entrance

Some productions have staged the entrance of the players in modern dress, with the actors wearing clothes that they would normally wear for rehearsal or for travelling. Other performances have made more theatrically bold decisions by featuring, for example, a *commedia dell'arte* (即兴喜剧) troupe (班子，团), acrobats (杂技演员) and musicians – even Elizabethan players with a lookalike Shakespeare!

- On page 2, you began a Director's Journal. Add to this now, making notes about how you would like the players to appear, what clothes they would wear and what props (道具) they would carry.

2 The farmer's eldest son (in pairs)

In lines 80–1, the Lord refers to a character from popular plays about courtship – the farmer's eldest son, who was well known for wooing the gentlewoman 'so well'.

- What other characters or stereotypes might you expect to see in plays about courtship and marriage? Look at the list below and choose an adjective for each person.

the _____ bride
the _____ groom
the _____ mother-in-law
the _____ father
the _____ sister

Write about it 写作练习

Layers of illusion

The Taming of the Shrew is filled with performances. Some of them are designed to deceive people, and some are part of the role play and display of everyday life. In the script opposite, the players arrive and receive a commission from the Lord to perform for Christopher Sly that evening.

- How would you use the stage space to show that some of the characters (from the Induction) are watching another performance (the play to be performed by the travelling players)? Write your ideas about how to stage this 'performance within a performance' as notes in your Director's Journal. Where will you place the two groups of players on the stage? How will you ensure that the audience doesn't get confused by these layers of performance?

---

1 So please = If it please
2 aptly fitted 演得恰到好处
3 naturally 自然，不做作
4 Soto 索托（英国剧作家约翰·弗莱彻 [John Fletcher, 1579—1625] 剧作《满足的女人》[*Woman Pleased*] 中的人物）
5 in happy time 正是时候
6 The rather for 特别因为
7 cunning 专长
8 doubtful of your modesties 拿不准你们的自制力
9 over-eyeing of 看到，目睹
10 break into some merry passion 忍不住笑起来
11 contain 克制
12 veriest antic 最奇特的怪胎
13 buttery 食物储藏室
14 want 缺少
15 affords 提供

Enter PLAYERS.

	Now, fellows, you are welcome.	75
PLAYERS	We thank your honour.	
LORD	Do you intend to stay with me tonight?	
1 PLAYER	So please[1] your lordship to accept our duty.	
LORD	With all my heart. This fellow I remember	
	Since once he played a farmer's eldest son –	80
	'Twas where you wooed the gentlewoman so well –	
	I have forgot your name, but sure that part	
	Was aptly fitted[2] and naturally[3] performed.	
2 PLAYER	I think 'twas Soto[4] that your honour means.	
LORD	'Tis very true; thou didst it excellent.	85
	Well, you are come to me in happy time[5],	
	The rather for[6] I have some sport in hand	
	Wherein your cunning[7] can assist me much.	
	There is a lord will hear you play tonight –	
	But I am doubtful of your modesties[8],	90
	Lest over-eyeing of[9] his odd behaviour	
	(For yet his honour never heard a play)	
	You break into some merry passion[10]	
	And so offend him; for I tell you, sirs,	
	If you should smile, he grows impatient.	95
1 PLAYER	Fear not, my lord, we can contain[11] ourselves	
	Were he the veriest antic[12] in the world.	
LORD	Go, sirrah, take them to the buttery[13]	
	And give them friendly welcome every one.	
	Let them want[14] nothing that my house affords[15].	100

Exit one with the Players

The Lord has a further idea. He will provide Sly with a 'wife' in the shape of a young page dressed as a woman. The Lord himself will act as the calming influence to dampen excessive hilarity.

剧情简介：爵爷又想出一个点子，他要给斯雷配个夫人，这个女人就由他的年轻侍童扮演。爵爷要亲自出场，压压他们过度的兴奋。

Themes 主题分析

A wife's duty (in small groups)

Bartholomew is the first example of many characters in the play pretending to be someone they are not. The Lord issues detailed instructions on how his page should play a humble and dutiful wife – a central theme in *The Taming of the Shrew*.

a One person reads through lines 101–24. The others note down the key words that suggest what the Lord expects from a dutiful wife.

b Work together to present a tableau that reflects the Lord's view of how a wife should behave towards her husband. Then put together a tableau that reflects other views of the role of a wife – perhaps showing how Christopher Sly sees women, or how wives are viewed in different cultural contexts from around the world.

Write about it 写作练习

The 'noble' wife of a 'drunken beggar'

The Lord gives elaborate instructions for Bartholomew to follow so that he can give a convincing performance as Sly's dutiful 'wife'. How do you think Bartholomew feels about enacting this deceit?

- Write his diary at the end of the day. What was it like pretending to be the 'noble' wife of a 'drunken beggar'? Where did he get his ideas for how such a noble wife would behave? How did he like using the stage trick mentioned in line 122?

1 Laughing with the Lord (in small groups)

a A volunteer slowly reads lines 127–34 as the Lord. The rest of the group become servants who are keen to win his favour. Whenever you have the chance, laugh at the idea of Sly and his 'wife' to show your approval of the Lord's wit. Notice that the Lord assumes that the absurdity of the situation will come not from a boy pretending to be a woman, but from a tinker thinking he is a lord.

b Script a conversation between the Lord and one of his servants, in which they discuss these ideas in relation to the trick they are playing on Sly. Remember that the Elizabethans had strong ideas about the appropriate social order, based on a chain of being, with God at the top of a strict hierarchical structure (等级结构).

1 **see him dressed** 把他装扮起来
2 **in all suits** 各个方面（suits 也指衣服）
3 **as … love** 如果他想让我今后更宠信他
4 **duty** 敬意
5 **lowly courtesy** 谦卑的行礼
6 **esteemèd him** 把自己当作
7 **commanded** 事先设计好
8 **shift** 目的
9 **in despite** 不由自主
10 **usurp** 假装
11 **gait** 步态
12 **Haply** 也许
13 **abate** 控制
14 **over-merry spleen** 高兴过度的冲动（以前人们认为脾[spleen]主管喜悦、愤怒、悲哀等强烈情感）
15 *Exeunt* 全体下

Sirrah, go you to Barthol'mew my page
And see him dressed[1] in all suits[2] like a lady.
That done, conduct him to the drunkard's chamber,
And call him 'madam', do him obeisance.
Tell him from me – as he will win my love[3] –   105
He bear himself with honourable action
Such as he hath observed in noble ladies
Unto their lords, by them accomplishèd.
Such duty[4] to the drunkard let him do
With soft low tongue and lowly courtesy[5],   110
And say, 'What is't your honour will command
Wherein your lady and your humble wife
May show her duty and make known her love?'
And then with kind embracements, tempting kisses,
And with declining head into his bosom,   115
Bid him shed tears, as being overjoyed
To see her noble lord restored to health,
Who for this seven years hath esteemèd him[6]
No better than a poor and loathsome beggar.
And if the boy have not a woman's gift   120
To rain a shower of commanded[7] tears,
An onion will do well for such a shift[8],
Which in a napkin being close conveyed
Shall in despite[9] enforce a watery eye.
See this dispatched with all the haste thou canst;   125
Anon I'll give thee more instructions.

Exit a Servingman

I know the boy will well usurp[10] the grace,
Voice, gait[11] and action of a gentlewoman.
I long to hear him call the drunkard 'husband',
And how my men will stay themselves from laughter   130
When they do homage to this simple peasant.
I'll in to counsel them. Haply[12] my presence
May well abate[13] the over-merry spleen[14]
Which otherwise would grow into extremes.

[*Exeunt*[15]]

Sly wakes up and the Lord's servants carry out their master's instructions. Sly is scornful, but they attempt to persuade the tinker that he is indeed a nobleman who is suffering from a delusion.

剧情简介： 斯雷醒来，爵爷的仆人执行主人的指令。斯雷鄙视众人，众人却想方设法使这个补锅匠相信自己其实是一个患有妄想症的爵爷。

Language in the play 剧中语言
Verse (韵文；诗体) and prose (散文；散体)

Sly speaks in prose, but the Servingmen and the Lord speak in verse. They also use more poetic language and more formal means of address ('thy', 'thee'). In addition, the Servingmen and the Lord use a rhetorical device called **anaphora***, in which a word or phrase is repeated at the beginning of successive clauses (see 'The language of *The Taming of the Shrew*', p. 190).

a What effect does the difference in prose and verse have on the audience's perception of Sly and of those playing the trick on him?

b What advice would you give the actors so that their actions match the language they are using? Write detailed stage directions for them at key points in the script opposite.

1 Comic moment (in small groups)

Sly tries to convince himself that he is not mad and that he really is 'old Sly's son', but in line 21 he breaks off suddenly. Is this because his surroundings suggest that he might be mistaken after all? Or is it because he is interrupted?

- In groups, write down how you would interpret this break in Sly's speech and exploit this potentially comic moment on the stage. You might find it useful to watch clips of other comic moments in Shakespeare's plays, or you could experiment with acting out this part of the scene yourself.

1 **other appurtenances** 其他用具（包括供斯雷享用的葡萄酒和蜜饯，也许还有乐器）
2 **small ale** 便宜的淡啤酒
3 **sack** （精酿）白葡萄酒或雪莉酒
4 **conserves** 蜜饯
5 **raiment** 服装
6 **Christophero** (Christopher 很做作的西班牙语读法)
7 **conserves of beef** 咸牛肉，腌牛肉
8 **doublets** 紧身外套
9 **overleather** 皮鞋面
10 **idle humour** 荒唐的幻想
11 **infusèd … spirit** 大脑被邪恶占据而充满如此可怕的幻觉
12 **Burton-heath** 荒野上的波顿（以及后面的温考特 [Wincot] 都是埃文河畔斯特拉特福镇 [Stratford-upon-Avon，莎士比亚出生地] 附近的村庄）
13 **cardmaker** 打铁梳子的
14 **by transmutation** 改行
15 **bear-herd** 驯熊人
16 **ale-wife** 酒馆老板娘
17 **on the score** 欠债
18 **sheer ale** 光是酒
19 **score me up for** 就算我是
20 **lying'st knave** 最会说瞎话的无赖
21 **bestraught** 疯了
22 **droop** 沮丧
23 **ancient thoughts** 原来（清醒）的头脑
24 **beck** 传唤

* **anaphora** 首语叠用，例如：The voice of the people is powerful, the voice of the people cannot be silenced, the voice of the people shakes the world.

Induction 2
The Lord's country house

Enter aloft [SLY] *with* ATTENDANTS — *some with apparel, basin and ewer, and other appurtenances[1] — and* LORD.

SLY	For God's sake, a pot of small ale[2]!
1 SERVINGMAN	Will't please your lordship drink a cup of sack[3]?
2 SERVINGMAN	Will't please your honour taste of these conserves[4]?
3 SERVINGMAN	What raiment[5] will your honour wear today?
SLY	I am Christophero[6] Sly – call not me 'honour' nor 'lordship'. I ne'er drank sack in my life, and if you give me any conserves, give me conserves of beef[7]. Ne'er ask me what raiment I'll wear, for I have no more doublets[8] than backs, no more stockings than legs, nor no more shoes than feet – nay, sometime more feet than shoes, or such shoes as my toes look through the overleather[9].
LORD	Heaven cease this idle humour[10] in your honour!
	O that a mighty man of such descent,
	Of such possessions and so high esteem,
	Should be infusèd with so foul a spirit[11]!
SLY	What, would you make me mad? Am not I Christopher Sly, old Sly's son of Burton-heath[12], by birth a pedlar, by education a cardmaker[13], by transmutation[14] a bear-herd[15], and now by present profession a tinker? Ask Marian Hacket, the fat ale-wife[16] of Wincot, if she know me not. If she say I am not fourteen pence on the score[17] for sheer ale[18], score me up for[19] the lying'st knave[20] in Christendom. What, I am not bestraught[21]! Here's –
3 SERVINGMAN	O, this it is that makes your lady mourn.
2 SERVINGMAN	O, this is it that makes your servants droop[22].
LORD	Hence comes it that your kindred shuns your house
	As beaten hence by your strange lunacy.
	O noble lord, bethink thee of thy birth.
	Call home thy ancient thoughts[23] from banishment,
	And banish hence these abject lowly dreams.
	Look how thy servants do attend on thee,
	Each in his office ready at thy beck[24].

Sly is offered many pleasures to choose from: music and relaxation, walking and riding, hawking and hunting, viewing erotic paintings. As the enticing pictures are described, the Lord introduces the topic of Sly's beautiful 'wife'.

 剧情简介：很多娱乐消遣供斯雷选择：欣赏音乐、放松身心、散步骑马、放鹰狩猎、春宫图观赏。说起春宫图，爵爷提起斯雷那位美丽的"夫人"。

1 Creating Lord Sly's bedchamber (in pairs)

The Servingmen try to convince Sly that he really is the noble owner of a great house. How could props and furniture help in this charade?

- Work as props assistants and make a list of all the items that might help to create the right illusion. There may be props for the actors to use, or larger items with which to dress the set. Allow your imagination full rein, and consider how you might make use of lighting, music, sounds – even smells! – in order to conjure up 'Sly's dream'.

2 The range of pleasures (whole class)

Two volunteers read aloud lines 31–42. One person should read the questions while the other reads out the answers in as enticing (诱人) a way as possible, laying out the goodies in front of Sly. To tempt him even further, the rest of the class should present a series of tableaux to represent the different forms of entertainment on offer. Don't hold back – make your tableaux excessive, over the top and fun!

Stagecraft 导演技巧

Wanton pictures (in threes)

The Lord said that he would seduce Sly with 'wanton pictures' (Induction 1, line 43), and these pictures are described in lines 45–56 opposite.

a Take parts and read the descriptions of the different pictures of mythical figures of love. Then experiment with how you would stage this part of the scene.

b Talk together about how Sly responds to all these classical references. Does he know what the Lord is talking about, or is he confused by the descriptions?

c Discuss how a feeling of sensuality (感官愉悦) could be created on stage during this part of the scene – through tone of voice, gestures or props.

d Why does the Lord suddenly tell Sly that he has 'a lady far more beautiful'? How might this change the atmosphere on stage? What effect would the Lord's words have on Sly?

1 **Hark** = Listen
2 **Apollo** 阿波罗（希腊神话中的音乐之神）
3 **lustful** 香艳
4 **Semiramis** 赛蜜拉蜜思（亚述女王，以骄奢淫逸闻名）
5 **trapped** 佩戴好马饰
6 **studded** 镶嵌
7 **welkin** 天空
8 **course** 放猎犬赶野兔
9 **breathèd** 健壮
10 **roe** 狍子
11 **straight** = immediately（马上）
12 **Adonis / Cytherea / Io / Daphne** 阿多尼斯，维纳斯，伊娥，达芙妮（都是希腊神话中的爱神，爵爷提到的"春宫图"中的神话人物）
13 **sedges** 莎草
14 **beguilèd and surprised** 被诱骗而猝不及防
15 **workmanly** 巧妙，精巧
16 **waning** 世风日下
17 **till** 在……之前
18 **yet** 仍然

THE TAMING OF THE SHREW INDUCTION 2

悍妇降服记

Wilt thou have music? Hark[1], Apollo[2] plays,   *Music*
And twenty cagèd nightingales do sing.
Or wilt thou sleep? We'll have thee to a couch
Softer and sweeter than the lustful[3] bed
On purpose trimmed up for Semiramis[4].   35
Say thou wilt walk, we will bestrow the ground.
Or wilt thou ride? Thy horses shall be trapped[5],
Their harness studded[6] all with gold and pearl.
Dost thou love hawking? Thou hast hawks will soar
Above the morning lark. Or wilt thou hunt?   40
Thy hounds shall make the welkin[7] answer them
And fetch shrill echoes from the hollow earth.

1 SERVINGMAN Say thou wilt course[8], thy greyhounds are as swift
As breathèd[9] stags, ay, fleeter than the roe[10].

2 SERVINGMAN Dost thou love pictures? We will fetch thee straight[11]   45
Adonis[12] painted by a running brook,
And Cytherea[12] all in sedges[13] hid,
Which seem to move and wanton with her breath
Even as the waving sedges play wi'th'wind.

LORD We'll show thee Io[12] as she was a maid,   50
And how she was beguilèd and surprised[14],
As lively painted as the deed was done.

3 SERVINGMAN Or Daphne[12] roaming through a thorny wood,
Scratching her legs that one shall swear she bleeds,
And at that sight shall sad Apollo weep,   55
So workmanly[15] the blood and tears are drawn.

LORD Thou art a lord, and nothing but a lord.
Thou hast a lady far more beautiful
Than any woman in this waning[16] age.

1 SERVINGMAN And till[17] the tears that she hath shed for thee   60
Like envious floods o'er-run her lovely face,
She was the fairest creature in the world –
And yet[18] she is inferior to none.

15

Wondering whether it is all a dream, Sly quickly decides that he is a lord after all. The servants tell him he has slept for fifteen years, saying strange things in his sleep.

 剧情简介：斯雷怀疑这一切只是一场梦，不过很快认定自己就是一个爵爷。仆人们说他已经昏睡了15年，睡梦里总说一些不着边际的话。

Language in the play 剧中语言

Sly's new language (in threes)

As Christopher Sly succumbs (抵挡不住) to the trick in lines 64–71, he begins to speak in **blank verse** (无韵诗；素体诗) (see p. 188). Read these lines aloud in unison and then discuss the following questions:

- Why do you think Shakespeare changes the language here?
- What tone of voice suits these lines best?
- What is the effect of Sly's line 'And once again a pot o'th'smallest ale' when contrasted with the lordly language he uses?

1 'I am a lord indeed' (by yourself)

a Re-read the script opposite. Now he is convinced of his true identity as a lord, how does Sly conduct himself towards the Servingmen? Apart from the fact that he now speaks in blank verse, are there any other ways that he tries to speak like a nobleman?

b In role as one of the Servingmen, write a note to a close friend telling them of the success of the trick and describing how Sly's behaviour changed at this point.

Themes 主题分析

Techniques of deception (in pairs)

The names of places and people, such as Wincot (line 18) and Peter Turph (line 90), fix Sly's world firmly in Shakespeare's Warwickshire. However, under instruction, the Servingmen claim these are names 'Which never were, nor no man ever saw'. This is a deliberate confusion of names and identity as a controlling strategy. Other such techniques include temptations, retelling the past and the invention of new identities.

a What other methods have been used for deceiving and controlling Sly in the Induction so far? Write out the three techniques listed above, then add your own ideas to the list.

b Put your list in order of least harmful to most harmful. Discuss with your partner why you think some aspects of this deception are comic and other aspects of it are dangerous.

1 **hither** = here
2 **smallest** 最便宜
3 **wit** 神志
4 **fifteen years** 15年（之前说是7年）
5 **fay** 信念
6 **of** = in
7 **idle words** 胡言乱语
8 **rail upon** 大骂
9 **present her at the leet** 把她告到本地衙门
10 **stone jugs** （缺斤短两的）石头酒杯
11 **sealed quarts** 带有官方印章的一夸脱的标准量杯
12 **amends** 恢复

THE TAMING OF THE SHREW INDUCTION 2
悍妇降服记

SLY　　　　　Am I a lord, and have I such a lady?
　　　　　　Or do I dream? Or have I dreamed till now?　　　　65
　　　　　　I do not sleep: I see, I hear, I speak,
　　　　　　I smell sweet savours and I feel soft things.
　　　　　　Upon my life, I am a lord indeed,
　　　　　　And not a tinker, nor Christopher Sly.
　　　　　　Well, bring our lady hither[1] to our sight,　　　　70
　　　　　　And once again a pot o'th'smallest[2] ale.
　　　　　　　　　　　　　　　　　　　　　　　[*Exit a Servingman*]
2 SERVINGMAN　Will't please your mightiness to wash your hands?
　　　　　　O, how we joy to see your wit[3] restored!
　　　　　　O, that once more you knew but what you are!
　　　　　　These fifteen years[4] you have been in a dream,　　　75
　　　　　　Or when you waked, so waked as if you slept.
SLY　　　　　These fifteen years! By my fay[5], a goodly nap.
　　　　　　But did I never speak of[6] all that time?
1 SERVINGMAN　O yes, my lord, but very idle words[7],
　　　　　　For though you lay here in this goodly chamber,　　80
　　　　　　Yet would you say ye were beaten out of door,
　　　　　　And rail upon[8] the hostess of the house,
　　　　　　And say you would present her at the leet[9]
　　　　　　Because she brought stone jugs[10] and no sealed quarts[11].
　　　　　　Sometimes you would call out for Cicely Hacket.　　85
SLY　　　　　Ay, the woman's maid of the house.
3 SERVINGMAN　Why, sir, you know no house, nor no such maid,
　　　　　　Nor no such men as you have reckoned up,
　　　　　　As Stephen Sly and old John Naps of Greece,
　　　　　　And Peter Turph and Henry Pimpernell,　　　　　90
　　　　　　And twenty more such names and men as these,
　　　　　　Which never were, nor no man ever saw.
SLY　　　　　Now Lord be thankèd for my good amends[12]!
ALL　　　　　Amen.

17

Sly is introduced to his 'wife' (Bartholomew). After some confusion over what to call 'her', he attempts to take 'her' to bed. Bartholomew's quick thinking saves both his honour and the whole charade.

剧情简介：斯雷见了他的"夫人"（巴特尔缪），一开始不知道如何称呼"她"，随后要拉"她"同房。巴特尔缪急中生智，巧妙脱身又保全了这场戏。

1 Bartholomew the 'wife'

There is plenty of potential for comedy when Bartholomew pretends to be Sly's wife, especially when Sly instructs 'her' to get undressed and come to bed.

- Look carefully at lines 114–20, then write an internal monologue of what is really going on in Bartholomew's mind. Does he throw himself into the charade, or is he timid and embarrassed?

Stagecraft 导演技巧

Boy actors (in small groups)

In Shakespeare's day, women were not allowed on stage – all female roles were played by boy actors. As a result, the comedy of Bartholomew dressing up as a woman and playing Sly's wife is more noticeable to a modern audience than it may have been in Shakespeare's day. In this scene, Bartholomew may have needed to emphasise the comedy by over-acting to draw attention to this kind of role reversal.

- Assuming that you have cast a man or boy as Bartholomew, talk about how he could play the script from line 95 to the end of the Induction. How would you want your Bartholomew to appear to Sly (and to the audience)? Is he a convincing 'woman' or is he a ludicrous (荒唐) figure clumping (脚步沉重地走) around the stage?

2 Stand or fall? (in pairs)

In lines 121–3, Sly makes a sexual joke that plays upon the innuendo (暗示) (double meaning) in the words 'stand' and 'fall'. Suggest gestures with which the actors could accompany these lines. You could also look through the rest of the play for other sexual puns (双关语). There are quite a lot of them!

1 thou … it 一会儿都有赏
2 How fares （表问候）
3 Marry 真的（表惊讶或强调的感叹词）
4 I fare well 我很好（这里的 fare是双关语，既回答上面的问候，又指他的饮食）
5 goodman 老公（这种称呼与lord身份不相称）
6 abandoned from your bed 不能与您同床共枕
7 Thrice noble 最最高贵
8 entreat 请求
9 expressly charged 明确关照过
10 In … malady 以免您旧病复发
11 stands for 可以当作
12 it stands so 问题是
13 tarry 等待

▼ How do you respond to this Sly, as he sits with the Lord and his friends?

Enter [BARTHOLOMEW, *a page, dressed as a*] *lady, with*
ATTENDANTS, [*one of whom gives Sly a pot of ale*].

SLY I thank thee, thou shalt not lose by it[1]. 95
BARTHOLOMEW How fares[2] my noble lord?
SLY Marry[3], I fare well[4], for here is cheer enough. [*He drinks.*] Where is my wife?
BARTHOLOMEW Here, noble lord, what is thy will with her?
SLY Are you my wife, and will not call me 'husband'? 100
    My men should call me 'lord'; I am your goodman[5].
BARTHOLOMEW My husband and my lord, my lord and husband,
    I am your wife in all obedience.
SLY I know it well — What must I call her?
LORD 'Madam.' 105
SLY 'Al'ce madam' or 'Joan madam'?
LORD 'Madam' and nothing else. So lords call ladies.
SLY Madam wife, they say that I have dreamed
    And slept above some fifteen year or more.
BARTHOLOMEW Ay, and the time seems thirty unto me, 110
    Being all this time abandoned from your bed[6].
SLY 'Tis much. Servants, leave me and her alone.
                    [*Exeunt Servingmen*]
    Madam, undress you and come now to bed.
BARTHOLOMEW Thrice noble[7] lord, let me entreat[8] of you
    To pardon me yet for a night or two, 115
    Or, if not so, until the sun be set.
    For your physicians have expressly charged[9],
    In peril to incur your former malady[10],
    That I should yet absent me from your bed.
    I hope this reason stands for[11] my excuse. 120
SLY Ay, it stands so[12] that I may hardly tarry[13] so long, but I would be loath to fall into my dreams again. I will therefore tarry in despite of the flesh and the blood.

Sly and his 'wife' settle to watch the play. Lucentio introduces himself as a well-born young man who has come to Padua with his servant Tranio to continue his education.

剧情简介：斯雷和"夫人"落座看戏。卢森修介绍自己出身名门，带着仆人川纽来帕多瓦求学。

1 Onstage audience (in pairs)

'Come, madam wife, sit by my side', says Sly (line 138) as he prepares to watch the play. Write detailed notes to the actors playing Sly and Bartholomew, advising them of what they will do for the rest of the play. In particular, consider the following:

- Where do Sly and his 'wife' sit? The stage directions at the start of Induction 2 suggest that the scene takes place 'aloft'. Would you place the actors from the Induction on a balcony or gallery (走廊)? Or to one side of the stage? Or at the back of the stage so that the audience can see their reactions throughout?

- How involved should Sly be in the unfolding action of the play? Is he watching at all or has he fallen asleep? Perhaps he is more concerned with his 'wife'?

2 'I am arrived'

This is where the story of *The Taming of the Shrew* begins. The way Shakespeare transports his audience to Padua may seem clumsy to a modern audience – Lucentio arrives and promptly explains what he is doing in Padua. However, the result is that the audience is immediately aware of the 'play-within-a-play' structure.

- Make a note of this as an example of overt theatricality (戏剧化), with an onstage audience watching the 'performance' of other people in the course of the play. Add to this list as you continue reading, noting further examples of theatricality. Also watch out for **asides** (旁白) – where characters talk directly to the real audience.

1 meet 适宜
2 congealed your blood 血流不畅（悲伤郁闷导致）
3 nurse of frenzy 滋生狂躁
4 mirth 欢乐
5 bars 预防
6 comonty （comedy之误）
7 gambold 小把戏；嬉闹
8 tumbling trick 翻跟斗之类的杂耍
9 history 故事
10 nursery of arts 文化与学术的摇篮
11 am arrived for 来到
12 well approved in all 事实证明各方面都很能干
13 breathe 逗留，暂歇
14 haply institute 也许开始
15 ingenuous 适合出身高贵的绅士

Themes 主题分析

Language, learning and knowledge

Lucentio refers to Padua as the 'nursery of the arts'. In Shakespeare's day, this city in northern Italy was home to a famous university and was a place of language, learning and knowledge.

- Write a paragraph explaining how this idea of education relates to the themes of trickery, deception and transformation that were raised in the Induction. Do you think it is educational to trick or deceive someone into seeing the world differently or behaving differently?

The Taming of the Shrew ACT 1 SCENE 1
悍妇降服记

Enter a MESSENGER.

MESSENGER Your honour's players, hearing your amendment,
Are come to play a pleasant comedy;   125
For so your doctors hold it very meet¹,
Seeing too much sadness hath congealed your blood²
And melancholy is the nurse of frenzy³ –
Therefore they thought it good you hear a play
And frame your mind to mirth⁴ and merriment,   130
Which bars⁵ a thousand harms and lengthens life.

SLY Marry, I will. Let them play it. Is not a comonty⁶ a Christmas gambold⁷ or a tumbling trick⁸?

BARTHOLOMEW No, my good lord, it is more pleasing stuff.

SLY What, household stuff?   135

BARTHOLOMEW It is a kind of history⁹.

SLY Well, we'll see't.
                                                                    [*Exit Messenger*]
Come, madam wife, sit by my side,
And let the world slip. We shall ne'er be younger.
                [*They sit down.*]
        [*A flourish of trumpets to announce the play.*]

Act 1 Scene 1
A street in Padua

Enter LUCENTIO *and his man* TRANIO.

LUCENTIO Tranio, since for the great desire I had
To see fair Padua, nursery of arts¹⁰,
I am arrived for¹¹ fruitful Lombardy,
The pleasant garden of great Italy,
And by my father's love and leave am armed   5
With his good will and thy good company –
My trusty servant well approved in all¹² –
Here let us breathe¹³ and haply institute¹⁴
A course of learning and ingenuous¹⁵ studies.

Lucentio talks of his father, a successful merchant, and of his own desire to study hard. Tranio suggests that they should not be too serious, nor forget that they must also enjoy themselves.

 剧情简介：卢森修说他父亲是一位成功的商人，又说起他自己很想刻苦学习。川纽建议不能过于认真，也不要忘了享受生活。

1 What's on Lucentio's mind? (in pairs)

a Lucentio packs a great deal into his first speech (lines 1–24). Read it through, alternating each line, then select a key word from each line. Discuss what this list suggests about Lucentio's interests, attitudes and state of mind.

b Use the key words you have identified to write a series of newspaper headlines in the *Padua News*. The headlines should let people know why this young nobleman has left his home town of Pisa to live in Padua.

Stagecraft 导演技巧

Start the play (in small groups)

Imagine you are directing this opening scene. You need to focus the audience's interest on the new story after the highly theatrical Induction. Talk together about how you might do this. Some directors try to make lines 1–45 funny (for example, by emphasising costumes, accents and props). Suggest at least three ideas for making the audience laugh out loud here.

2 Aristotle versus Ovid (in pairs)

In lines 25–40, Tranio mentions classical authors to convince Lucentio of the validity of his argument that serious study should be balanced with fun and entertainment. Aristotle was a Greek philosopher who taught that happiness can be achieved only through virtuous living. Ovid was a Roman poet popular among the Elizabethans for his love poetry. For Tranio, Aristotle represents academic discipline and logic, whereas Ovid represents imagination, story-telling and pleasure. In lines 39–40, Tranio tells Lucentio:

No profit grows where is no pleasure tane:
In brief, sir, study what you most affect.

- Do you agree with Tranio? Write a letter to a younger student giving them advice about their studies and telling them what you think is the right balance in order to succeed, as well as to enjoy life.

1 traffic 生意
2 Bentivolii 本提沃利（意大利的一个大家族）
3 serve … deck 求学上进、端正品行以不负厚望
4 apply 追求
5 plash 水坑，泥潭
6 satiety 满足
7 *Mi perdonato* 恕我冒昧（意大利语）
8 affected 倾向于
9 stoics 斯多葛们（禁欲主义者）
10 stocks 木块（与stoics谐音，讽刺像木头一样缺乏情感）
11 checks 戒律
12 Ovid 奥维德（43 BC—17 AD, 古罗马诗人，与倡导苦修式学术研究的亚里士多德形成对比）
13 abjured 冷落
14 Balk logic 争执，辩论
15 quicken 使活泼有生气
16 metaphysics 哲学
17 stomach 食欲；爱好
18 tane = taken
19 affect 喜爱
20 Gramercies 多谢
21 Biondello 卞代娄（卢森修一个不在场的仆人）

	Pisa renownèd for grave citizens	10
	Gave me my being and my father first,	
	A merchant of great traffic[1] through the world,	
	Vincentio, come of the Bentivolii[2].	
	Vincentio's son, brought up in Florence,	
	It shall become to serve all hopes conceived	15
	To deck[3] his fortune with his virtuous deeds.	
	And therefore, Tranio, for the time I study,	
	Virtue and that part of philosophy	
	Will I apply[4] that treats of happiness	
	By virtue specially to be achieved.	20
	Tell me thy mind, for I have Pisa left	
	And am to Padua come as he that leaves	
	A shallow plash[5] to plunge him in the deep	
	And with satiety[6] seeks to quench his thirst.	
TRANIO	*Mi perdonato*[7], gentle master mine,	25
	I am in all affected[8] as yourself,	
	Glad that you thus continue your resolve	
	To suck the sweets of sweet philosophy.	
	Only, good master, while we do admire	
	This virtue and this moral discipline,	30
	Let's be no stoics[9] nor no stocks[10], I pray,	
	Or so devote to Aristotle's checks[11]	
	As Ovid[12] be an outcast quite abjured[13].	
	Balk logic[14] with acquaintance that you have	
	And practise rhetoric in your common talk;	35
	Music and poesy use to quicken[15] you;	
	The mathematics and the metaphysics[16] –	
	Fall to them as you find your stomach[17] serves you.	
	No profit grows where is no pleasure tane[18]:	
	In brief, sir, study what you most affect[19].	40
LUCENTIO	Gramercies[20], Tranio, well dost thou advise.	
	If, Biondello[21], thou wert come ashore,	
	We could at once put us in readiness	
	And take a lodging fit to entertain	
	Such friends as time in Padua shall beget.	45

Lucentio and Tranio stand aside and listen as Baptista declares he will not allow his daughter Bianca to marry before Katherina, her elder sister. Katherina quarrels with Hortensio, one of Bianca's suitors. Lucentio is very attracted to Bianca.

 剧情简介：卢森修和川纽站在一旁，听巴普提斯塔宣称他不允许二女儿碧昂卡先于长女凯特芮娜出嫁。凯特芮娜与碧昂卡的一位追求者郝坦修争吵。卢森修被碧昂卡深深吸引了。

Stagecraft 导演技巧

Watching 'some show to welcome us to town'

Once again the theatricality of the situation is emphasised as Lucentio and Tranio become another onstage audience.

- How would you stage this? Make notes in your Director's Journal describing where you would position these characters. Do they melt into the background or is the audience constantly aware of them? What difference might that make?

1 First impressions of Katherina (in pairs)

The men clearly think that Katherina is unruly and bad-tempered. But in performance what initial impression might she make?

- One partner reads Katherina's lines aloud, while the other makes moves and gestures to emphasise her 'shrewishness'. Afterwards, swap roles and repeat the exercise with a calm and reasonable Katherina.
- Talk together about the different effects created by these versions. Which reading do you think best suits the script opposite?

2 'the other's silence' (in pairs)

Katherina breaks social convention by standing up for herself and insulting the men. In contrast, Bianca says nothing and is described by Lucentio as having 'Maid's mild behaviour and sobriety' (line 71).

- Take parts as Katherina and Bianca and create a tableau that contrasts these two women. Afterwards, describe your character's thoughts and feelings about the men on stage. What do you think of their interpretation of you?

Characters 人物分析

The stereotypical shrew (in small groups)

- Compile a list of how other people describe Katherina. Find examples of her behaviour that reveal her to be an unruly woman (start with words such as 'shrewd', 'froward', 'curst', 'ill-favoured'). Add to this list as you continue reading through the play.
- Do you think Katherina is a social rebel? An angry woman? A lonely outcast? A rejected daughter? A rebellious misfit (与别人合不来的人)? Or some combination of these?

1 *pantaloon* 愚蠢可笑的老头儿（意大利喜剧中常见的丑角，总妨碍年轻恋人结合）
2 *show* 表演
3 *importune* 强求
4 *bestow* 嫁出
5 *court* 追求
6 *cart her* 用车拉她游街（当时惩罚野女人的方式；cart与上文的court谐音）
7 *stale* 妓女（也指笑柄）
8 *mates* 卑鄙的家伙（臭男人）
9 *Iwis* 当然
10 *comb your noddle* 砸您的头
11 *paint* （用鲜血）染
12 *pastime toward* 要有好戏看了
13 *stark mad* 简直是疯了
14 *froward* 倔强泼辣
15 *sobriety* 端庄文静
16 *Mum!* 安静！
17 *gaze your fill* 看个够

THE TAMING OF THE SHREW ACT 1 SCENE 1
悍妇降服记

Enter BAPTISTA *with his two daughters* KATHERINA *and* BIANCA;
GREMIO, *a pantaloon*¹, *and* HORTENSIO, *suitor to Bianca.*

	But stay awhile, what company is this?	
TRANIO	Master, some show² to welcome us to town.	
	Lucentio and Tranio stand by.	
BAPTISTA	Gentlemen, importune³ me no farther	
	For how I firmly am resolved you know –	
	That is, not to bestow⁴ my youngest daughter	50
	Before I have a husband for the elder.	
	If either of you both love Katherina,	
	Because I know you well and love you well,	
	Leave shall you have to court⁵ her at your pleasure.	
GREMIO	To cart her⁶ rather! She's too rough for me.	55
	There, there, Hortensio, will you any wife?	
KATHERINA	[*To Baptista*] I pray you, sir, is it your will	
	To make a stale⁷ of me amongst these mates⁸?	
HORTENSIO	'Mates', maid? How mean you that? No mates for you	
	Unless you were of gentler, milder mould.	60
KATHERINA	I'faith, sir, you shall never need to fear.	
	Iwis⁹ it is not halfway to her heart –	
	But if it were, doubt not her care should be	
	To comb your noddle¹⁰ with a three-legged stool	
	And paint¹¹ your face and use you like a fool.	65
HORTENSIO	From all such devils, good Lord deliver us!	
GREMIO	And me too, good Lord!	
TRANIO	[*Aside to Lucentio*]	
	Husht, master, here's some good pastime toward¹²;	
	That wench is stark mad¹³, or wonderful froward¹⁴.	
LUCENTIO	[*Aside to Tranio*] But in the other's silence do I see	70
	Maid's mild behaviour and sobriety¹⁵.	
	Peace, Tranio.	
TRANIO	[*Aside to Lucentio*]	
	Well said, master. Mum!¹⁶ And gaze your fill¹⁷.	

剧情简介：姐妹俩拌了几句嘴。巴普提斯塔让碧昂卡进屋，请两个追求者给她找家庭教师。凯特芮娜离开，坚称自己无论何时，来去自由。

Characters

The good father (in threes)

a Baptista says he will be 'liberal / To mine own children in good bringing up.' What impressions have you formed so far of Baptista as a father? What kind of relationship does he have with his two daughters? Discuss this in your groups.

b Create a family portrait in tableau form, to show the relationships between Baptista and his daughters, and between Katherina and Bianca. Make sure your tableau demonstrates what you have learned about the personalities of these characters so far. You might also like to sketch or write out your ideas.

1 Two sisters (in pairs)

In lines 78–83, Katherina and Bianca have what seems to be a rather bad-tempered exchange.

a Read the lines to each other several times, thinking about the different ways in which you can say them and how you want to portray the sisters.

b Write two detailed stage directions for Katherina and Bianca as they each make their exit, to demonstrate their mood and feelings at this point in the play.

◀ Experiment with ways of delivering Katherina's parting exclamation: 'Ha!'

1 make good　兑现
2 peat　宠坏的孩子；乖孩子
3 put finger in the eye　戳眼睛（假装哭）
4 Minerva　密涅瓦（罗马神话中的智慧女神）
5 Signor　先生，阁下
6 strange　严厉
7 mew　关起来（猎鹰换羽时要用笼子关起来）
8 bear the penance　承担过错
9 music, instruments and poetry　音乐、乐器和诗歌（在莎士比亚时代只有极少数贵族女士才精通）
10 Prefer　推荐
11 cunning　有才能
12 commune　商量
13 appointed hours　被别人安排时间
14 belike　好像，仿佛

The Taming of the Shrew Act 1 Scene 1
悍妇降服记

BAPTISTA	Gentlemen, that I may soon make good[1]
	What I have said – Bianca, get you in.
	And let it not displease thee, good Bianca,
	For I will love thee ne'er the less, my girl.
KATHERINA	A pretty peat[2]! It is best put finger in the eye[3], and she knew why.
BIANCA	Sister, content you in my discontent.
	Sir, to your pleasure humbly I subscribe.
	My books and instruments shall be my company,
	On them to look and practise by myself.
LUCENTIO	[*Aside*] Hark, Tranio, thou mayst hear Minerva[4] speak!
HORTENSIO	Signor[5] Baptista, will you be so strange[6]?
	Sorry am I that our good will effects
	Bianca's grief.
GREMIO	Why will you mew[7] her up,
	Signor Baptista, for this fiend of hell,
	And make her bear the penance[8] of her tongue?
BAPTISTA	Gentlemen, content ye. I am resolved.
	Go in, Bianca.

[*Exit Bianca*]

And, for I know she taketh most delight
In music, instruments and poetry[9],
Schoolmasters will I keep within my house
Fit to instruct her youth. If you, Hortensio,
Or Signor Gremio you, know any such,
Prefer[10] them hither; for to cunning[11] men
I will be very kind, and liberal
To mine own children in good bringing up.
And so farewell. Katherina, you may stay,
For I have more to commune[12] with Bianca. *Exit*

KATHERINA Why, and I trust I may go too, may I not?
What, shall I be appointed hours[13] as though, belike[14],
I knew not what to take and what to leave? Ha! *Exit*

Gremio and Hortensio discuss their common problem: they have no chance of marrying Bianca until Katherina is married. They agree to work together to find a husband for her.

 剧情简介：葛莱缪和郝坦修探讨他们共同的难题：凯特芮娜不出嫁，他们就别想娶碧昂卡。他们商量好要联手给凯特芮娜找个丈夫。

1 Proverbs

Gremio and Hortensio use many proverbs when discussing how to get Katherina married off so they can woo Bianca.

a Read through lines 105–36 and note down as many proverbs as you can. When you have finished, write a modern equivalent for each one.

b Why do you think Shakespeare gave these characters so many proverbs? What is their effect? Do they show Gremio and Hortensio as wise men of the world, or as two-dimensional characters who have no original thoughts of their own?

2 Gremio and Hortensio (in small groups)

a Flick back through this scene to remind yourself about these two suitors. Remember that the rich old lover and the poor young lover in disguise are stock characters (固定角色；模式化人物) from the Italian *commedia dell'arte*, but they may not necessarily conform to those stereotypes. How would you portray them and what props would you give them to add new dimensions to their characters?

b List your impressions of Gremio and Hortensio in terms of age, looks, ways of speaking, wealth, dress, opinions and attitudes. Pool your ideas and see how similar your interpretations are.

3 Inner voices (in fours)

The competing suitors have joined forces, but what are they really thinking?

- Two of you read lines 111–27, a sentence at a time. The other pair 'shadows' them by suggesting at the end of each sentence what Gremio and Hortensio are secretly thinking.

Language in the play 剧中语言
Insulting language

- How do Gremio and Hortensio talk about Katherina? Look for language that refers to cattle markets and to instruments of social punishment. What does this language reveal about how the two men regard Katherina? What does it tell us about their personalities? Is this sort of language commonly used to describe women today?

- Use these questions as a starting point for a discussion on how perceptions of women have changed (or not) since Shakespeare wrote this play.

1 devil's dam 魔鬼他娘（悍妇的原型）
2 blow our nails 静观其变
3 fast it fairly out 过好自己的日子
4 Our … sides 我们俩都失败了
5 light on 遇到
6 wish 推荐
7 brooked parle 有商量的余地
8 advice 反思
9 toucheth 关系到
10 labour and effect 努力促成
11 so very a fool 不折不扣的傻子
12 Tush 闭嘴；得啦；呸
13 alarums 责骂
14 with all faults 连带着缺点（牛市用语，表示出售的牛都会有些毛病）
15 lief 愿意
16 high cross 立在城镇中心市场上的十字架（当时在斯特拉特福这样的乡镇常见犯人受惩罚的场景）
17 bar in law 法律设置的障碍（这里指巴普提斯塔立下的长女先嫁的规矩）
18 Happy man be his dole! 愿胜者有福！

THE TAMING OF THE SHREW ACT 1 SCENE 1
悍妇降服记

GREMIO You may go to the devil's dam[1]! Your gifts are so good here's none will hold you. There! Love is not so great, Hortensio, but we may blow our nails[2] together and fast it fairly out[3]. Our cake's dough on both sides[4]. Farewell. Yet, for the love I bear my sweet Bianca, if I can by any means light on[5] a fit man to teach her that wherein she delights, I will wish[6] him to her father.

HORTENSIO So will I, Signor Gremio. But a word, I pray. Though the nature of our quarrel yet never brooked parle[7], know now, upon advice[8], it toucheth[9] us both – that we may yet again have access to our fair mistress and be happy rivals in Bianca's love – to labour and effect[10] one thing specially.

GREMIO What's that, I pray?

HORTENSIO Marry, sir, to get a husband for her sister.

GREMIO A husband? A devil!

HORTENSIO I say a husband.

GREMIO I say a devil. Think'st thou, Hortensio, though her father be very rich, any man is so very a fool[11] to be married to hell?

HORTENSIO Tush[12], Gremio. Though it pass your patience and mine to endure her loud alarums[13] – why, man, there be good fellows in the world, and a man could light on them, would take her with all faults[14], and money enough.

GREMIO I cannot tell. But I had as lief[15] take her dowry with this condition: to be whipped at the high cross[16] every morning.

HORTENSIO Faith, as you say, there's small choice in rotten apples. But come, since this bar in law[17] makes us friends, it shall be so far forth friendly maintained till by helping Baptista's eldest daughter to a husband we set his youngest free for a husband – and then have to't afresh. Sweet Bianca! Happy man be his dole![18] He that runs fastest gets the ring. How say you, Signor Gremio?

GREMIO I am agreed, and would I had given him the best horse in Padua to begin his wooing that would thoroughly woo her, wed her, and bed her, and rid the house of her. Come on.

Exeunt Gremio and Hortensio

Lucentio has fallen in love at first sight with Bianca and asks Tranio to help him. Tranio tries to bring his master down to earth, reminding him of the problem of Katherina.

剧情简介：卢森修对碧昂卡一见钟情，请川纽帮他。川纽提醒主人要立足现实，凯特芮娜是个难题。

1 'I burn! I pine, I perish' (in pairs)

What has Lucentio been doing to prompt Tranio's lines 137–8? His sudden love for Bianca is expressed in a way that modern audiences might find rather extreme (line 147).

- Take turns to sculpt each other into statues that represent Lucentio. Try to mould your partner into a pose that reflects how he might have looked to prompt (提示) Tranio's question: 'is it possible / That love should of a sudden take such hold?'

Language in the play 剧中语言
The language of love

a Lucentio's language is conventional and predictable. Try to find examples of the following in his lines opposite:

- His knowledge of the classics, which he uses in a way that echoes the extravagant expression of literary lovers throughout the ages.
- His use of conventions of love poetry to describe Bianca (her breath, her lips, her modesty, her beauty).

b How would you present Lucentio on stage? What kind of response would you hope to elicit from an audience through his language and behaviour? Write your ideas in a paragraph using embedded quotations and referring closely to the script opposite.

1 *love-in-idleness* 三色紫罗兰（据说有迷情功效；字面意思为"闲中生爱"）
2 *secret* 亲信
3 *Anna* 安娜（迦太基女王荻朵[Dido]的妹妹和智囊）
4 *rated* 通过责骂来驱除
5 *Redime … minimo* 用尽可能小的代价赎回自己被俘虏的身体（拉丁语）
6 *so longly* 如此长时间
7 *pith* 关键问题
8 *daughter of Agenor* 阿基诺之女欧罗芭（Europa，以美貌著称）
9 *Jove* 乔武（罗马神话中最高的神，因爱慕欧罗芭而化成公牛，将她带到克里特岛[Crete]）
10 *strand* 海岸
11 *din* 大声吵闹
12 *trance* 入迷，恍惚
13 *curst and shrewd* 脾气火爆又乖戾
14 *Because* 以便，为的是
15 *annoyed with* 被打扰

THE TAMING OF THE SHREW ACT 1 SCENE 1
悍妇降服记

TRANIO	I pray sir, tell me, is it possible
	That love should of a sudden take such hold?
LUCENTIO	O Tranio, till I found it to be true
	I never thought it possible or likely.
	But see! while idly I stood looking on,
	I found the effect of love-in-idleness[1],
	And now in plainness do confess to thee
	That art to me as secret[2] and as dear
	As Anna[3] to the Queen of Carthage was –
	Tranio, I burn! I pine, I perish, Tranio,
	If I achieve not this young modest girl.
	Counsel me, Tranio, for I know thou canst;
	Assist me, Tranio, for I know thou wilt.
TRANIO	Master, it is no time to chide you now;
	Affection is not rated[4] from the heart.
	If love have touched you, naught remains but so:
	Redime te captum quam queas minimo[5].
LUCENTIO	Gramercies, lad. Go forward. This contents;
	The rest will comfort, for thy counsel's sound.
TRANIO	Master, you looked so longly[6] on the maid,
	Perhaps you marked not what's the pith[7] of all.
LUCENTIO	O yes, I saw sweet beauty in her face,
	Such as the daughter of Agenor[8] had,
	That made great Jove[9] to humble him to her hand
	When with his knees he kissed the Cretan strand[10].
TRANIO	Saw you no more? Marked you not how her sister
	Began to scold and raise up such a storm
	That mortal ears might hardly endure the din[11]?
LUCENTIO	Tranio, I saw her coral lips to move,
	And with her breath she did perfume the air.
	Sacred and sweet was all I saw in her.
TRANIO	Nay, then, 'tis time to stir him from his trance[12].
	I pray, awake, sir. If you love the maid
	Bend thoughts and wits to achieve her. Thus it stands:
	Her elder sister is so curst and shrewd[13]
	That, till the father rid his hands of her,
	Master, your love must live a maid at home,
	And therefore has he closely mewed her up,
	Because[14] she will not be annoyed with[15] suitors.

140
145
150
155
160
165
170
175

Lucentio and Tranio arrive at the same solution to enable Lucentio to win Bianca: Lucentio will become Bianca's schoolteacher. They exchange clothes, and Tranio adopts Lucentio's identity.

 剧情简介：卢森修和川纽同时想到了一个能让卢森修赢得碧昂卡芳心的办法：卢森修去做碧昂卡的教师。二人互换了衣物，川纽变身为卢森修。

Stagecraft 导演技巧
Master and servant (in pairs)

Lucentio frequently asks his servant Tranio for 'counsel' or advice. The cunning and worldly servant is another stock character from the Italian *commedia dell'arte* tradition, whose role is to explain the plot to his lovesick master.

- In your Director's Journal, write notes for the actors playing these two characters in a modern production. To what extent does Tranio take the upper hand? Do you see Lucentio as an intelligent man blinded by love, or do you think he is rather dim-witted?

1 Changing clothes (in small groups)

As Lucentio and Tranio swap clothes, there is great opportunity for farcical (荒唐) stage business.

a Work out how the exchange of clothes should be enacted. In particular, think about the effects of any onstage spectators at this point (previous productions have used passing nuns, policemen, waiters and an early entrance by Biondello). Write detailed stage directions for everything that would be happening at this point.

b Experiment with reading lines 193–208, exchanging clothes as you do so. Can you fit the lines to undressing and dressing again?

Themes 主题分析
Clothes and identity

Shakespeare's stage did not make use of elaborate scenery or stage mechanics, but the actors did have lavish (华丽) costumes. This is one reason for the interest Shakespeare shows in clothes as part of the plot (in the form of disguises and identity swapping) and as part of the **imagery** (the metaphorical references to clothes to explore the theme of appearance and reality).

- Begin compiling a list of references to clothes and of imagery that relates to clothing in the play. Start with what you have seen so far in this act. Add to this list as you continue reading, bearing in mind the following question: how do these references to clothing link to the ideas of appearance and reality, disguise, and social roles or status that are raised in the play?

1 art thou not advised 你听没听到
2 hand 部分
3 inventions 想法；计划
4 meet and jump in one 不谋而合
5 device 办法；计划
6 Keep house （在家）招待客人
7 ply his book 研究学问
8 *Basta!* 够了！（意大利语）
9 I have it full 我已经完全想好了
10 in my stead 代替我
11 port 生活方式
12 hatched 决定了
13 Uncase thee 脱下你的外衣
14 coloured hat and cloak （伊丽莎白时代，绅士多穿色彩艳丽的衣服）
15 sith = since （既然）
16 serviceable to 尽心服侍

THE TAMING OF THE SHREW ACT 1 SCENE 1
悍妇降服记

LUCENTIO   Ah, Tranio, what a cruel father's he!
But art thou not advised[1] he took some care
To get her cunning schoolmasters to instruct her?

TRANIO   Ay, marry, am I, sir – and now 'tis plotted!

LUCENTIO   I have it, Tranio!

TRANIO   Master, for my hand[2],   180
Both our inventions[3] meet and jump in one[4].

LUCENTIO   Tell me thine first.

TRANIO   You will be schoolmaster
And undertake the teaching of the maid –
That's your device[5].

LUCENTIO   It is. May it be done?

TRANIO   Not possible. For who shall bear your part   185
And be in Padua here Vincentio's son,
Keep house[6], and ply his book[7], welcome his friends,
Visit his countrymen and banquet them?

LUCENTIO   *Basta!*[8] Content thee, for I have it full[9].
We have not yet been seen in any house,   190
Nor can we be distinguished by our faces
For man or master. Then it follows thus:
Thou shalt be master, Tranio, in my stead[10];
Keep house and port[11] and servants as I should.
I will some other be – some Florentine,   195
Some Neapolitan or meaner man of Pisa.
'Tis hatched[12] and shall be so. Tranio, at once
Uncase thee[13]; take my coloured hat and cloak[14].
            [*They exchange clothes.*]
When Biondello comes, he waits on thee,
But I will charm him first to keep his tongue.   200

TRANIO   So had you need.
In brief, sir, sith[15] it your pleasure is,
And I am tied to be obedient –
For so your father charged me at our parting:
'Be serviceable to[16] my son', quoth he,   205
Although I think 'twas in another sense –
I am content to be Lucentio,
Because so well I love Lucentio.

Biondello, another servant, is confused when he sees that his master and Tranio have exchanged clothes. Lucentio invents a story that it is a disguise to prevent his arrest for murder. Biondello is sworn to secrecy.

剧情简介：卢森修的另一个仆人卞代娄见到互换了装束的主人和川纽，迷惑不解。卢森修谎称他杀了人，为摆脱追捕而乔装打扮。卞代娄发誓保密。

Language in the play 剧中语言
Iambic pentameter (抑扬五音步)

You will have noticed that some characters speak in prose and others speak in verse. In lines 216–24, Lucentio addresses his servant Biondello in blank verse. He uses unrhymed lines in **iambic pentameter**, with carefully placed stressed and unstressed syllables that create a rhythm like a heartbeat (da DUM, da DUM, da DUM, da DUM, da DUM).

a Read lines 216–24 aloud with this rhythm in mind – either walking around the room or tapping a beat on the table.

b Why do you think Shakespeare gives Lucentio blank verse for his elaborate explanation to Biondello? What effect does the language have on the servant (see line 225)?

1 Another servant (in pairs)

a Lucentio doesn't seem to trust Biondello as much as he trusts Tranio. Does this show in the way Lucentio speaks to each of them? Discuss this in your pairs.

b Read aloud lines 216–28 together in the following three ways:
- in whispers, as if they conceal a vital secret
- loudly, as if they are military orders
- with humour, as if they are a practical joke.

Then discuss the effects each version has and decide which you think works best.

Write about it 写作练习
Another suitor for Bianca? (in pairs)

Lucentio hints that he has good reasons for ordering Tranio to become a further suitor for Bianca (line 238).

- Work together to write a **soliloquy** (独白) for Lucentio to deliver after the other characters leave the stage. In it, he should explain why he thinks this is a good idea (use what you know of his plans so far to help you). Write the soliloquy in the style of language that Lucentio uses in the script opposite. Take turns to read your soliloquy aloud to another pair.

1 thralled 俘获
2 wounded eye 受伤的眼球（即眼球被爱神丘比特的箭射中）
3 fellow 伙伴（服侍同一个主子的仆人）
4 Pray = Please
5 what's the news 出了什么事
6 frame your manners 改变您的行为举止
7 count'nance 外貌体态；举止
8 descried 被认出
9 as becomes 得体
10 Ay = Yes
11 Ne'er a whit 一点儿也不
12 not a jot 一个字也别（提）
13 The better for him! 他倒占了便宜！
14 use your manners 规规矩矩
15 rests 还有……（要办）
16 execute （要）办
17 Sufficeth 就够了

LUCENTIO	Tranio, be so, because Lucentio loves,	
	And let me be a slave t'achieve that maid	210
	Whose sudden sight hath thralled[1] my wounded eye[2].	

Enter BIONDELLO.

	Here comes the rogue. Sirrah, where have you been?	
BIONDELLO	Where have I been? Nay, how now, where are you?	
	Master, has my fellow[3] Tranio stolen your clothes or you stolen his,	
	or both? Pray[4], what's the news[5]?	215
LUCENTIO	Sirrah, come hither. 'Tis no time to jest,	
	And therefore frame your manners[6] to the time.	
	Your fellow Tranio here, to save my life,	
	Puts my apparel and my count'nance[7] on,	
	And I for my escape have put on his;	220
	For in a quarrel since I came ashore	
	I killed a man, and fear I was descried[8].	
	Wait you on him, I charge you, as becomes[9],	
	While I make way from hence to save my life.	
	You understand me?	
BIONDELLO	Ay[10], sir. Ne'er a whit[11].	225
LUCENTIO	And not a jot[12] of 'Tranio' in your mouth:	
	Tranio is changed into Lucentio.	
BIONDELLO	The better for him![13] Would I were so too.	
TRANIO	So could I, faith, boy, to have the next wish after –	
	That Lucentio indeed had Baptista's youngest daughter.	230
	But, sirrah, not for my sake but your master's, I advise	
	You use your manners[14] discreetly in all kind of companies.	
	When I am alone, why then I am Tranio,	
	But in all places else your master Lucentio.	
LUCENTIO	Tranio, let's go.	235
	One thing more rests[15] that thyself execute[16]:	
	To make one among these wooers. If thou ask me why,	
	Sufficeth[17] my reasons are both good and weighty.	

Exeunt

Christopher Sly seems to be wearying of the play. In Scene 2, Petruchio – newly arrived from Verona – quarrels with his servant Grumio outside the house of his friend Hortensio. He strikes Grumio.

剧情简介：克瑞斯特夫·斯雷似乎看戏看得有点儿倦了。第二场，刚从维罗纳来的珀楚秋在好友郝坦修的家门口和自己的仆人葛儒缪争吵起来。珀楚秋打了葛儒缪。

Stagecraft 导演技巧
The disappearance of Sly

a Many critics have wondered why, once the play-within-a-play begins, Sly disappears completely (together with his 'wife', servants and the Lord), except for a brief appearance here at the end of Scene 1.

- Is this because the purpose of the Induction was simply to set the scene and establish the thematic concerns for the more important performance about the taming of the shrew? What common themes have you noticed so far?

b Some productions remain true to the original, but in others the players in the 'taming' story have directed particular lines to Sly, and he has even joined in the dialogue.

- What effect could this sort of interaction between Sly (from the Induction) and characters from the 'taming' story have on the audience? Would it allow Sly to comment on what is going on, or would it offer opportunities for comic interruptions?

c Sometimes the actor playing Sly doubles as Petruchio and the actress playing the Hostess (who throws Sly out of the ale house) doubles as Katherina.

- This would explain why Sly seems to disappear. But what comment might the director be making by linking the drunken Sly who dreams he is a lord with Petruchio, and the angry Hostess with Katherina the shrew?

1 *Presenters* 评介人（以观众身份介绍、解释剧情或加以评论的角色）
2 nod 打盹儿
3 mind 观看
4 Saint Anne 圣安妮（圣母马利亚的母亲，耶稣的外祖母）
5 *mark* 注意
6 of all 尤其
7 trow 相信
8 rebused 冒犯（葛儒缪本想说abused）
9 knock me 给我打
10 rap 敲打
11 pate 头
12 I should … worst 我知道如果我先打您，您一定会更狠地打我
13 and = if
14 ring it 摇铃（ring与wring谐音）
15 *sol-fa* 唱曲（sol-fa，又写作solfa或sol fa，既是名词，表示音阶名称，也可以是谓词，表示唱出sol-fa音阶 [do、re、mi、fa、sol、la、si] 来）

Language in the play 剧中语言
Knock, knock (in pairs)

Elizabethans thoroughly enjoyed wordplay such as **puns** (words with double meanings, see p. 189). In the script opposite, Petruchio and Grumio play on different meanings of the word 'knock'. Shakespeare may also have intended Grumio to understand 'here' in line 8 as 'ear'.

- Read lines 1–19 and lines 27–40. At each mention of 'knocking', one of you mimes (演哑剧) what Petruchio means and the other mimes what Grumio means.

The Taming of the Shrew Act 1 Scene 2
悍妇降服记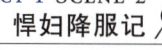

The Presenters[1] above speaks.

LORD	My lord, you nod[2]; you do not mind[3] the play.	
SLY	Yes, by Saint Anne[4], do I. A good matter surely. Comes there any more of it?	240
BARTHOLOMEW	My lord, 'tis but begun.	
SLY	'Tis a very excellent piece of work, madam lady. Would 'twere done!	

They sit and mark[5].

Act 1 Scene 2
Outside Hortensio's house

Enter PETRUCHIO *and his man* GRUMIO.

PETRUCHIO Verona, for a while I take my leave
To see my friends in Padua, but of all[6]
My best belovèd and approvèd friend,
Hortensio: and I trow[7] this is his house.
Here, sirrah Grumio, knock, I say.   5

GRUMIO Knock, sir? Whom should I knock? Is there any man has rebused[8] your worship?

PETRUCHIO Villain, I say, knock me[9] here soundly.

GRUMIO Knock you here, sir? Why, sir, what am I, sir, that I should knock you here, sir?   10

PETRUCHIO Villain, I say, knock me at this gate,
And rap[10] me well, or I'll knock your knave's pate[11]!

GRUMIO My master is grown quarrelsome. I should knock you first,
And then I know after who comes by the worst[12].

PETRUCHIO Will it not be?   15
Faith, sirrah, and[13] you'll not knock, I'll ring it[14].
I'll try how you can *sol-fa*[15], and sing it.
He wrings him by the ears.

GRUMIO Help, mistress, help! My master is mad.

PETRUCHIO Now knock when I bid you, sirrah villain.

Hortensio welcomes Petruchio. Grumio complains about Petruchio's 'knocking' but Hortensio urges peace between master and servant. Petruchio explains that he is broadening his mind and looking for a wife.

 剧情简介：郝坦修欢迎珀楚秋，葛儒缪抱怨珀楚秋的"敲打"，郝坦修劝主仆二人和好。珀楚秋解释他此行目的是想见见世面，再讨个老婆。

Characters 人物分析

'We will compound this quarrel' (in pairs)

a Hortensio tries to settle the disagreement between Petruchio and Grumio. Read how each gives his side of the story in lines 20–44, then re-enact the event in lines 5–19 using the following prompts:

- Grumio innocently misunderstands and Petruchio treats him harshly.
- Grumio deliberately misunderstands in order to annoy Petruchio, and Petruchio responds out of frustration.

b Discuss how each interpretation reflects on the characters. What does this show about their relationship? Is Petruchio demanding and cruel, or frustrated and soft-hearted? Is Grumio aggravating (故意惹恼) or simple-minded and childish?

Language in the play 剧中语言

Language and status

Petruchio and Hortensio speak in verse and also in Italian, showing their education and status (although when Petruchio speaks to his servant, he uses prose). In contrast, Grumio speaks in prose and mistakes the Italian for Latin, showing that he has no education in either language.

a How would you advise actors playing these characters to speak and act to match the distinction made by their language?

b In pairs, read the lines twice, varying the delivery and using appropriate gestures.

1 What kind of person is Petruchio? (in pairs)

a Read aloud lines 47–55 and make notes detailing what you discover about Petruchio's character and his plans while in Padua. What image is Petruchio presenting of himself – that of a romantic stranger or a mercenary (贪财) adventurer?

b Why does Petruchio mention his father's death in line 51 (and then again in lines 98 and 185)? Might this indicate his loss and loneliness, or his dismissive indifference? Experiment with ways of performing these lines, adapting tone, volume and gesture to suit your impression of Petruchio at this point in the play.

1 *Con … trovato* 今日得见，三生有幸（意大利语）
2 *Alla … Petruchio* 欢迎尊贵的珀楚秋先生光临寒舍（意大利语）
3 compound 和解
4 ledges 声称
5 two … out 过分了（当时流行牌戏one-and-thirty，two and thirty在牌面上多出一个点 [pip]）
6 pledge 担保人
7 heavy chance 不幸事件
8 'twixt = between
9 ancient 长期
10 pleasant 风趣
11 in a few 简单地说
12 maze 迷宫
13 Happily 幸运
14 Crowns 金币或银币

The Taming of the Shrew Act 1 Scene 2
悍妇降服记

Enter HORTENSIO.

HORTENSIO How now, what's the matter? My old friend Grumio and my good friend Petruchio! How do you all at Verona?

PETRUCHIO Signor Hortensio, come you to part the fray?
Con tutto il cuore ben trovato[1], may I say.

HORTENSIO *Alla nostra casa ben venuto*
Molto honorato signor mio Petruchio[2].
Rise, Grumio, rise. We will compound[3] this quarrel.

GRUMIO Nay, 'tis no matter, sir, what he ledges[4] in Latin. If this be not a lawful cause for me to leave his service – look you, sir: he bid me knock him and rap him soundly, sir. Well, was it fit for a servant to use his master so, being perhaps, for aught I see, two and thirty, a pip out[5]?
Whom would to God I had well knocked at first,
Then had not Grumio come by the worst.

PETRUCHIO A senseless villain! Good Hortensio,
I bade the rascal knock upon your gate
And could not get him for my heart to do it.

GRUMIO Knock at the gate? O heavens! Spake you not these words plain: 'Sirrah, knock me here, rap me here, knock me well, and knock me soundly'? And come you now with 'knocking at the gate'?

PETRUCHIO Sirrah, be gone, or talk not, I advise you.

HORTENSIO Petruchio, patience. I am Grumio's pledge[6].
Why this' a heavy chance[7] 'twixt[8] him and you –
Your ancient[9], trusty, pleasant[10] servant Grumio.
And tell me now, sweet friend, what happy gale
Blows you to Padua here from old Verona?

PETRUCHIO Such wind as scatters young men through the world
To seek their fortunes farther than at home
Where small experience grows. But, in a few[11],
Signor Hortensio, thus it stands with me:
Antonio my father is deceased
And I have thrust myself into this maze[12],
Happily[13] to wive and thrive as best I may.
Crowns[14] in my purse I have, and goods at home,
And so am come abroad to see the world.

Hortensio promises Petruchio a rich wife, and Petruchio declares he will marry anyone who has money. Hortensio describes Katherina's good and bad points. Petruchio is eager to meet her at once.

剧情简介：郝坦修答应给珀楚秋找个富有的妻子，珀楚秋称只要有钱不管是谁他都愿意娶。郝坦修描述了凯特芮娜的优点和缺点，珀楚秋表示想马上见到她。

Characters

Love or money? (in sixes)

Two volunteers slowly read aloud Petruchio's lines 45–55 and 62–73. Everyone else listens carefully. Whenever you hear a word connected with money, 'echo' it in a whisper. Repeat the activity with a different pair of readers, but this time echo every word connected with love. Afterwards, discuss what connection there is between love and money – and what Petruchio's words reveal about his character.

1 Hortensio's motives (in pairs)

What *exactly* is Hortensio up to in lines 56–61? Read his lines with emphasis to show what he might be thinking. Then write an aside for him in order to reveal more of his plans to the audience. Remember that an aside is a dramatic device that gives important insights into a character's thoughts and feelings.

▼ Katherina's behaviour prompts harsh words and sometimes rough treatment from characters such as her father (far left) and Petruchio (holding Katherina).

1 come roundly　直截了当地说
2 shrewd　暴躁粗鲁；爱指使人
3 ill-favoured　脾气坏（一般指相貌丑陋，但这里指脾气不好）
4 burden　音乐伴奏；副歌
5 As … dance　我求婚为的是钱财
6 foul　丑陋
7 Florentius　弗罗伦修斯（英国诗人约翰·高尔 [John Gower, 1330—1408] 的《恋人的告白》[Confessio Amantis] 中的骑士，为了活命娶了一个丑老太婆）
8 Sibyl　悉碧尔（神话中原本美貌的女预言家，用她的爱情向阿波罗交换永生时忘记要求永葆青春，始终老而不死）
9 Xanthippe　赞蒂琵（古希腊哲学家苏格拉底之妻，以凶悍闻名）
10 edge　热切，强烈
11 swelling Adriatic seas　波涛汹涌的亚德里亚海
12 aglet-baby　雕刻的小人儿
13 trot　丑老太婆
14 nothing … withal　金钱先行，路路畅通 (withal = in addition)
15 intolerable curst　脾气坏得让人无法忍受
16 board　追求
17 crack　相撞，爆炸

HORTENSIO	Petruchio, shall I then come roundly[1] to thee	
	And wish thee to a shrewd[2] ill-favoured[3] wife?	
	Thou'dst thank me but a little for my counsel –	
	And yet I'll promise thee she shall be rich,	
	And very rich. But th'art too much my friend,	60
	And I'll not wish thee to her.	
PETRUCHIO	Signor Hortensio, 'twixt such friends as we	
	Few words suffice, and therefore, if thou know	
	One rich enough to be Petruchio's wife –	
	As wealth is burden[4] of my wooing dance[5] –	65
	Be she as foul[6] as was Florentius'[7] love,	
	As old as Sibyl[8], and as curst and shrewd	
	As Socrates' Xanthippe[9] or a worse,	
	She moves me not, or not removes at least	
	Affection's edge[10] in me, were she as rough	70
	As are the swelling Adriatic seas[11].	
	I come to wive it wealthily in Padua;	
	If wealthily, then happily in Padua.	
GRUMIO	Nay, look you sir, he tells you flatly what his mind is. Why, give him gold enough and marry him to a puppet or an aglet-baby[12] or an old trot[13] with ne'er a tooth in her head, though she have as many diseases as two and fifty horses. Why, nothing comes amiss, so money comes withal[14].	75
HORTENSIO	Petruchio, since we are stepped thus far in,	
	I will continue that I broached in jest.	80
	I can, Petruchio, help thee to a wife	
	With wealth enough, and young, and beauteous,	
	Brought up as best becomes a gentlewoman.	
	Her only fault – and that is faults enough –	
	Is that she is intolerable curst[15],	85
	And shrewd and froward so beyond all measure	
	That, were my state far worser than it is,	
	I would not wed her for a mine of gold!	
PETRUCHIO	Hortensio, peace. Thou know'st not gold's effect.	
	Tell me her father's name and 'tis enough,	90
	For I will board[16] her though she chide as loud	
	As thunder when the clouds in autumn crack[17].	

Petruchio is instantly attracted by Hortensio's description of Katherina. Hortensio admits his own interest in Bianca. He asks Petruchio to introduce him, disguised as a potential music teacher, to Baptista.

剧情简介：听了郝坦修对凯特芮娜的介绍，珀楚秋立刻有了兴趣。郝坦修坦言他自己对碧昂卡的好感，他想化装成音乐教师，请珀楚秋把自己介绍给巴普提斯塔。

1 Who's who? (in fives)

- Stand or sit in a circle. One person slowly reads Hortensio's lines 111–22. The others point to a particular person in the group every time a certain character is referred to (by name, or as he, she, I, and so on). It sounds complicated, but try it. You'll find it's easy to pick up. Afterwards, repeat the exercise with a different reader.
- In your groups, discuss what this activity reveals about the plot at this point, and also what it tells us about Hortensio.

2 Stereotyping (刻板印象) (in threes)

'Katherine the curst' say Hortensio and Grumio – and so Katherina is pigeon-holed (将某人轻率分类) by the men. Think up similar labels for other characters that have appeared so far in the play:

- Bianca the …
- Petruchio the …
- Baptista the …
- Tranio the …
- Sly the …

Language in the play 剧中语言
Romantic love

Hortensio and Bianca's other suitors use conventions of love poetry when talking about her. The romanticism of their language, and their descriptions of her as a 'jewel' or as 'treasure' that is locked away, contrast sharply with the language used to describe Katherina. One common feature of love poetry was the description of different parts of the beloved's body (eyes, lips, breath, hands or heart) using flattering **metaphors** (隐喻) or **similes** (明喻) (see p. 188).

- Look online to find a version of Shakespeare's Sonnet 130, which uses this feature of romantic poetry but also makes fun of it.
- Compose either a poem that Hortensio might write to Bianca or a poem that Petruchio might write to Katherina. Consider modernising your own poem by writing it as song lyrics or creating a rap version.

1	give you over	跟您告别
2	thither	= there
3	humour	兴致，劲头
4	A'	= On
5	And	= If
6	rail in his rope-tricks	用一串粗话咒骂（这里的rope-tricks 既是rhetoric之讹，又是tricks worthy of the rope [该判绞刑]的骂法）
7	stand	质疑，抵抗
8	throw a figure	破口大骂（figure指修辞手法）
9	disfigure … cat	把她吓得目瞪口呆，招架不住
10	keep	无法靠近的堡垒
11	other more	其他爱慕者
12	do me grace	帮我个忙
13	Well seen	精通
14	make love	求爱；谈情说爱

THE TAMING OF THE SHREW ACT 1 SCENE 2
悍妇降服记

HORTENSIO	Her father is Baptista Minola,	
	An affable and courteous gentleman.	
	Her name is Katherina Minola,	95
	Renowned in Padua for her scolding tongue.	
PETRUCHIO	I know her father, though I know not her,	
	And he knew my deceasèd father well.	
	I will not sleep, Hortensio, till I see her,	
	And therefore let me be thus bold with you	100
	To give you over¹ at this first encounter –	
	Unless you will accompany me thither²?	
GRUMIO	I pray you, sir, let him go while the humour³ lasts. A'⁴ my word, and she knew him as well as I do, she would think scolding would do little good upon him. She may perhaps call him half a score knaves or so – why, that's nothing. And⁵ he begin once, he'll rail in his rope-tricks⁶. I'll tell you what, sir, and she stand⁷ him but a little, he will throw a figure⁸ in her face and so disfigure her with it that she shall have no more eyes to see withal than a cat⁹. You know him not, sir.	105 110
HORTENSIO	Tarry, Petruchio, I must go with thee,	
	For in Baptista's keep¹⁰ my treasure is.	
	He hath the jewel of my life in hold,	
	His youngest daughter, beautiful Bianca,	
	And her withholds from me and other more¹¹ –	115
	Suitors to her and rivals in my love –	
	Supposing it a thing impossible,	
	For those defects I have before rehearsed,	
	That ever Katherina will be wooed.	
	Therefore this order hath Baptista tane,	120
	That none shall have access unto Bianca	
	Till Katherine the curst have got a husband.	
GRUMIO	'Katherine the curst'!	
	A title for a maid of all titles the worst.	
HORTENSIO	Now shall my friend Petruchio do me grace¹²	125
	And offer me disguised in sober robes	
	To old Baptista as a schoolmaster	
	Well seen¹³ in music, to instruct Bianca,	
	That so I may by this device at least	
	Have leave and leisure to make love¹⁴ to her	130
	And unsuspected court her by herself.	

43

Petruchio, Hortensio and Grumio eavesdrop on Gremio. He is giving instructions to Lucentio (disguised as Cambio) on how to behave when teaching Bianca.

 剧情简介：珀楚秋、郝坦修、葛儒缪偷听葛莱缪说话。葛莱缪正在指导卢森修（假扮坎毕欧）教碧昂卡时如何注意自己的言谈举止。

1 'O this learning, what a thing it is!' (in pairs)

Gremio seems delighted to have found Cambio (Lucentio). We, of course, know that he is not a real schoolteacher, but Lucentio does not appear to have had any problem pretending to be one so far.

- First improvise (即兴表演) and then write down the conversation that took place when Gremio interviewed 'Cambio'. Remember that Lucentio is very anxious to secure the job, and Gremio is equally keen to gain the services of someone who will please Baptista. Bear in mind your earlier opinion about whether Lucentio is as heroic and intelligent as he thinks he is, as well as how old and foolish Gremio actually is.

> ### Language in the play 剧中语言
> **Rhetoric and repetition**
>
> a Lines 153–6 contain features of language that have great comic effect. Identify the repetition of language features and the use of sound echoes in the script opposite.
>   - Look out for anaphora (where a word or phrase is repeated at the *beginning* of successive clauses) and **epistrophe*** (where a word or phrase is repeated at the *end* of a series of clauses).
>   - Look out also for repetitions during the asides of each of the characters – remember, repetition could also be evident in their tone and gestures.
>
> b How would you stage lines 153–6 to use these language features to greatest comic effect?

2 They stand aside (in small groups)

For most of this scene, there are two (possibly three) groups on the stage:

- Hortensio, Petruchio and Grumio
- Lucentio and Gremio
- Sly, his 'wife' and the others (if they are still watching).

How would you stage this? Work out two (or three) tableaux, one for each group of characters, which show something about the relationships between those in the group. Bear in mind that Grumio is a servant. Would his social status make a difference to his position in the group?

---

1 *Cambio* （意大利语，意为"交换"）
2 knavery 骗人的行为
3 proper stripling 帅小伙儿（葛儒缪故意讽刺）
4 amorous 多情种
5 perused 细看了
6 note 书单
7 see that at any hand 无论怎样都要保证
8 liberality 慷慨、出手大方
9 mend it with a largess 增加一份钱
10 still in place 一直在场
11 woodcock 傻子，缺心眼，笨鸟
12 Trow you = Do you know
13 Fit for her turn 正适合她

* epistrophe 尾词重复，例如：We are born to sorrow, pass our time in sorrow, end our days in sorrow.

THE TAMING OF THE SHREW ACT 1 SCENE 2
悍妇降服记

Enter GREMIO, *and* LUCENTIO *disguised* [*as Cambio¹, a schoolmaster*].

GRUMIO Here's no knavery²! See, to beguile the old folks, how the young folks lay their heads together. Master, master, look about you! Who goes there, ha?

HORTENSIO Peace, Grumio. It is the rival of my love. 135
Petruchio, stand by a while.

GRUMIO A proper stripling³, and an amorous⁴!
[*They stand aside.*]

GREMIO O, very well, I have perused⁵ the note⁶.
Hark you, sir, I'll have them very fairly bound –
All books of love, see that at any hand⁷ – 140
And see you read no other lectures to her:
You understand me. Over and beside
Signor Baptista's liberality⁸
I'll mend it with a largess⁹. Take your paper too
And let me have them very well perfumed, 145
For she is sweeter than perfume itself
To whom they go to. What will you read to her?

LUCENTIO Whate'er I read to her I'll plead for you
As for my patron, stand you so assured
As firmly as yourself were still in place¹⁰ – 150
Yea and perhaps with more successful words
Than you, unless you were a scholar, sir.

GREMIO O this learning, what a thing it is!

GRUMIO [*Aside*] O this woodcock¹¹, what an ass it is!

PETRUCHIO [*Aside*] Peace, sirrah. 155

HORTENSIO [*Aside*] Grumio, mum.
[*Coming forward.*]
God save you, Signor Gremio.

GREMIO And you are well met, Signor Hortensio.
Trow you¹² whither I am going? To Baptista Minola.
I promised to inquire carefully
About a schoolmaster for the fair Bianca, 160
And by good fortune I have lighted well
On this young man, for learning and behaviour
Fit for her turn¹³, well read in poetry
And other books – good ones, I warrant ye.

45

Hortensio tells Gremio that he has found somebody prepared to marry Katherina. Gremio is amazed, but Petruchio assures him that he knows about Katherina's faults and is still determined to wed her.

剧情简介：郝坦修告诉葛莱缪他已经找到愿意娶凯特芮娜的人，葛莱缪惊奇不已，但珀楚秋向他保证已经了解凯特芮娜的缺点并执意娶她。

1 Petruchio's past (in small groups)

Petruchio is introduced to the other characters as the man prepared to take on Katherina. What impression does he want to create?

a Stand in a circle and read Petruchio's lines 192–204 through twice. The first time, stress the verbs; the second time, emphasise all the words concerned with sound.

b Discuss whether you think Petruchio is just boasting or whether some of his claims are true. Does it even matter? Work together to rewrite his speech, imagining he is talking to a room full of women.

▶ Is this how you imagine Petruchio? Why or why not? What line from the script opposite do you think he might be saying?

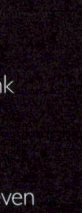

1 another 另一位教师
2 bags 钱袋子
3 vent 谈论
4 speak me fair 对我客客气气
5 indifferent good 同样有好处
6 Upon … liking 如果咱们出的钱财令他满意
7 What countryman? 您老家在哪儿？
8 lives for me 全是我的
9 were = would be
10 if … name 如果您真想娶她，那就大胆去吧
11 Will … her （此话源自两个俗语：better to be half hanged than ill wed [与其成怨偶，不如半入土]; wedding and hanging go by destiny [婚姻与绞索都是命中注定]）
12 daunt 吓倒，使气馁
13 puffed up with winds 被风吹得卷起大浪
14 chafèd 恼怒

Language in the play 剧中语言
Petruchio's speech

Petruchio makes use of anaphora in his impassioned speech in lines 192–204. How would you advise an actor playing Petruchio to use gestures to emphasise this device and build up a vivid picture of his exploits? Write out your ideas as notes in your Director's Journal, ready for a meeting with the actor.

Write about it 写作练习
Grumio's commentary

Grumio is an expert in formulating witty and critical comments about the other characters. Write out a few comments that Grumio might offer as asides while Petruchio is speaking in the script opposite. (For prompts, see lines 170 and 191, and also lines 137 and 154.)

HORTENSIO	'Tis well. And I have met a gentleman	165
	Hath promised me to help me to another[1],	
	A fine musician to instruct our mistress.	
	So shall I no whit be behind in duty	
	To fair Bianca, so beloved of me.	
GREMIO	Beloved of me, and that my deeds shall prove.	170
GRUMIO	[*Aside*] And that his bags[2] shall prove.	
HORTENSIO	Gremio, 'tis now no time to vent[3] our love.	
	Listen to me, and if you speak me fair[4],	
	I'll tell you news indifferent good[5] for either.	
	Here is a gentleman whom by chance I met,	175
	[*Presents Petruchio.*]	
	Upon agreement from us to his liking[6],	
	Will undertake to woo curst Katherine,	
	Yea, and to marry her, if her dowry please.	
GREMIO	So said, so done, is well.	
	Hortensio, have you told him all her faults?	180
PETRUCHIO	I know she is an irksome, brawling scold.	
	If that be all, masters, I hear no harm.	
GREMIO	No? Say'st me so, friend? What countryman?[7]	
PETRUCHIO	Born in Verona, old Antonio's son.	
	My father dead, my fortune lives for me[8],	185
	And I do hope good days and long to see.	
GREMIO	O sir, such a life with such a wife were[9] strange.	
	But if you have a stomach, to't a God's name[10]!	
	You shall have me assisting you in all.	
	But will you woo this wildcat?	
PETRUCHIO	Will I live?	190
GRUMIO	Will he woo her? Ay, or I'll hang her[11].	
PETRUCHIO	Why came I hither but to that intent?	
	Think you a little din can daunt[12] mine ears?	
	Have I not in my time heard lions roar?	
	Have I not heard the sea, puffed up with winds[13],	195
	Rage like an angry boar chafèd[14] with sweat?	

Petruchio continues to recount his past exploits and bravery. Gremio is impressed. However, Hortensio and Gremio are suspicious of Tranio's interest in the Minola family.

 剧情简介：珀楚秋接着讲述了他当年的功绩和勇猛，葛莱缪很钦佩。然而，郝坦修和葛莱缪发现川纽对米讷拉家很感兴趣，心生怀疑。

1 The lovers: competitive men (in small groups)

Lines 212–30 are complicated but fascinating:

- Hortensio and Gremio are jealous of any interest shown in Bianca by Tranio.
- This is the first time that Tranio will play the part of his master Lucentio.
- Lucentio is on the sidelines, egging on (怂恿，唆使) Tranio.

a In your Director's Journal, write notes about how you would direct this section to ensure that the audience can see how each character attempts to assert his authority over the others. (Some productions have even staged comic fights at this point.)

b Casting decisions will, of course, have a significant influence on the play. For example, what are the relative ages of the competing suitors? How suitable are they as potential husbands? Would a woman really be interested in any of them? Talk together about how you would cast the characters that appear in the script opposite.

Characters 人物分析

Comic pairs (in pairs)

Concentrate on a pair of characters (for example, Hortensio and Gremio). Create a comic tableau to show how the pair see themselves. Then turn it around, and depict how the other characters might see them. Show your tableaux to the class.

Stagecraft 导演技巧

Shared lines (in small groups)

Lines 212–30 contain many shared lines – and shared **rhyming couplets** (押韵二行连句；对偶句) (see p. 189) – between the characters.

a Read through this passage again, thinking about the effect created by lines being shared between two competitive and jealous men. Talk together about the effect created by the rhyming couplets they share.

b How would you want the characters to speak and act these lines on stage? Write detailed directions to help the actors.

1 ordnance 大炮
2 pitchèd battle 两军对阵
3 'larums 战场上紧急备战的号令
4 fear boys 吓唬小孩儿
5 bugs 小妖精
6 fears none 什么都不怕
7 charge 费用
8 readiest 最快
9 He … mean? (卞代娄这样说是为了让其他人一下子明白川纽想要找哪家)
10 Even he 正是他
11 What have you to do? 这跟您有什么关系？
12 at any hand 无论如何
13 chiders 爱骂人的人
14 ere = before

48

	Have I not heard great ordnance¹ in the field,	
	And heaven's artillery thunder in the skies?	
	Have I not in a pitchèd battle² heard	
	Loud 'larums³, neighing steeds and trumpets' clang?	200
	And do you tell me of a woman's tongue,	
	That gives not half so great a blow to hear	
	As will a chestnut in a farmer's fire?	
	Tush, tush, fear boys⁴ with bugs⁵!	
GRUMIO	For he fears none⁶.	
GREMIO	Hortensio, hark.	205
	This gentleman is happily arrived,	
	My mind presumes, for his own good and yours.	
HORTENSIO	I promised we would be contributors	
	And bear his charge⁷ of wooing, whatsoe'er.	
GREMIO	And so we will – provided that he win her.	210
GRUMIO	I would I were as sure of a good dinner.	

Enter TRANIO [*disguised as Lucentio*] *and* BIONDELLO.

TRANIO	Gentlemen, God save you. If I may be bold,	
	Tell me, I beseech you, which is the readiest⁸ way	
	To the house of Signor Baptista Minola?	
BIONDELLO	He that has the two fair daughters – is't he you mean?⁹	215
TRANIO	Even he¹⁰, Biondello.	
GREMIO	Hark you, sir, you mean not her to –	
TRANIO	Perhaps him and her, sir. What have you to do?¹¹	
PETRUCHIO	Not her that chides, sir, at any hand¹², I pray.	
TRANIO	I love no chiders¹³, sir. Biondello, let's away.	220
LUCENTIO	[*Aside*] Well begun, Tranio.	
HORTENSIO	Sir, a word ere¹⁴ you go.	
	Are you a suitor to the maid you talk of, yea or no?	
TRANIO	And if I be, sir, is it any offence?	
GREMIO	No, if without more words you will get you hence.	
TRANIO	Why, sir, I pray, are not the streets as free	225
	For me as for you?	
GREMIO	But so is not she.	
TRANIO	For what reason, I beseech you?	
GREMIO	For this reason, if you'll know –	
	That she's the choice love of Signor Gremio.	
HORTENSIO	That she's the chosen of Signor Hortensio.	230

Tranio announces his intention to become a suitor to Bianca. Petruchio tells Tranio of his own interest in Katherina and of Baptista's resolution that Katherina must marry before her sister.

 剧情简介：川纽宣布他要向碧昂卡求婚。珀楚秋告诉川纽，他自己对凯特芮娜很感兴趣，而且巴普提斯塔决心要先嫁长女凯特芮娜。

1 Tranio's 'performance' (in pairs)

One person reads Tranio's lines from the script opposite. The other echoes those parts where Tranio seems to be playing the gentleman. Take turns to say the lines with suitable gestures. How skilled an actor is Tranio? How much does he enjoy his role?

2 'I know he'll prove a jade' (in sixes)

Take a part each and read lines 212–42 several times. How well does Tranio carry off his impersonation (装扮) of his master Lucentio? As a result, how do you think Lucentio should speak line 242? Is he pleased with his servant's performance, or is he worried or annoyed?

▼ Gremio complains that Tranio will 'out-talk us all'. Try reading the script opposite seriously and ponderously (生硬地), then very quickly, with the characters cutting into one another's speeches. Which do you think works best?

1 Softly 慢慢来，别着急
2 Do me this right 劳驾
3 all 完全
4 Fair Leda's daughter 丽达的美貌女儿（指因其美貌引发特洛伊战争的海伦 [Helen]）
5 Paris 帕里斯（诱拐海伦的特洛伊王子）
6 speed 成功
7 out-talk 比……更能说
8 give him head 让他说下去试试
9 prove a jade 没有后劲（如同劣马）
10 beauteous modesty 文雅而温柔
11 let her go by 不要再提她了
12 Alcides 阿尔喀德斯（即赫丘力 [Hercules]，完成了12项"不可能完成的"任务。葛莱缪意指珀楚秋任务更加艰巨）
13 in sooth 明确
14 hearken for 想求婚

THE TAMING OF THE SHREW ACT 1 SCENE 2

悍妇降服记

TRANIO	Softly¹, my masters! If you be gentlemen,	
	Do me this right² – hear me with patience.	
	Baptista is a noble gentleman	
	To whom my father is not all³ unknown,	
	And were his daughter fairer than she is,	235
	She may more suitors have, and me for one.	
	Fair Leda's daughter⁴ had a thousand wooers;	
	Then well one more may fair Bianca have.	
	And so she shall: Lucentio shall make one,	
	Though Paris⁵ came in hope to speed⁶ alone.	240
GREMIO	What, this gentleman will out-talk⁷ us all!	
LUCENTIO	Sir, give him head⁸. I know he'll prove a jade⁹.	
PETRUCHIO	Hortensio, to what end are all these words?	
HORTENSIO	Sir, let me be so bold as ask you,	
	Did you yet ever see Baptista's daughter?	245
TRANIO	No, sir, but hear I do that he hath two,	
	The one as famous for a scolding tongue	
	As is the other for beauteous modesty¹⁰.	
PETRUCHIO	Sir, sir, the first's for me; let her go by¹¹.	
GREMIO	Yea, leave that labour to great Hercules,	250
	And let it be more than Alcides'¹² twelve.	
PETRUCHIO	Sir, understand you this of me in sooth¹³:	
	The youngest daughter, whom you hearken for¹⁴,	
	Her father keeps from all access of suitors	
	And will not promise her to any man	255
	Until the elder sister first be wed.	
	The younger then is free, and not before.	

51

Tranio thanks Petruchio for his determination to wed Katherina. He offers to reward Petruchio if he wins Katherina. Everyone goes off to eat and drink together.

 剧情简介：川纽感谢珀楚秋决心娶凯特芮娜为妻，他许诺说，如果珀楚秋向凯特芮娜求婚成功，他将有重谢。众人下去一同吃喝。

1 Eat and drink as friends (in small groups)

All the characters leave the stage and intend to relax together.

- Improvise a short scene to show what happens at this gathering. Do you think they will remain friends, or will there be disagreements? To what extent will money be important? It is worth noting that the deceitfulness of lawyers (lines 271–2) was legendary, so perhaps this gives a clue to what happens.

2 Impatient servants (in pairs)

Shakespeare links Grumio and Biondello through their shared line 273. These two characters seem very anxious to leave. Do you think they are hungry? Or greedy? Or simply bored?

- With your partner, improvise a few lines of dialogue as they leave the stage, allowing the servants to comment on their masters and on what has happened since they arrived in Padua. What might Grumio say about Petruchio, and what does Biondello think of his master Lucentio and his fellow servant Tranio?

1 **stead** 有助于
2 **do this feat** 完成这一壮举（把她搞到手）
3 **whose hap shall be** 无论是哪个幸运儿
4 **ingrate** 忘恩负义
5 **conceive** 明白事理
6 **gratify** 报答
7 **rest generally beholding** 全指望着，全都受惠
8 **contrive** 度过，消磨
9 **quaff carouses** 为……干杯
10 **motion** 提议
11 **I … venuto** 我来为您洗尘（*ben venuto*是welcome的意大利文形式）

Stagecraft 导演技巧

A right song and dance (in pairs)

Productions sometimes conclude this scene with a song-and-dance routine.

- Talk together about the wisdom of this decision. How would it affect the mood? If you were to end the scene in this way, what style of music and dance would you choose?

Characters 人物分析

Who's who? (in fours)

Act 1 introduces a number of characters. Several of these characters are in love, some adopt disguises during the course of the act, and some have particular relationships with each other.

- Draw a diagram to show as clearly as possible who's who, who is pretending to be someone else, and the chief relationships among the characters.

THE TAMING OF THE SHREW ACT 1 SCENE 2
悍妇降服记

TRANIO	If it be so, sir, that you are the man	
	Must stead[1] us all, and me amongst the rest,	
	And if you break the ice and do this feat[2] –	260
	Achieve the elder, set the younger free	
	For our access – whose hap shall be[3] to have her	
	Will not so graceless be to be ingrate[4].	
HORTENSIO	Sir, you say well, and well you do conceive[5];	
	And since you do profess to be a suitor,	265
	You must, as we do, gratify[6] this gentleman	
	To whom we all rest generally beholding[7].	
TRANIO	Sir, I shall not be slack; in sign whereof,	
	Please ye we may contrive[8] this afternoon	
	And quaff carouses[9] to our mistress' health,	270
	And do as adversaries do in law,	
	Strive mightily, but eat and drink as friends.	
GRUMIO BIONDELLO	} O excellent motion[10]! Fellows, let's be gone.	
HORTENSIO	The motion's good indeed, and be it so.	
	Petruchio, I shall be your *ben venuto*[11].	275

Exeunt

The Taming of the Shrew
悍妇降服记

Looking back at Act 1 第1幕回顾
Activities for groups or individuals

1 Where is Padua?

Not surprisingly, the 'play-within-a-play' has been set in a range of Italianate settings, from the lovingly re-created Renaissance Italy of the 1976 Zeffirelli movie, through Mafia stereotypes, to present-day trattorias (意大利餐馆) with pizzas, ice cream and cappuccinos. Padua has also been relocated to the American Wild West, a 1950s Midwest small-town community, Canada, North Africa and the East End of London. Other settings have included a bullring (斗牛场), a wrestling ring and (perhaps inevitably, given where Induction 1 is set) a tavern and a wine bar.

- Where would you set the 'play-within-a-play' and why? Sketch or build a model of the staging you would use, and write a detailed description of the set design and props you plan to include.

2 What do the sisters look like?

From the start of Act 1, this play sets up a series of contrasts between acceptable social behaviour and that which is considered unacceptable. Katherina is 'too rough', 'stark mad', 'wonderful froward', whereas Bianca behaves with 'mild behaviour and sobriety' – exactly as a well-bred young woman was supposed to behave in Elizabethan times.

a Create a table comparing the sisters and noting their similarities and differences. Use evidence from the play so far. How do you think this contrast affects their relationship?

b What else might affect their relationship? Look at the images of Bianca and Katherina on the opposite page. How physically different do you think the sisters should be? How much older is Katherina? Is one taller than the other?

c Write a couple of paragraphs exploring the relationship between the sisters, the impact it has on their behaviour and its significance in the play. Remember to find evidence from the play to support your ideas.

3 Different kinds of men

Lucentio uses a striking image to convey his desire for experience as he arrives in Padua:

> And am to Padua come as he that leaves
> A shallow plash to plunge him in the deep
> And with satiety seeks to quench his thirst.
>
> Act 1 Scene 1, lines 22–4

Petruchio speaks with typical force:

> And I have thrust myself into this maze,
> Happily to wive and thrive as best I may.
>
> Act 1 Scene 2, lines 52–3

- Copy and complete the table below to compare and contrast the two men in as many ways as you can, particularly in their attitudes towards women, love, money and servants, as well as in their first appearances on the stage. You can add to this list if you want to.

	Lucentio	Petruchio
Attitude to women		
Attitude to love		
Attitude to money		
Attitude to servants		
First appearances		

Katherina has tied Bianca's hands, and is cross-questioning her about which suitor she loves the most. Bianca tries to pacify her, but Katherina strikes her. Baptista rescues Bianca and reprimands Katherina.

剧情简介：凯特芮娜绑住碧昂卡双手，盘问她最喜欢哪个求婚者。碧昂卡想抚慰姐姐，凯特芮娜却打了她。巴普提斯塔救下碧昂卡，并训斥凯特芮娜。

1 Stage directions – explicit and implicit (in pairs)

Imagine you have been cast as Bianca and Katherina in a new production of the play. Use the following activities to help you explore lines 1–28.

a Read through the passage and identify to each other all the obvious stage directions to guide you.

b As one person reads the lines, the other suggests appropriate gestures and moves for every line. Together, run through the passage without words, just making these movements.

c In role as one of the actors, write a description of how you hope the audience will respond to your portrayal of the character you have chosen in this key scene. Would you want the audience to feel sorry for Bianca or sympathetic towards Katherina? What else do you want them to think?

2 Father and daughters (in threes)

After Baptista enters at line 23, this becomes one of the rare moments in the play when only the Minola family is present. The single stage direction here is 'He unties her hands' (line 24), so we have plenty of freedom to imagine what all three might be doing.

- Prepare a tableau of Baptista, Katherina and Bianca at this moment. Take turns to break out of the frozen moment to answer the question (while still in role): 'What is your relationship with the other members of your family?'

1	gauds	首饰穿戴
2	raiment	衣服
3	petticoat	衬裙
4	dissemble	骗人，说谎
5	fancy	喜欢
6	Minion	死丫头
7	affect	喜欢
8	but you shall have him	如果没有别的办法让你得到他
9	fair	穿金戴银
10	envy	恨
11	prithee	求你了
12	ply thy needle	去做你的针线活儿
13	meddle not with her	别理她
14	hilding	一无是处
15	cross	惹……生气

▶ Does this Bianca reflect your own ideas of how this character should be played? Why, or why not?

Act 2 Scene 1
Baptista's house

Enter KATHERINA *and* BIANCA [*with her hands tied*].

BIANCA Good sister, wrong me not, nor wrong yourself
To make a bondmaid and a slave of me.
That I disdain. But for these other gauds[1] —
Unbind my hands, I'll pull them off myself,
Yea, all my raiment[2], to my petticoat[3], 5
Or what you will command me will I do,
So well I know my duty to my elders.

KATHERINA Of all thy suitors here I charge thee tell
Whom thou lov'st best. See thou dissemble[4] not.

BIANCA Believe me, sister, of all the men alive 10
I never yet beheld that special face
Which I could fancy[5] more than any other.

KATHERINA Minion[6], thou liest! Is't not Hortensio?

BIANCA If you affect[7] him, sister, here I swear
I'll plead for you myself but you shall have him[8]. 15

KATHERINA O then, belike, you fancy riches more:
You will have Gremio to keep you fair[9].

BIANCA Is it for him you do envy[10] me so?
Nay then, you jest, and now I well perceive
You have but jested with me all this while. 20
I prithee[11], sister Kate, untie my hands.
[*Katherina*] *strikes her.*

KATHERINA If that be jest, then all the rest was so.

Enter BAPTISTA.

BAPTISTA Why, how now, dame! Whence grows this insolence?
Bianca, stand aside. Poor girl, she weeps.
[*He unties her hands.*]
Go, ply thy needle[12]; meddle not with her[13]. 25
For shame, thou hilding[14] of a devilish spirit!
Why dost thou wrong her that did ne'er wrong thee?
When did she cross[15] thee with a bitter word?

Baptista sends Bianca into the house. Katherina leaves, talking of favouritism and revenge. Petruchio tells Baptista of his interest in Katherina, and presents Hortensio (disguised as Litio) as Bianca's tutor.

剧情简介：巴普提斯塔让碧昂卡进屋，凯特芮娜边走边说父亲偏心，说要报复。珀楚秋告诉巴普提斯塔他对凯特芮娜有好感，并引荐了郝坦修（假扮理修）给碧昂卡当老师。

1 Sibling rivalry?

a In line 18, Bianca suggests that Katherina envies her. Do you think this is true? If so, is it because of Bianca's good looks, the attention she gets from men or the favouritism of their father?

b Quickly read over the start of this scene up to line 36 opposite. List three feelings Katherina might have towards her sister and father. Then write a diary entry for her to reveal her true feelings towards her family.

Write about it 写作练习
Quarrelling sisters

Both sisters leave the stage here in quick succession, as Bianca runs off, hotly pursued by Katherina.

- Write a paragraph describing what has happened in the lead-up to this exit as if it were an episode in a novel or short story. Remember to describe the sort of behaviour that would have been acted out on stage to accompany the script. Think about whether Bianca might truly have been an innocent victim of Katherina's violence, or whether she actually gives as good as she gets, and is equally aggressive to her sister behind Baptista's back.

Characters 人物分析
Petruchio presents himself (in pairs)

This is a very important moment for Petruchio. He needs to impress Baptista in order to win approval for his courtship of Katherina. How might he do this? For example, in some productions Petruchio arrives with an enormous bunch of flowers. Would your Petruchio exploit his arrogance or his charm?

a Talk together about how to perform the first part of this speech (lines 45–52). Do you think there is a difference in how Petruchio would be understood in today's society compared to how he might have been presented on Shakespeare's stage?

b Write a paragraph or two describing how you would perform these lines in your own production, and how you would like the other characters (and the audience) to respond to Petruchio.

---

1 flouts 嘲笑
2 suffer me 让我做我想做的
3 dance barefoot 光着脚跳舞（据英国旧俗，在姐妹的婚礼上光脚跳舞的女子可以找到丈夫）
4 lead apes in hell 牵只猴子下地狱（因为没有孩子领着去天堂，只能牵猴子下地狱）
5 mean 下等
6 Good morrow = Good morning
7 orderly 按部就班
8 forward 急切；冒昧
9 oft = often
10 entrance to my entertainment 为回报您的款待
11 Cunning 精通
12 sciences 知识，技能

KATHERINA	Her silence flouts[1] me, and I'll be revenged.
	Flies after Bianca.
BAPTISTA	What, in my sight? Bianca, get thee in.
	Exit [Bianca]
KATHERINA	What, will you not suffer me[2]? Nay, now I see
	She is your treasure, she must have a husband.
	I must dance barefoot[3] on her wedding day
	And, for your love to her, lead apes in hell[4].
	Talk not to me! I will go sit and weep
	Till I can find occasion of revenge. [*Exit*]
BAPTISTA	Was ever gentleman thus grieved as I?
	But who comes here?

Enter GREMIO, LUCENTIO *in the habit of a mean*[5] *man [disguised as Cambio],* PETRUCHIO *with [*HORTENSIO *disguised as Litio,]* TRANIO *[disguised as Lucentio,] with his boy [*BIONDELLO*] bearing a lute and books.*

GREMIO	Good morrow[6], neighbour Baptista.
BAPTISTA	Good morrow, neighbour Gremio. God save you, gentlemen.
PETRUCHIO	And you, good sir. Pray have you not a daughter
	Called Katherina, fair and virtuous?
BAPTISTA	I have a daughter, sir, called Katherina.
GREMIO	You are too blunt; go to it orderly[7].
PETRUCHIO	You wrong me, Signor Gremio. Give me leave.
	[*To Baptista*] I am a gentleman of Verona, sir,
	That hearing of her beauty and her wit,
	Her affability and bashful modesty,
	Her wondrous qualities and mild behaviour,
	Am bold to show myself a forward[8] guest
	Within your house, to make mine eye the witness
	Of that report which I so oft[9] have heard.
	And for an entrance to my entertainment[10],
	I do present you with a man of mine,
	[*Presents Hortensio.*]
	Cunning[11] in music and the mathematics,
	To instruct her fully in those sciences[12],
	Whereof I know she is not ignorant.
	Accept of him, or else you do me wrong.
	His name is Litio, born in Mantua.

Baptista welcomes Petruchio, and accepts Gremio's gift of Cambio (Lucentio) as a teacher for Bianca. Tranio declares that he wants to be considered as a suitor for Bianca.

 剧情简介：巴普提斯塔欢迎珀楚秋，接受葛莱缪的好意推荐，让坎毕欧（卢森修假扮）做碧昂卡的老师。川纽宣布要向碧昂卡求婚。

1 Plain speaking (in small groups)

'I speak but as I find', says Baptista (line 65). Plain speaking is usually considered a virtue, but even plain speakers do not always express their real thoughts.

a Consider each character here in turn and discuss whether they 'speak as they find' all the time, or whether they sometimes conceal what they really think.

b Choose three points in the script opposite and write out stage directions to suggest what gestures or actions the actors might use to reveal what the characters are really thinking at those moments.

Language in the play 剧中语言

Rhyming couplets (by yourself)

a Find the rhyming couplet shared by Petruchio and Gremio in the script opposite. Why is 'doing' rhymed with 'wooing'? Why is this significant, considering what each man is implying about the other's chances of success in love?

b In notes to the actors playing these two characters, describe how you would want this moment to be staged for greatest dramatic or comic effect.

1 your turn 您这样的人物
2 Saving your tale 恕我直言
3 poor petitioners 请愿人
 （poor为客套话）
4 Backare! 靠后站！（仿拉丁语）
5 marvellous 非常
6 I would fain be doing 我急于把事情办妥
7 grateful 受欢迎
8 gentle 尊贵
9 walk like a stranger 站在那儿像个外人
10 upon knowledge of 您得知……之后

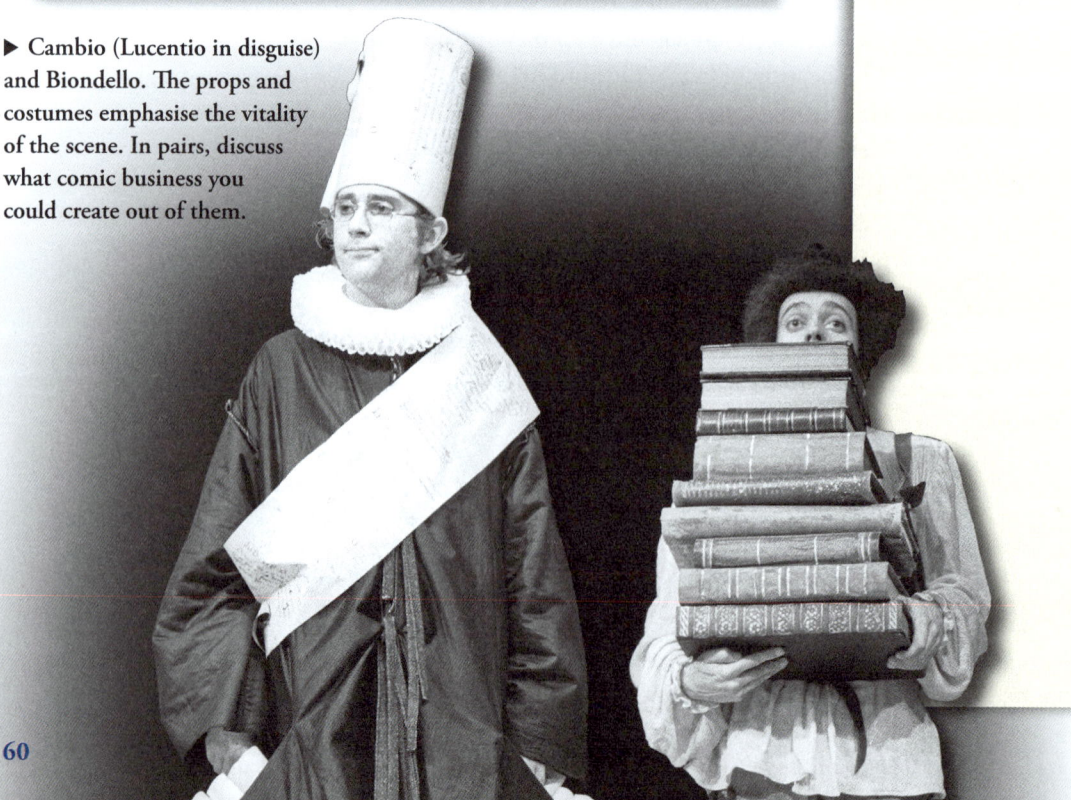

▶ Cambio (Lucentio in disguise) and Biondello. The props and costumes emphasise the vitality of the scene. In pairs, discuss what comic business you could create out of them.

BAPTISTA	Y'are welcome, sir, and he for your good sake,	60
	But for my daughter Katherine, this I know:	
	She is not for your turn[1], the more my grief.	
PETRUCHIO	I see you do not mean to part with her,	
	Or else you like not of my company.	
BAPTISTA	Mistake me not; I speak but as I find.	65
	Whence are you, sir? What may I call your name?	
PETRUCHIO	Petruchio is my name, Antonio's son,	
	A man well known throughout all Italy.	
BAPTISTA	I know him well. You are welcome for his sake.	
GREMIO	Saving your tale[2], Petruchio, I pray	70
	Let us that are poor petitioners[3] speak too.	
	Backare![4] You are marvellous[5] forward.	
PETRUCHIO	O pardon me, Signor Gremio, I would fain be doing[6].	
GREMIO	I doubt it not, sir, but you will curse your wooing.	
	[*To Baptista*] Neighbour, this is a gift very grateful[7], I am sure of it. To express the like kindness, myself, that have been more kindly beholding to you than any, freely give unto you this young scholar [*Presents Lucentio.*] that hath been long studying at Rheims, as cunning in Greek, Latin and other languages as the other in music and mathematics. His name is Cambio. Pray accept his service.	75 80
BAPTISTA	A thousand thanks, Signor Gremio. Welcome, good Cambio. [*To Tranio*] But, gentle[8] sir, methinks you walk like a stranger[9]. May I be so bold to know the cause of your coming?	
TRANIO	Pardon me, sir, the boldness is mine own	
	That, being a stranger in this city here,	85
	Do make myself a suitor to your daughter,	
	Unto Bianca, fair and virtuous.	
	Nor is your firm resolve unknown to me	
	In the preferment of the eldest sister.	
	This liberty is all that I request	90
	That, upon knowledge of[10] my parentage,	
	I may have welcome 'mongst the rest that woo,	
	And free access and favour as the rest,	
	And toward the education of your daughters	
	I here bestow a simple instrument	95
	And this small packet of Greek and Latin books.	
	[*Biondello steps forward with the lute and books.*]	
	If you accept them, then their worth is great.	

Baptista welcomes Tranio (Lucentio) and the 'teachers' leave to meet their pupils. Petruchio and Baptista discuss the financial details of Katherina's marriage. Baptista warns that he must first win her love.

  剧情简介：巴普提斯塔欢迎川纽（卢森修），两位"教师"离开去见学生。珀楚秋和巴普提斯塔商量凯特芮娜结婚的具体财产安排。巴普提斯塔警告他必须先赢得凯特芮娜的芳心。

1 Negotiating the dowry (in pairs)

a Look carefully at lines 117–23, where the financial arrangements concerning Katherina's marriage are described. How does Baptista make the extraordinarily large offer and how does Petruchio respond? Do you think Baptista is really prepared to provide such a large dowry? Why does he suddenly talk about love in line 125?

b Experiment with staging these negotiations about money. Read the passage through again, this time on your feet and using the following three actions: *approach*, *retreat* or *manoeuvre*. Use these at appropriate times as you read your character's lines and ask yourselves the questions below:

- Why might you approach someone or something in everyday life?
- Why might you retreat from something or someone?
- Why might you manoeuvre or reposition yourself in the same space?

1 **presently** 立刻
2 **in possession** 结婚当天
3 **twenty thousand crowns** 两万克朗（非常丰厚的嫁妆，这里有可能是开玩笑：只有出大钱才能把大女儿嫁出去）
4 **assure ... widowhood** 保证我死后她拥有寡妇的权利
5 **specialties** 契约
6 **covenants** 合约字据

Themes 主题分析

Love: 'the special thing' (in pairs)

Amidst the complex marriage arrangements involving dowries, contracts, family background and possible widowhood, 'love' is the final – but most important – consideration.

a Talk about why you think Baptista feels obliged to mention the importance of obtaining Katherina's love when discussing marriage arrangements with Petruchio (lines 124–5).

b Using your knowledge of these two characters so far, write a paragraph explaining how successful you think Petruchio will be in meeting the challenge of winning Katherina's love.

Stagecraft 导演技巧

Noises off stage (in small groups)

Later on in the scene, at line 137, Hortensio arrives on stage '*with his head broke*' after an encounter with Katherina.

- Prepare the audience for this with some offstage noises and snatches of dialogue at comically suitable points during Petruchio and Baptista's conversation (lines 110–37). How might these two characters react to the disturbance off stage?

BAPTISTA	Lucentio is your name. Of whence, I pray?	
TRANIO	Of Pisa, sir, son to Vincentio.	
BAPTISTA	A mighty man of Pisa. By report	100

    I know him well. You are very welcome, sir.
    [*To Hortensio*] Take you the lute, [*To Lucentio*] and you the
        set of books;
    You shall go see your pupils presently[1].
    Holla, within!

           Enter a SERVANT.

           Sirrah, lead these gentlemen
    To my daughters, and tell them both   105
    These are their tutors. Bid them use them well.
           [*Exeunt Servant, Hortensio, Lucentio*]
    We will go walk a little in the orchard
    And then to dinner. You are passing welcome,
    And so I pray you all to think yourselves.

PETRUCHIO   Signor Baptista, my business asketh haste,   110
    And every day I cannot come to woo.
    You knew my father well, and in him me,
    Left solely heir to all his lands and goods,
    Which I have bettered rather than decreased.
    Then tell me, if I get your daughter's love,   115
    What dowry shall I have with her to wife?

BAPTISTA   After my death, the one half of my lands,
    And in possession[2] twenty thousand crowns[3].

PETRUCHIO   And for that dowry I'll assure her of
    Her widowhood[4], be it that she survive me,   120
    In all my lands and leases whatsoever.
    Let specialties[5] be therefore drawn between us,
    That covenants[6] may be kept on either hand.

BAPTISTA   Ay, when the special thing is well obtained,
    That is, her love, for that is all in all.   125

Petruchio confirms his determination to woo Katherina. Hortensio returns injured, and describes Katherina's violent response to her music lesson, but Petruchio appears undaunted.

 剧情简介：珀楚秋确认他一定要向凯特芮娜求婚。郝坦修受伤返回，讲述凯特芮娜在音乐课上的野蛮行径，但珀楚秋不为所惧。

Language in the play 剧中语言

Romantic skirmishes (in small groups)

a Read carefully through Petruchio's speech in lines 126–33. Together, sketch or use symbols to show the visual images that Petruchio conjures up through his language. What is he actually saying here?

b What is the impact of this war-like imagery on the audience? What does it suggest about Petruchio's attitude to romance? Discuss how this is developed by the imagery used to describe Katherina in lines 135 and 141–2.

1. peremptory 强硬
2. to the proof 全副盔甲
3. *broke* 受伤流血
4. promise 保证
5. prove a soldier 证明是个好战士
6. break her to the lute 教她学会弹琴
7. frets 琴品（另有"烦躁"的意思）
8. bowed her hand 弯着她的手（教她）
9. fume 恼火
10. pate 头顶
11. pillory （夹住犯人头和手的）枷锁
12. rascal fiddler 流氓琴师
13. twangling Jack 沿街卖艺的要饭花子
14. studied 算计好
15. lusty 勇猛，刚烈
16. chat 聊天，谈心

1 A 'twangling Jack' (in pairs)

Work out a series of three tableaux to tell Hortensio's story (lines 145–55). Then see if you can identify the main characters in the tableau in the image below.

Characters 人物分析

Public voice versus inner thoughts

What does Petruchio think when he hears what has happened to Hortensio? In role as Petruchio, describe:

- what you want others to think when you say lines 156–8 (your public voice)
- what you really think (your inner thoughts).

PETRUCHIO	Why, that is nothing, for I tell you, father,	
	I am as peremptory¹ as she proud-minded,	
	And where two raging fires meet together	
	They do consume the thing that feeds their fury.	
	Though little fire grows great with little wind,	130
	Yet extreme gusts will blow out fire and all.	
	So I to her, and so she yields to me,	
	For I am rough and woo not like a babe.	
BAPTISTA	Well mayst thou woo, and happy be thy speed!	
	But be thou armed for some unhappy words.	135
PETRUCHIO	Ay, to the proof², as mountains are for winds,	
	That shakes not though they blow perpetually.	

Enter Hortensio with his head broke³.

BAPTISTA	How now, my friend! Why dost thou look so pale?	
HORTENSIO	For fear, I promise⁴ you, if I look pale.	
BAPTISTA	What, will my daughter prove a good musician?	140
HORTENSIO	I think she'll sooner prove a soldier⁵!	
	Iron may hold with her, but never lutes.	
BAPTIST	Why then, thou canst not break her to the lute⁶?	
HORTENSIO	Why no, for she hath broke the lute to me.	
	I did but tell her she mistook her frets⁷	145
	And bowed her hand⁸ to teach her fingering,	
	When, with a most impatient devilish spirit,	
	'Frets, call you these?' quoth she, 'I'll fume⁹ with them!'	
	And with that word she struck me on the head,	
	And through the instrument my pate¹⁰ made way,	150
	And there I stood amazèd for a while,	
	As on a pillory¹¹, looking through the lute,	
	While she did call me rascal fiddler¹²	
	And twangling Jack¹³, with twenty such vile terms,	
	As had she studied¹⁴ to misuse me so.	155
PETRUCHIO	Now, by the world, it is a lusty¹⁵ wench!	
	I love her ten times more than e'er I did.	
	O how I long to have some chat¹⁶ with her.	

Baptista comforts Hortensio. Left alone, Petruchio describes how he plans to woo Katherina. When she arrives, he 'flatters' her and speaks of her reputation for mildness.

 剧情简介：巴普提斯塔安慰郝坦修。独自一人时，珀楚秋讲述他打算如何向凯特芮娜求婚。凯特芮娜到来，珀楚秋"赞美"她温顺贤良的好名声。

1 Getting the audience on side (in pairs)

In lines 165–76, Petruchio is alone on stage and makes clear his basic strategy for 'wooing' Katherina – to use language to disorientate and disconcert her.

- Talk together about whether you think Petruchio's approach will succeed. Remember that during this soliloquy, the audience finds out more about his plans and is given an insight into his motivations and character. How might members of the audience respond to him, and what effect might this knowledge have on their opinion of him?

1 Proceed in practice 继续教
2 attend 等候
3 spirit 热情
4 rail 骂人
5 clear 清纯美丽
6 volubility 能言善辩
7 piercing 感人
8 pack 打包走人，滚开
9 banns （贴在教堂等公众场所的）结婚预告
10 bonny 美丽可爱
11 dainties 美味佳肴（也称 cates，与Kate同音）
12 consolation 安慰
13 sounded 称赞
14 moved 打动

Stagecraft 导演技巧

Meeting for the first time

a Petruchio and Katherina are alone on stage the first time they meet. What might happen here? Consider whether:
- they fall in love at first sight
- Katherina is angry because her father made her come out
- they pretend not to be attracted to each other
- Petruchio is intimidated by Katherina
- Katherina is afraid of being alone with him
- they are secretly interested in each other and enjoy the verbal skirmish that follows.

b In your Director's Journal, write a description of how you think the characters should behave and what they are thinking and feeling during this first meeting. Note how Petruchio 'feeds' Katherina some good lines in the dialogue here – and in the rest of the scene. He seems to relish her performance as much as his own.

Write about it 写作练习

Kate … Kate … Kate (by yourself)

What is Katherina doing while she listens to Petruchio's speech in lines 181–90? Why does he say her name so many times? Is he trying to get her attention? Or is she trying to say something and he is making sure she can't get a word in?

- Write four stage directions at the word 'Kate' to help the actor know what to do. Then write a paragraph explaining what you want this part of the script to reveal about her character.

THE TAMING OF THE SHREW ACT 2 SCENE 1
悍妇降服记

BAPTISTA [*To Hortensio*]
Well, go with me, and be not so discomfited.
Proceed in practice¹ with my younger daughter; 160
She's apt to learn and thankful for good turns.
Signor Petruchio, will you go with us,
Or shall I send my daughter Kate to you?

PETRUCHIO I pray you do. I'll attend² her here –

[*Exeunt all but Petruchio*]

And woo her with some spirit³ when she comes! 165
Say that she rail⁴, why then I'll tell her plain
She sings as sweetly as a nightingale.
Say that she frown, I'll say she looks as clear⁵
As morning roses newly washed with dew.
Say she be mute and will not speak a word, 170
Then I'll commend her volubility⁶
And say she uttereth piercing⁷ eloquence.
If she do bid me pack⁸, I'll give her thanks
As though she bid me stay by her a week.
If she deny to wed, I'll crave the day 175
When I shall ask the banns⁹, and when be married.

Enter Katherina.

But here she comes, and now, Petruchio, speak.
Good morrow, Kate, for that's your name, I hear.

KATHERINA Well have you heard, but something hard of hearing –
They call me Katherine that do talk of me. 180

PETRUCHIO You lie, in faith, for you are called plain Kate,
And bonny¹⁰ Kate, and sometimes Kate the curst.
But Kate, the prettiest Kate in Christendom,
Kate of Kate-Hall, my super-dainty Kate –
For dainties¹¹ are all Kates – and therefore, Kate, 185
Take this of me, Kate of my consolation¹²:
Hearing thy mildness praised in every town,
Thy virtues spoke of and thy beauty sounded¹³ –
Yet not so deeply as to thee belongs –
Myself am moved¹⁴ to woo thee for my wife. 190

Katherina and Petruchio argue wittily, trying to outdo each other. She is eventually driven to strike him. He promises to return the blow if she hits him again.

  剧情简介：凯特芮娜和珀楚秋机智诙谐地争论，都想压倒对方。最后凯特芮娜气急败坏打了珀楚秋。珀楚秋说如果她再动手，他一定还手。

1 Provide the action (in pairs)

a In this play, Shakespeare provides many clues for the actors to suggest when actions and gestures are needed. As you read through the script opposite, decide when you might use the following actions:

- taking centre stage
- turning your back on the other person
- blocking the other's movement away
- slapping
- advancing or retreating
- tripping up the other person
- avoiding a punch.

b Insert as many stage directions as you can into a copy of the script opposite. Then experiment with bringing to life your version of the scene.

2 Sharing the verse

Petruchio and Katherina's dialogue here is in verse. Notice how certain lines are shared between them (193–4, 202, 210, 213). Read the whole page aloud in two ways (remember that shared lines often indicate that characters are speaking quickly or drawing closer to each other):

- Use the shared lines to keep the rhythm and increase the pace of the scene.
- Break the rhythm of the line and add pauses between the shared lines to slow down the pace.

What difference does it make when the cues are picked up quickly and the rhythm of each line is retained?

Language in the play 剧中语言
Outrageous punning (in pairs)

- The script opposite is full of puns. Use the glossary to help you find as many as you can. Write them out as a list.
- For each of the puns you find, work out what insults Petruchio and Katherina are using with the same word. Then create a couple of tableaux to represent their punning. (Petruchio's pun in lines 212–13 is particularly rude – and may be why she hits him!)

1 **movable** 易变的人（也指动产）
2 **joint stool** 小木凳（通常比喻容易被忽视的人）
3 **bear** 载物载人（即任人骑；也有"生养"之意）
4 **jade** 劣马（也指性能力低下的男人）
5 **burden** 指责（也有"使怀孕"的意思）
6 **light** 苗条（也指轻浮放荡）
7 **swain** 乡巴佬（也指情人）
8 **as … be** 像边缘完整的钱币一样一点儿也不轻（最初的银币常被人偷偷切去边，造成分量不足）
9 **buzz** 谣言（珀楚秋暗示他听说凯特芮娜名声不好）
10 **tane** 被抓住了（猎鹰术语，指在飞行中抓住）
11 **buzzard** 训练不成功的鹰（也指什么也学不会的笨人）
12 **turtle** 斑鸠（爱与和平的象征）
13 **tales** 谣言（与前文的tail为同音双关；tail也暗指女性私处）
14 **try** 检验
15 **arms** 盾形纹章（绅士身份的象征）
16 **put me in thy books** 把我封为绅士（也有"接受我对你的爱意"之意）

KATHERINA	'Moved' – in good time! Let him that moved you hither
	Remove you hence. I knew you at the first
	You were a movable[1].
PETRUCHIO	Why, what's a movable?
KATHERINA	A joint stool[2].
PETRUCHIO	Thou hast hit it. Come sit on me.
KATHERINA	Asses are made to bear[3], and so are you.
PETRUCHIO	Women are made to bear, and so are you.
KATHERINA	No such jade[4] as you, if me you mean.
PETRUCHIO	Alas, good Kate, I will not burden[5] thee,
	For, knowing thee to be but young and light[6] –
KATHERINA	Too light for such a swain[7] as you to catch,
	And yet as heavy as my weight should be[8].
PETRUCHIO	'Should be'! Should – buzz[9]!
KATHERINA	Well tane[10], and like a buzzard[11].
PETRUCHIO	O slow-winged turtle[12], shall a buzzard take thee?
KATHERINA	Ay, for a turtle, as he takes a buzzard.
PETRUCHIO	Come, come, you wasp! I'faith you are too angry.
KATHERINA	If I be waspish, best beware my sting.
PETRUCHIO	My remedy is then to pluck it out.
KATHERINA	Ay, if the fool could find it where it lies.
PETRUCHIO	Who knows not where a wasp does wear his sting?
	In his tail.
KATHERINA	In his tongue.
PETRUCHIO	Whose tongue?
KATHERINA	Yours, if you talk of tales[13], and so farewell.
	[She turns to go.]
PETRUCHIO	What, with my tongue in your tail? Nay, come again.
	Good Kate, I am a gentleman –
KATHERINA	That I'll try[14].
	She strikes him.
PETRUCHIO	I swear I'll cuff you if you strike again.
	[He holds her.]
KATHERINA	So may you lose your arms[15].
	If you strike me, you are no gentleman,
	And if no gentleman, why then no arms.
PETRUCHIO	A herald, Kate? O put me in thy books[16].

Line numbers: 195, 200, 205, 210, 215

> The battle between Katherina and Petruchio continues. He describes her, using terms that are the exact opposite of her reputation.
> 剧情简介：凯特芮娜和珀楚秋继续唇枪舌剑。珀楚秋对凯特芮娜的评价与她一贯的名声完全相反。

Language in the play 剧中语言

Quick-fire exchanges (in small groups)

a Many lines in this scene alternate rapidly between Katherina and Petruchio to increase pace and tension. They are an example of **stichomythia** (针锋对话) and are usually spoken quickly and sharply on stage, with rhythmic intensity. As you read these lines aloud, make a list of words that describe how you feel – and how the audience might feel on hearing these lines.

b Lines 219–24 contain much **alliteration*** (words that emphasise the repetition of consonants). Find as many examples as you can, and talk together about what effects the actors could create with these words, adding force to the quarrel.
How do these 'sound echoes' affect the quick-fire exchanges between the two?

1 A battle of wits (in pairs)

Lines 224–31 contain fast-paced dialogue between Katherina and Petruchio. The lines reach a climax as Katherina tries to leave.

a How would you stage lines 230–1? Why is Katherina quiet at this point? How has Petruchio managed to keep her attention for so long?

b Think about what happens from this point to the end of the page. Then write two stage directions to help the actors convey the way the relationship between their characters is developing. Make sure you extend the stage direction '*He lets her go*' at line 241.

1 crest 纹章上的装饰（也指鸟头上的一撮毛）
2 coxcomb 小丑的帽子（像鸡冠）
3 combless 心满意足
4 craven 胆小且斗败了的公鸡
5 crab 海棠果（一种味酸的野苹果；也指面带怒容的人）
6 Well … one 新手猜得很准
7 scape 逃避
8 chafe 惹怒
9 coy 傲慢；害羞
10 very 彻头彻尾
11 gamesome 好玩儿，顽皮
12 askance 鄙夷
13 halt 瘸
14 whom thou keep'st command 对你自己的仆人指手画脚吧
15 Dian 荻阿娜（狩猎与贞洁女神）
16 sportful 多情

* alliteration 头韵，指诗句里两个或多个词的第一个辅音相同，如 *sing a song of sixpence*，类似中文的双声。

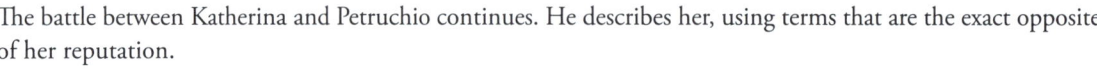

THE TAMING OF THE SHREW ACT 2 SCENE 1
悍妇降服记

KATHERINA What is your crest[1] – a coxcomb[2]?
PETRUCHIO A combless[3] cock, so Kate will be my hen. 220
KATHERINA No cock of mine; you crow too like a craven[4].
PETRUCHIO Nay, come, Kate, come; you must not look so sour.
KATHERINA It is my fashion when I see a crab[5].
PETRUCHIO Why, here's no crab, and therefore look not sour.
KATHERINA There is, there is. 225
PETRUCHIO Then show it me.
KATHERINA   Had I a glass I would.
PETRUCHIO What, you mean my face?
KATHERINA   Well aimed of such a young one[6].
PETRUCHIO Now, by Saint George, I am too young for you.
KATHERINA Yet you are withered.
PETRUCHIO   'Tis with cares.
KATHERINA   I care not.
PETRUCHIO Nay, hear you, Kate – in sooth you scape[7] not so. 230
KATHERINA I chafe[8] you if I tarry. Let me go.
PETRUCHIO Nay, not a whit. I find you passing gentle.
      'Twas told me you were rough and coy[9] and sullen,
      And now I find report a very[10] liar,
      For thou art pleasant, gamesome[11], passing courteous, 235
      But slow in speech, yet sweet as springtime flowers.
      Thou canst not frown, thou canst not look askance[12],
      Nor bite the lip as angry wenches will,
      Nor hast thou pleasure to be cross in talk,
      But thou with mildness entertain'st thy wooers, 240
      With gentle conference, soft and affable.
      [*He lets her go.*]
      Why does the world report that Kate doth limp?
      O sland'rous world! Kate like the hazel twig
      Is straight and slender, and as brown in hue
      As hazel-nuts and sweeter than the kernels. 245
      O let me see thee walk. Thou dost not halt[13].
KATHERINA Go, fool, and whom thou keep'st command[14].
PETRUCHIO Did ever Dian[15] so become a grove
      As Kate this chamber with her princely gait?
      O be thou Dian, and let her be Kate, 250
      And then let Kate be chaste and Dian sportful[16]!

Petruchio tells Katherina he intends to marry her and tame her. Baptista returns, anxious to know what has happened. Katherina accuses her father of lack of care for her in wanting her to marry Petruchio.

剧情简介：珀楚秋告诉凯特芮娜有意娶她，还要驯服她。巴普提斯塔赶回来，急于知道发生的一切。凯特芮娜指责父亲对她不关心，要把她嫁给珀楚秋。

Stagecraft 导演技巧

Stage directions (in pairs)

Read through Petruchio's lines 256–67 together, giving the word 'Kate' different kinds of emphasis. Think about whose side you are on at any particular moment. Then discuss how your sympathies change throughout this speech.

Themes 主题分析

Taming techniques

What taming techniques has Petruchio used so far? Find examples from the list below in this act. Can you think of any other techniques?

- verbal battles
- flattery and compliments
- misunderstanding what Katherina means
- physical force
- contrariness
- reasonable appeals to Katherina
- mockery of romantic notions
- witty skirmishes.

1 Baptista replies (in pairs)

Katherina replies to Baptista's rather offhand (漫不经心) comment, 'in your dumps?' (line 273) with an attack on him as a father.

- One person reads Katherina's speech while the other attempts a reply. Then swap over. Try to come up with different 'attacks' and 'responses'.

2 Katherina's perspective

What is Katherina really thinking at lines 274–8? How might her private thoughts differ from what she says out loud? Write her diary entry, recording her reactions to what is happening, her feelings towards Petruchio and her plans for the future.

1 extempore 临时想出来，即兴
2 mother-wit 娘胎里带来的（即天生的）智慧
3 Witless else her son 因为她儿子自己没有一点儿智慧
4 keep you warm 只知道暖和，再没任何智慧
5 will you, nill you 不管您愿不愿意
6 for your turn 正好适合您
7 wild Kate （与wildcat谐音）
8 Conformable 温顺
9 speed 进展
10 in your dumps 不开心，垂头丧气
11 mad-cap ruffian 狂妄的恶棍
12 swearing Jack 满口脏话的流氓
13 face the matter out 鲁莽强硬，以为厚颜无耻就可以把事情搞定

THE TAMING OF THE SHREW ACT 2 SCENE 1

悍妇降服记

KATHERINA   Where did you study all this goodly speech?
PETRUCHIO   It is extempore[1], from my mother-wit[2].
KATHERINA   A witty mother! Witless else her son[3].
PETRUCHIO   Am I not wise?
KATHERINA   Yes, keep you warm[4].   255
PETRUCHIO   Marry, so I mean, sweet Katherine, in thy bed.
And therefore, setting all this chat aside,
Thus in plain terms: your father hath consented
That you shall be my wife, your dowry 'greed on,
And will you, nill you[5], I will marry you.   260
Now Kate, I am a husband for your turn[6],
For, by this light whereby I see thy beauty –
Thy beauty that doth make me like thee well –
Thou must be married to no man but me,
For I am he am born to tame you, Kate,   265
And bring you from a wild Kate[7] to a Kate
Conformable[8] as other household Kates.

Enter Baptista, Gremio and Tranio.

Here comes your father. Never make denial –
I must and will have Katherine to my wife.

BAPTISTA   Now, Signor Petruchio, how speed[9] you with my daughter?   270
PETRUCHIO   How but well, sir? How but well?
It were impossible I should speed amiss.
BAPTISTA   Why, how now, daughter Katherine, in your dumps[10]?
KATHERINA   Call you me 'daughter'? Now I promise you
You have showed a tender fatherly regard   275
To wish me wed to one half lunatic,
A mad-cap ruffian[11] and a swearing Jack[12]
That thinks with oaths to face the matter out[13].

Petruchio claims that Katherina loves him. However 'curst' she appears in public, she is very different in private. Baptista agrees to the match, and Petruchio leaves to prepare for the wedding.

剧情简介：珀楚秋声称凯特芮娜爱他，无论在公共场合多像个泼妇，私下里她并不这样。巴普提斯塔答应了这桩婚事，珀楚秋告辞去筹备婚礼。

Stagecraft 导演技巧

What does Kate do? (in pairs)

Every director must decide how to interpret Katherina's silence in the script opposite. Is she speechless with rage? Or is she simply unable to hear what is being said properly?

a Read the passage aloud, with Petruchio keeping as much as he can from Katherina. Then read it again with Petruchio making sure that Katherina *does* hear. What difference do these two stagings make?

b In your Director's Journal, describe how you would stage the script opposite. Where would you place the actors? How would you advise them to behave? Remember to address the following directorial choices as you do so:

- In line 313, Petruchio asks Katherina to kiss him. Shakespeare does not indicate how Katherina responds. What would you have her do?
- At the end of the scene, what stage business could you provide for their exit? For example, in some productions Petruchio picks up Katherina and carries her off; in others, Katherina marches off in a temper. Which do you prefer?

1 Parting comments (in small groups)

Supply Katherina with a characteristic parting comment before she exits (look at line 288 for a good example). Then read through lines 306–13 and finish with your addition to the script.

1 **for policy** 故意装出来
2 **hot** = hot-tempered
3 **Grissel** 格蕊塞尔（薄伽丘[Giovanni Boccaccio, 1313—1375]《十日谈》[*Decameron*]中萨鲁佐侯爵[Marquis of Saluzzo]之妻，对丈夫百依百顺，忍受其一切折磨而毫无怨言）
4 **Lucrece** 鲁克瑞斯（罗马传说中的贞妇，被塔尔昆王[King Tarquin]强奸后自杀以保全家族的荣誉）
5 **'greed** = agreed
6 **speeding** 成功
7 **goodnight our part** 我们可以跟梦想说再见了（也可能表示"我们不用支付珀楚秋任何费用了"）
8 **twain** 两个
9 **vied** 翻番，再加倍
10 **'Tis a world** 这太神奇了
11 **meacock** 胆小，温顺
12 **adieu** 再见
13 **apace** 很快

THE TAMING OF THE SHREW ACT 2 SCENE 1
悍妇降服记

PETRUCHIO   Father, 'tis thus: yourself and all the world
             That talked of her have talked amiss of her.   280
             If she be curst, it is for policy¹,
             For she's not froward, but modest as the dove;
             She is not hot², but temperate as the morn;
             For patience she will prove a second Grissel³,
             And Roman Lucrece⁴ for her chastity.   285
             And, to conclude, we have 'greed⁵ so well together
             That upon Sunday is the wedding day.
KATHERINA   I'll see thee hanged on Sunday first!
GREMIO   Hark, Petruchio, she says she'll see thee hanged first.
TRANIO   Is this your speeding⁶? Nay then, goodnight our part⁷.   290
PETRUCHIO   Be patient, gentlemen. I choose her for myself.
             If she and I be pleased, what's that to you?
             'Tis bargained 'twixt us twain⁸, being alone,
             That she shall still be curst in company.
             I tell you, 'tis incredible to believe   295
             How much she loves me – O the kindest Kate!
             She hung about my neck, and kiss on kiss
             She vied⁹ so fast, protesting oath on oath,
             That in a twink she won me to her love.
             O you are novices! 'Tis a world¹⁰ to see   300
             How tame, when men and women are alone,
             A meacock¹¹ wretch can make the curstest shrew.
             Give me thy hand, Kate. I will unto Venice,
             To buy apparel 'gainst the wedding day.
             Provide the feast, father, and bid the guests.   305
             I will be sure my Katherine shall be fine.
BAPTISTA   I know not what to say, but give me your hands.
             God send you joy, Petruchio! 'tis a match.
GREMIO }
TRANIO }   Amen say we. We will be witnesses.

PETRUCHIO   Father, and wife, and gentlemen, adieu¹².   310
             I will to Venice – Sunday comes apace¹³.
             We will have rings, and things, and fine array,
             And kiss me, Kate, 'We will be married a' Sunday.'
                       Exeunt Petruchio and Katherina [separately]

Gremio and Tranio argue about the strength of their love for Bianca. Baptista tells them that the person who brings the greatest wealth into the marriage will win. Gremio lists his assets.

 剧情简介：葛莱缪和川纽争论各自对碧昂卡的爱慕程度。巴普提斯塔告诉他们谁为婚姻出钱最多谁就会胜出。葛莱缪列举了他的财产。

Language in the play 剧中语言
The love merchant

a Lines 315–20 are full of references to money and merchandise, including a reference to 'a desperate mart'. Why should Baptista think what he is doing is risky? List other references to finances in these lines. What do they suggest to you about Baptista's attitude to his family? Does this match what you know of his character so far?

b Find Baptista's monosyllabic (单音节) line as he attempts to settle the strife between Bianca's suitors. Experiment with ways of saying this line in the context of the whole speech. How does Shakespeare use this line of single syllables to create feeling and atmosphere?

Themes 主题分析
Love and rivalry

Lines 322–9 represent the classic theme of rivalry between an old lover and a young lover.

- Write notes in your Director's Journal about how you would stage this exchange to highlight the theme. What props and costume would you give each character? What use would you make of the end-line rhymes and the shared line (327)? What gestures and expressions would you use to mark these features? Would you want it to be comic or cruel?

1 | clapped up | 匆匆搞定
2 | desperate mart | 有极高风险的买卖
3 | commodity | 商品（指凯特芮娜）
4 | fretting | （货物压在手里）变陈旧或被损坏（也指令人厌烦）
5 | Skipper | 毛头小子，毫无责任感的花花公子
6 | compound this strife | 解决这场冲突
7 | dower | 彩礼
8 | lave | 洗
9 | Tyrian tapestry | 泰尔的织毯（泰尔 [Tyre] 是古代腓尼基 [Phoenicia] 的重要港口城市，以染料和纺织物出名）
10 | coffers | 钱柜
11 | arras counterpoints | 织毯床罩
12 | tents | 帷幔
13 | bossed | 绣着
14 | Valance | 床帷的穗
15 | Pewter and brass | 白镴（锡铅合金）和黄铜
16 | milch-kine | 奶牛
17 | pail | 牛奶桶
18 | answerable to this portion | 跟这个家业配套
19 | struck in years | 上了年纪

1 The rich lover (in small groups)

Gremio's list of his wealth is detailed. He takes real delight in his possessions.

- Plan a promotional video for Gremio (perhaps for a dating agency), using his speech opposite and any other information you have gathered about him from the play so far. Act it out if you can.

2 Bianca and love (in pairs)

At no point in arranging Bianca's marriage does Baptista mention the importance of love. Yet he does so in connection with Katherina's marriage (lines 124–5).

- Interview Baptista (one of you in role) in order to learn his motives for this difference in his attitude to the two marriages.

GREMIO	Was ever match clapped up[1] so suddenly?	
BAPTISTA	Faith, gentlemen, now I play a merchant's part,	315
	And venture madly on a desperate mart[2].	
TRANIO	'Twas a commodity[3] lay fretting[4] by you.	
	'Twill bring you gain, or perish on the seas.	
BAPTISTA	The gain I seek is quiet in the match.	
GREMIO	No doubt but he hath got a quiet catch!	320
	But now, Baptista, to your younger daughter:	
	Now is the day we long have lookèd for;	
	I am your neighbour and was suitor first.	
TRANIO	And I am one that love Bianca more	
	Than words can witness, or your thoughts can guess.	325
GREMIO	Youngling, thou canst not love so dear as I.	
TRANIO	Greybeard, thy love doth freeze.	
GREMIO	But thine doth fry.	
	Skipper[5], stand back! 'Tis age that nourisheth.	
TRANIO	But youth in ladies' eyes that flourisheth.	
BAPTISTA	Content you, gentlemen; I will compound this strife[6].	330
	'Tis deeds must win the prize, and he of both	
	That can assure my daughter greatest dower[7]	
	Shall have my Bianca's love.	
	Say, Signor Gremio, what can you assure her?	
GREMIO	First, as you know, my house within the city	335
	Is richly furnishèd with plate and gold,	
	Basins and ewers to lave[8] her dainty hands;	
	My hangings all of Tyrian tapestry[9];	
	In ivory coffers[10] I have stuffed my crowns,	
	In cypress chests my arras counterpoints[11],	340
	Costly apparel, tents[12] and canopies,	
	Fine linen, Turkey cushions bossed[13] with pearl,	
	Valance[14] of Venice gold in needlework,	
	Pewter and brass[15], and all things that belongs	
	To house or housekeeping. Then at my farm	345
	I have a hundred milch-kine[16] to the pail[17],	
	Six score fat oxen standing in my stalls,	
	And all things answerable to this portion[18].	
	Myself am struck in years[19] I must confess,	
	And if I die tomorrow this is hers,	350
	If whilst I live she will be only mine.	

Tranio and Gremio make their rival bids for Bianca. Baptista finds Tranio's offer the more attractive and awards him Bianca, subject to confirmation of the dowry. Wedding dates are arranged.

 剧情简介：川纽和葛莱缪为碧昂卡竞价，巴普提斯塔更满意川纽的出价，答应聘礼下定后便将碧昂卡许配给他，并定下婚礼日期。

Stagecraft 导演技巧

Internal stage directions

Lines 360 and 365 are internal stage directions, prompting some kind of noise or gesture from the characters. The lines also mirror each other in their structure (remember, anaphora is where a word or phrase is repeated at the beginning of successive sentences).

- How would you advise the actors to speak and act at these points for greatest comic effect? Write notes giving practical advice to the actors and explaining why your ideas will work.

Write about it

Bianca's point of view (in small groups)

We don't know what Bianca thinks about the way she is being traded by the men and 'sold' to the highest bidder. Imagine that she has overheard the entire conversation from line 330 onwards.

a Take parts as Baptista, Tranio, Gremio and Bianca, and read lines 330–87 aloud. At key points in the script, allow Bianca time to give a commentary on their 'business deal'.

b Write a brief letter from Bianca to a close friend, describing how she feels about this and about each of the men on stage. Remember, she will probably relate parts of what she has overheard, so identify some lines she might quote in her letter.

1 list = listen
2 ducats 达克（一种曾在欧洲通行的意大利金币）
3 Of = In, From
4 jointure （我死后留给她的）赡养费
5 pinched 给……压力
6 argosy 大商船
7 in Marsellis' road 停靠在马赛的港湾
8 galliasses 货轮
9 tight galleys 结实的帆船
10 out-vied 被超过（原指牌戏中叫牌被超过）
11 cavil 鸡毛蒜皮

▶ In what ways does this picture match your idea of Tranio disguised as his master Lucentio? How would you cast and costume him?

THE TAMING OF THE SHREW ACT 2 SCENE 1
悍妇降服记

TRANIO   That 'only' came well in. Sir, list[1] to me:
         I am my father's heir and only son.
         If I may have your daughter to my wife,
         I'll leave her houses three or four as good   355
         Within rich Pisa walls as any one
         Old Signor Gremio has in Padua,
         Besides two thousand ducats[2] by the year
         Of[3] fruitful land, all which shall be her jointure[4].
         What, have I pinched[5] you, Signor Gremio?   360

GREMIO   Two thousand ducats by the year of land?
         [*Aside*] My land amounts not to so much in all! –
         That she shall have, besides an argosy[6]
         That now is lying in Marsellis' road[7]. –
         What, have I choked you with an argosy?   365

TRANIO   Gremio, 'tis known my father hath no less
         Than three great argosies, besides two galliasses[8]
         And twelve tight galleys[9]. These I will assure her,
         And twice as much whate'er thou off'rest next.

GREMIO   Nay, I have offered all. I have no more,   370
         And she can have no more than all I have.
         If you like me, she shall have me and mine.

TRANIO   Why, then the maid is mine from all the world
         By your firm promise. Gremio is out-vied[10].

BAPTISTA I must confess your offer is the best,   375
         And, let your father make her the assurance,
         She is your own; else, you must pardon me.
         If you should die before him, where's her dower?

TRANIO   That's but a cavil[11]. He is old, I young.

GREMIO   And may not young men die as well as old?   380

BAPTISTA Well, gentlemen, I am thus resolved.
         On Sunday next you know
         My daughter Katherine is to be married.
         Now, on the Sunday following shall Bianca
         Be bride to you, if you make this assurance.   385
         If not, to Signor Gremio.
         And so I take my leave, and thank you both.

Gremio comments on the foolishness of Tranio's father in giving away all his money to his son. Tranio realises that as 'Lucentio' he must find a 'Vincentio', his 'father'.

 剧情简介：葛莱缪认为川纽的父亲把所有的钱都给儿子，是做了一件蠢事。川纽意识到，作为"卢森修"他必须找一个"文森修"来当他的"父亲"。

Characters 人物分析

Insulted and insulting (in pairs)

Gremio and Tranio freely insult each other:

- Gremio calls Tranio a 'young gamester' and says that his father is a fool for giving him so much money.
- In line 352, Tranio suggests that if Bianca is stupid enough to marry Gremio, it will not be long before she is unfaithful.

Are these insults warranted and do they have any basis in truth? What do you think of each character's opinion of the other, and of the way they engage in such insulting behaviour?

1 Set foot under thy table 靠你的施舍过活
2 toy 笑话；岂有此理
3 faced it 虚张声势吹牛皮
4 card of ten 面值小的牌
5 supposed 冒牌
6 get 产生
7 sire 父亲

1 Tranio reports back to Lucentio (in pairs)

Improvise a conversation between Lucentio and Tranio about the progress of his negotiations to win Bianca's hand in marriage:

- How will Tranio tell his master about this new twist in the plot?
- How might Lucentio respond?
- What plan will they hatch to 'get a sire'?

In the course of this improvised conversation, include a prediction of what might happen in the next act.

2 Sentences in single syllables (in small groups)

This act contains many one-line sentences that have only single-syllable words in them. The last monosyllabic line is in the script opposite at line 394: 'Yet I have faced it with a card of ten.'

a Read this line aloud several times to experiment with ways of emphasising the monosyllables. Then read lines 389 and 397 out loud. How do these lines contrast with each other?

b Make your own list of monosyllabic lines from the play so far, then talk together about how Shakespeare uses these sentences to create feeling and atmosphere. How do they help us understand the characters?

GREMIO	Adieu, good neighbour.	
		Exit Baptista
	Now I fear thee not.	
	Sirrah, young gamester, your father were a fool	
	To give thee all and in his waning age	390
	Set foot under thy table[1]. Tut, a toy[2]!	
	An old Italian fox is not so kind, my boy.	*Exit*
TRANIO	A vengeance on your crafty withered hide!	
	Yet I have faced it[3] with a card of ten[4].	
	'Tis in my head to do my master good:	395
	I see no reason but supposed[5] Lucentio	
	Must get[6] a father called supposed Vincentio.	
	And that's a wonder – fathers commonly	
	Do get their children, but in this case of wooing	
	A child shall get a sire[7], if I fail not of my cunning.	*Exit* 400

THE TAMING OF THE SHREW
悍妇降服记

Looking back at Act 2 第2幕回顾
Activities for groups or individuals

1 Sly's comments

What do you think Sly's reaction would be to what he has witnessed so far? In some productions, extra 'stage business' is added to include Sly applauding, reacting with distaste or commenting on what he thinks should happen on stage.

- Choose four key moments in Act 2 and improvise appropriate comments from Sly.

2 A new aside for Kate

In Shakespeare's play, Katherina says nothing in response to marrying Petruchio. But at about the same time as Shakespeare's version was first staged, another play called *The Taming of a Shrew* was published. This included an aside in which Katherina reveals her motives for marrying Petruchio: 'But yet I will consent and marry him / For I methinks have lived too long a maid.' Another adaptation of the play included a different aside for Kate: 'A plague upon his impudence! I'm vexed – / I'll marry my revenge, but I will tame him.'

a Which aside do you think is most convincing – one of these two or the one that you made up yourself on page 74?

b Write a paragraph discussing why directors and actors after Shakespeare may have wanted to include a reference to Katherina's motivation for marrying Petruchio. How important is it to understand Katherina's perspective?

3 Plot and sub-plot

The audience's attention in this act alternates between the main plot (with Petruchio and Katherina) and the sub-plot (which centres on Bianca). To explore the similarities and differences between these two plots, copy the chart, opposite (above) and add to it with more characteristics for each group of characters. Try to find examples or quotations from the play as you do so.

Petruchio and Katherina	Bianca and her suitors
Down-to-earth physicality	Romantic ideals
'Taming' and the battle of the sexes	Romance and conventions of love
Imagery of falconry, taming of wild animals and hunting	References to classical lovers, art and poetry
Stock characters from English folk tales (e.g. ...)	Stock characters from Italian comedy (e.g. ...)

4 Put a spin on it

Divide into groups. Each group chooses a different major character and looks back at their speeches and behaviour in this act (remember that several characters are pretending to be someone else). In role as this character, take turns to answer questions from the rest of the group. These questions should interrogate (询问) the character, their actions and motives. They must also be supported by evidence from the script. Present your findings to the other groups and encourage them to ask questions that will help you take your exploration of this character further.

5 What's funny?

Act 2 contains a number of episodes that are often very funny in the theatre.

- Select three or four short extracts from this act and discuss what you think a modern audience would find funny about them. Explore different ways in which your chosen scenes could be directed; for example, by emphasising its 'darker' aspects: is one of the characters unhappy? Do the extracts highlight an unpleasant side to any character?

The two suitors, disguised as teachers, compete for Bianca's attention. She reminds them that she is not a schoolchild, and chooses Cambio (Lucentio) for her first lesson rather than Litio (Hortensio).

剧情简介：假扮教师的两位追求者为赢得碧昂卡相互竞争。碧昂卡提醒他俩自己不是小学生，然后选择让卡毕欧（卢森修），而非理修（郝理修），给她上第一课。

1 'as I please myself' (in pairs)

Take it in turns to read Bianca's lines 16–23.

- The first time, read it in a relaxed way as if you were trying to calm the quarrel. Then identify some quotations that show how Bianca might enjoy being the centre of attention.
- The second time round, read the speech as angrily and selfishly as you can. Then identify some quotations that suggest Bianca may have learnt some lessons from her demanding sister!

Characters 人物分析

Bianca – innocent or coy (故作羞涩)?

a Is Bianca really the submissive daughter she seems to be? Consider her comment to her 'tutors' in Act 3 Scene 1, lines 18–20. Is there any suggestion that Bianca is not quite the modest girl Lucentio thinks she is?

b Think about how physical actions and gestures could reveal more about Bianca's character. Then write two stage directions for lines 16–23 to direct an actor playing Bianca.

1	forbear	收敛，克制
2	forward	冒失，放肆
3	wrangling pedant	爱争辩的学究
4	prerogative	优先权
5	lecture	课
6	Preposterous	本末倒置
7	usual pain	正常工作
8	give me leave	允许我
9	serve in	来点儿（音乐）
10	braves	侮辱，无礼
11	breeching	穿着短裤（指年纪轻总被罚的学生）
12	'pointed = appointed	（规定好）
13	the whiles	片刻，一会儿
14	Conster	翻译

▼ What does the characters' body language reveal about them?

2 Compare the 'love' scenes (in pairs)

Look back at how Petruchio first sets about wooing Katherina in Act 2 Scene 1. How does that wooing scene compare with the one portrayed opposite? Write notes to advising two young actors on how to develop a convincing portrayal of romantic love between Bianca and Lucentio.

Act 3 Scene 1
Baptista's house

Enter LUCENTIO [*as Cambio*], HORTENSIO [*as Litio*] *and* BIANCA.

LUCENTIO	Fiddler, forbear[1]! You grow too forward[2], sir.	
	Have you so soon forgot the entertainment	
	Her sister Katherine welcomed you withal?	
HORTENSIO	But, wrangling pedant[3], this is	
	The patroness of heavenly harmony.	5
	Then give me leave to have prerogative[4],	
	And when in music we have spent an hour,	
	Your lecture[5] shall have leisure for as much.	
LUCENTIO	Preposterous[6] ass, that never read so far	
	To know the cause why music was ordained!	10
	Was it not to refresh the mind of man	
	After his studies or his usual pain[7]?	
	Then give me leave[8] to read philosophy	
	And, while I pause, serve in[9] your harmony.	
HORTENSIO	Sirrah! I will not bear these braves[10] of thine!	15
BIANCA	Why, gentlemen, you do me double wrong	
	To strive for that which resteth in my choice.	
	I am no breeching[11] scholar in the schools:	
	I'll not be tied to hours nor 'pointed[12] times	
	But learn my lessons as I please myself.	20
	And, to cut off all strife, here sit we down.	
	Take you your instrument; play you the whiles[13];	
	His lecture will be done ere you have tuned.	
HORTENSIO	You'll leave his lecture when I am in tune?	
LUCENTIO	That will be never. Tune your instrument.	25
BIANCA	Where left we last?	
LUCENTIO	Here, madam. [*He reads.*]	
	Hic ibat Simois, hic est Sigeia tellus,	
	Hic steterat Priami regia celsa senis.	
BIANCA	Conster[14] them.	30

Lucentio reveals his true identity to Bianca, who, though cautious, offers him hope. After two unsuccessful attempts, Hortensio wins the right to begin his music lesson.

 剧情简介：卢森修向碧昂卡透露了自己的真实身份，碧昂卡尽管小心翼翼，还是让他心存希望。两次失败后，郝坦修终于获得给碧昂卡上音乐课的机会。

Stagecraft 导演技巧

Latin games (in pairs)

Lucentio reveals his love for Bianca in a carefully guarded manner, hidden amongst Latin phrases (lines 31–5). Bianca replies in the same way (lines 39–42).

a As one student reads the lines, pausing at each full stop or semi-colon, the other describes Lucentio's emotional reaction at each point.

b Write notes in your Director's Journal explaining how you would stage this part of the script. Consider the following:
- Does Lucentio alter his delivery at particular points?
- Does he touch Bianca? If so, how does she respond?
- Does Hortensio overhear any part of this secret conversation?

1 Rivals (in small groups)

Throughout the script opposite, the rivalry between the two lovers grows.

- In your groups, take turns as either Hortensio or Lucentio in the hot-seat. Answer questions from the rest of the group about how confident you feel that you can win Bianca's love, and about your plans for gaining her affections and outwitting your rival.

Language in the play 剧中语言

Dramatic irony and musical imagery

a Experiment with reading Hortensio's and Lucentio's asides, to explore their character and emotions. What does the audience know that the other character is not aware of?

b Identify the musical jokes and insults prompted by Hortensio's disguise as a music tutor in lines 37–8, 43–4 and 57. How does this language affect the comedy of the situation as it develops?

1 **bearing my port** 假扮我
2 **pantaloon** （指葛莱缪）
3 **treble jars** 高音太刺耳
4 **Spit in the hole** 再去调调音（引自谚语 spit in your hands and take better hold [掌中吐唾沫，抓得更牢靠]）
5 **take heed** 注意，提防
6 **bass** 低音
7 **base knave** 低贱的无赖
8 **Pedascule** 书虫（轻蔑的叫法）
9 **Aeacides / Ajax** 艾西迪斯，爱杰克斯（特洛伊战争中的希腊勇士）
10 **else** 否则
11 **pleasant** 开玩笑，闹着玩
12 **three parts** 需要三位歌手的和音（郝坦修暗示卢森修是不受欢迎的第三者）
13 **withal** = as well
14 **but** = unless

THE TAMING OF THE SHREW ACT 3 SCENE 1
悍妇降服记

LUCENTIO *Hic ibat* – as I told you before; *Simois* – I am Lucentio; *hic est* – son unto Vincentio of Pisa; *Sigeia tellus* – disguised thus to get your love. *Hic steterat* – and that Lucentio that comes a-wooing; *Priami* – is my man Tranio; *regia* – bearing my port[1]; *celsa senis* – that we might beguile the old pantaloon[2]. 35

HORTENSIO Madam, my instrument's in tune.

BIANCA Let's hear. [*He plays.*] O fie! The treble jars[3].

LUCENTIO Spit in the hole[4], man, and tune again.

BIANCA Now let me see if I can conster it. *Hic ibat Simois* – I know you not; *hic est Sigeia tellus* – I trust you not; *Hic steterat Priami* – take heed[5] he hear us not; *regia* – presume not; *celsa senis* – despair not. 40

HORTENSIO Madam, 'tis now in tune.
        [*He plays again.*]

LUCENTIO   All but the bass[6].

HORTENSIO The bass is right; 'tis the base knave[7] that jars.
    [*Aside*] How fiery and forward our pedant is! 45
    Now, for my life, the knave doth court my love.
    Pedascule[8], I'll watch you better yet.

BIANCA In time I may believe, yet I mistrust.

LUCENTIO Mistrust it not, for sure Aeacides[9]
    Was Ajax[9], called so from his grandfather. 50

BIANCA I must believe my master, else[10], I promise you,
    I should be arguing still upon that doubt.
    But let it rest. Now, Litio, to you.
    Good master, take it not unkindly, pray,
    That I have been thus pleasant[11] with you both. 55

HORTENSIO [*To Lucentio*]
    You may go walk, and give me leave awhile.
    My lessons make no music in three parts[12].

LUCENTIO Are you so formal, sir? Well, I must wait –
    [*Aside*] And watch withal[13], for, but[14] I be deceived,
    Our fine musician groweth amorous. 60

Hortensio attempts to woo Bianca during a 'lesson', but she rejects him. Bianca is summoned to prepare for Katherina's wedding, so Lucentio also leaves. Hortensio is suspicious of them both.

剧情简介：郝坦修"上课"时向碧昂卡求爱，遭到拒绝。碧昂卡被唤去准备凯特芮娜的婚礼，于是卢森修也离开。郝坦修对他们俩产生了怀疑。

1 Update the gamut

Directors have often been unable to resist updating Bianca's recital of the 'gamut'. For example, in recent productions it has been set to a tune from a big production musical and delivered as a rap.

- What would you do to make this part of the script more interesting or amusing?

1 rudiments 基础知识
2 gamut 正规音阶
3 pithy 简练
4 effectual 有效
5 clef 谱号
6 nice 挑剔；反复无常
7 pry into 打听，窥探
8 stale 诱鸟，召回猎鹰的诱饵
9 Seize thee that list! 让任何想得到你的人得手吧！
10 ranging 见异思迁（原指猎鹰偏离目标）
11 be quit with 撇开，摆脱
12 changing 另觅佳人

▼ In pairs, discuss the sort of pupil Bianca appears to be in this production.

2 Hortensio's suspicions (in pairs)

a In lines 84–9, Hortensio voices his suspicions about Lucentio and describes how he would respond if he thought Bianca had eyes for anyone but him. Imagine that Bianca overheard these words. Compose a few lines she might give in response.

b Read the lines aloud to each other in different ways – angrily, jealously, sadly, viciously. Do you think Hortensio is sincere in his love for Bianca? What kind of husband or lover would he make?

3 Dramatic exits

Hortensio is given a rhyming couplet as he leaves the stage, but notice how the words at the end of these two lines are linked in meaning as well as in rhyme (if Bianca will 'range', then Hortensio will 'change').

- Make up similar rhyming couplets for Bianca and Lucentio as they each make their exits, commenting on the events that have just taken place.

The Taming of the Shrew Act 3 Scene 1
悍妇降服记

HORTENSIO   Madam, before you touch the instrument
To learn the order of my fingering,
I must begin with rudiments[1] of art,
To teach you gamut[2] in a briefer sort,
More pleasant, pithy[3] and effectual[4]   65
Than hath been taught by any of my trade;
And there it is in writing, fairly drawn.

BIANCA   Why, I am past my gamut long ago.

HORTENSIO   Yet read the gamut of Hortensio.

BIANCA   [*Reads*]
'*Gamut* I am, the ground of all accord: 70
A re, to plead Hortensio's passion;
B mi, Bianca, take him for thy lord;
C fa ut, that loves with all affection;
D sol re, one clef[5], two notes have I;
E la mi, show pity or I die.'   75
Call you this 'gamut'? Tut, I like it not!
Old fashions please me best. I am not so nice[6]
To change true rules for odd inventions.

Enter a SERVANT.

SERVANT   Mistress, your father prays you leave your books,
And help to dress your sister's chamber up.   80
You know tomorrow is the wedding-day.

BIANCA   Farewell, sweet masters both, I must be gone.
[*Exeunt Bianca and Servant*]

LUCENTIO   Faith, mistress, then I have no cause to stay.   [*Exit*]

HORTENSIO   But I have cause to pry into[7] this pedant:
Methinks he looks as though he were in love.   85
Yet if thy thoughts, Bianca, be so humble
To cast thy wand'ring eyes on every stale[8],
Seize thee that list![9] If once I find thee ranging[10]
Hortensio will be quit with[11] thee by changing[12].   *Exit*

The wedding day has arrived, the family and guests are ready, but Petruchio is missing. Katherina complains bitterly about her treatment and, although Tranio tries to cheer her up, she leaves in tears.

剧情简介：婚礼的日子到了，亲友宾客均已到场，却不见珀楚秋的踪影。凯特芮娜苦苦抱怨她竟被如此对待，川纽想让她高兴起来，但她还是哭着离开。

Stagecraft 导演技巧

What sort of wedding is it? (in pairs)

The way in which a production stages the wedding morning creates opportunities for comedy and manipulates the audience into making significant judgments about the characters. With a partner, discuss how a director might stage lines 1–26 as the guests wait for the bridegroom. Consider:

- what Katherina is wearing
- the gestures and tones used by Baptista and Katherina in the script opposite
- what the other characters are doing and saying while they wait for Petruchio.

1	forsooth	确实
2	rudesby	无礼的粗人
3	spleen	喜怒无常
4	wooed ... leisure	(谚语 to marry in haste and repent at leisure [结婚太匆忙，闲来悔断肠])
5	frantic	疯狂
6	be noted for	以……闻名
7	merry	幽默风趣
8	Lo	= Look
9	means but well	完全出于好意

1 Responses to Katherina (in fours)

If Katherina is so much against marrying Petruchio, why is she now waiting in her wedding dress? Write a brief response to that question. Afterwards, each person chooses a character from those on stage during the wedding morning. Explain to the others how much sympathy your character feels for Katherina as she waits for the missing Petruchio.

Characters 人物分析

'Petruchio means but well'

Look carefully at Tranio's portrait of Petruchio in lines 21–5. Contrast it with the way in which Katherina has just described him (lines 8–20). Copy and complete the table below with quotations from the play so far that confirm either or both of these views. Add other descriptions of Petruchio and suggest a few aspects of his personality not mentioned by either Tranio or Katherina.

Tranio's descriptions	Katherina's descriptions	Other descriptions
He 'means but well'	'mad-brain rudesby'	

Act 3 Scene 2
Outside Baptista's house

Enter BAPTISTA, GREMIO, TRANIO [*disguised as Lucentio*], KATHERINA, BIANCA, [LUCENTIO *disguised as Cambio,*] *other* GUESTS *and* ATTENDANTS.

BAPTISTA	[*To Tranio*] Signor Lucentio, this is the 'pointed day
	That Katherine and Petruchio should be married,
	And yet we hear not of our son-in-law.
	What will be said? What mockery will it be
	To want the bridegroom when the priest attends 5
	To speak the ceremonial rites of marriage!
	What says Lucentio to this shame of ours?
KATHERINA	No shame but mine. I must, forsooth[1], be forced
	To give my hand, opposed against my heart,
	Unto a mad-brain rudesby[2], full of spleen[3], 10
	Who wooed in haste and means to wed at leisure[4].
	I told you, I, he was a frantic[5] fool,
	Hiding his bitter jests in blunt behaviour.
	And to be noted for[6] a merry[7] man,
	He'll woo a thousand, 'point the day of marriage, 15
	Make feast, invite friends, and proclaim the banns,
	Yet never means to wed where he hath wooed.
	Now must the world point at poor Katherine
	And say, 'Lo[8], there is mad Petruchio's wife
	If it would please him come and marry her!' 20
TRANIO	Patience, good Katherine, and Baptista too.
	Upon my life, Petruchio means but well[9],
	Whatever fortune stays him from his word.
	Though he be blunt, I know him passing wise;
	Though he be merry, yet withal he's honest. 25
KATHERINA	Would Katherine had never seen him though!

Exit weeping [*followed by Bianca and others*]

As Baptista sympathises with Katherina, Biondello brings news of the bridegroom's approach. He describes Petruchio's fantastic appearance. Grumio is dressed in a similarly strange manner.

 剧情简介：正当巴普提斯塔对凯特芮娜表示同情的时候，卞代娄带来消息说新郎马上到。他描述了珀楚秋的奇异打扮，葛儒缪也打扮得怪模怪样。

Stagecraft 导演技巧
'Go, girl' (in pairs)

Katherina makes her exit at line 26 and her father says 'I cannot blame thee now to weep'.

- Talk together about how Katherina might leave the stage. Is she alone? If someone accompanies her, do they go out of curiosity or to offer genuine support? What effect might this have on the characters left on stage? And on the audience?

1 Biondello's language (in large groups)

Biondello gives a very detailed picture of Petruchio, his horse and Grumio. Everything is described with great invention and relish, and Biondello includes all the horse diseases he can think of for the sake of comic exaggeration.

a Read lines 41–62 round the group (speak only up to a punctuation mark, then allow the next person to take over). Do this two or three times to gain fluency. Afterwards, write three pieces of advice for an actor on how to perform these lines on stage – what pace, tone and gestures should they use?

b The description of Petruchio's horse presents a particular problem for the actor. Should he attempt to make the meaning clear to the audience using physical gestures or mime? Within your groups, split into pairs. Each pair should perform three or four lines from Biondello's description. Use vocal and facial expressions, gestures, mimes – anything to help you convey the meaning. Then choose a particular style (slowly, quickly, amused, shocked) and perform it again for the whole group.

Write about it 写作练习
Gossip and scandal

Use Biondello's description in lines 41–56 to write a letter from one of the wedding guests to a close friend. How did you feel as Katherina waited alone at the altar (圣坛)? Describe Petruchio's late and chaotic arrival and his bizarre appearance. Try to explain to your friend what you think Petruchio is doing. Is he, as Tranio said, someone who 'means but well'?

1 jerkin 马甲，短夹克
2 turned 里外反穿（这样省得洗）
3 candle-cases 破得都可以当蜡烛盒
4 chapeless 没有剑鞘
5 points 把紧身裤袜系在紧身上衣上的吊带
6 hipped 因髋骨受伤而跛
7 of no kindred 不配套
8 glanders 因患马鼻疽而下巴肿、流鼻涕
9 lampass / fashions 动物的口疾
10 windgalls … fives 马身上其他肿瘤和肿胀部分
11 stark spoiled 被完全摧毁
12 staggers 导致头迷眼花、四肢不稳的病
13 begnawn with the bots 肠道有虫子噬咬
14 shoulder-shotten 肩膀脱臼
15 near-legged before 前腿向内弯曲
16 half-cheeked bit 戴歪的马嚼子
17 headstall / girth / crupper 马笼头，肚带，臀兜带（马具）
18 pieced with packthread 用绳线修补过
19 lackey 男仆，侍从
20 caparisoned 装束
21 kersey 羊毛
22 boot-hose 与马靴配套的长袜
23 gartered … list 用红色和蓝色的破布条做吊袜带

THE TAMING OF THE SHREW ACT 3 SCENE 2
悍妇降服记

BAPTISTA Go, girl. I cannot blame thee now to weep,
For such an injury would vex a very saint,
Much more a shrew of thy impatient humour.

Enter BIONDELLO.

BIONDELLO Master, master, news! And such old news as you never heard of!

BAPTISTA Is it new and old too? How may that be?

BIONDELLO Why, is it not news to hear of Petruchio's coming?

BAPTISTA Is he come?

BIONDELLO Why no, sir.

BAPTISTA What then?

BIONDELLO He is coming.

BAPTISTA When will he be here?

BIONDELLO When he stands where I am and sees you there.

TRANIO But say, what to thine old news?

BIONDELLO Why, Petruchio is coming in a new hat and an old jerkin[1]; a pair of old breeches thrice turned[2]; a pair of boots that have been candle-cases[3], one buckled, another laced; an old rusty sword tane out of the town armoury, with a broken hilt and chapeless[4]; with two broken points[5]; his horse hipped[6] – with an old mothy saddle and stirrups of no kindred[7] – besides, possessed with the glanders[8] and like to mose in the chine; troubled with the lampass[9], infected with the fashions[9], full of windgalls, sped with spavins, rayed with the yellows, past cure of the fives[10], stark spoiled[11] with the staggers[12], begnawn with the bots[13], swayed in the back and shoulder-shotten[14], near-legged before[15], and with a half-cheeked bit[16] and a headstall[17] of sheep's leather, which, being restrained to keep him from stumbling, hath been often burst and now repaired with knots; one girth[17] six times pieced, and a woman's crupper[17] of velour, which hath two letters for her name fairly set down in studs, and here and there pieced with packthread[18].

BAPTISTA Who comes with him?

BIONDELLO O sir, his lackey[19], for all the world caparisoned[20] like the horse, with a linen stock on one leg and a kersey[21] boot-hose[22] on the other, gartered with a red and blue list[23]; an old hat and the humour of forty fancies pricked in't for a feather; a monster, a very monster in apparel, and not like a Christian footboy or a gentleman's lackey.

Biondello distracts Baptista with more wordplay until Petruchio makes his entrance. Petruchio appears puzzled by the amazement that greets him.

剧情简介：卞代娄继续耍嘴皮子转移巴普提斯塔的注意力，直到珀楚秋上场。迎接他的众人目瞪口呆，珀楚秋却看上去疑惑不解。

Stagecraft 导演技巧

The arrival of Petruchio and Grumio (in pairs)

Shakespeare deliberately delays Petruchio and Grumio's entrance to intensify the shock, surprise and comedy.

a Work up detailed stage directions for the script opposite and then stage your own entrance for these characters. Experiment with pose and gesture. Think about movements that the two men could make as they enter that might add to the comedy.

b Look back at how Biondello describes Petruchio and Grumio in lines 41–62, then talk about ways in which you could costume them for a modern-dress production.

1 pricks 促使
2 mean-apparelled 穿着寒酸
3 all one 一回事
4 Saint Jamy = Saint James
5 gallants 穿着时髦的小伙子
6 Were it better 即使我穿得好一点儿
7 Gentles 先生们
8 monument 预兆
9 prodigy 征兆
10 unprovided 毫无准备
11 doff this habit 脱掉这身穿戴
12 estate 身份，地位
13 occasion of import 重要事情

◀ This is how Petruchio and Grumio looked in one production. What effect do you think their entrance would have had on the other characters?

1 Internal stage directions (in pairs)

a Petruchio and Baptista share two lines of script upon Petruchio's arrival. Experiment with different ways of reading these lines, then discuss how you would stage this interchange. Write notes to the actors playing these characters, giving them advice about what to do here.

b Petruchio's rhetorical questions give some indication of how the rest of the characters should behave. Use these internal stage directions to advise the other actors what they should be doing at this point.

TRANIO	'Tis some odd humour pricks¹ him to this fashion,	
	Yet oftentimes he goes but mean-apparelled².	
BAPTISTA	I am glad he's come, howsoe'er he comes.	65
BIONDELLO	Why, sir, he comes not.	
BAPTISTA	Didst thou not say he comes?	
BIONDELLO	Who? That Petruchio came?	
BAPTISTA	Ay, that Petruchio came.	
BIONDELLO	No, sir, I say his horse comes with him on his back.	70
BAPTISTA	Why, that's all one³.	
BIONDELLO	Nay, by Saint Jamy⁴,	
	I hold you a penny,	
	A horse and a man	
	Is more than one,	75
	And yet not many.	

Enter PETRUCHIO *and* GRUMIO.

PETRUCHIO	Come, where be these gallants⁵? Who's at home?	
BAPTISTA	You are welcome, sir.	
PETRUCHIO	And yet I come not well.	
BAPTISTA	And yet you halt not.	
TRANIO	Not so well apparelled	
	As I wish you were.	80
PETRUCHIO	Were it better⁶, I should rush in thus.	
	But where is Kate? Where is my lovely bride?	
	How does my father? Gentles⁷, methinks you frown,	
	And wherefore gaze this goodly company	
	As if they saw some wondrous monument⁸,	85
	Some comet or unusual prodigy⁹?	
BAPTISTA	Why, sir, you know this is your wedding-day.	
	First were we sad, fearing you would not come,	
	Now sadder that you come so unprovided¹⁰.	
	Fie, doff this habit¹¹, shame to your estate¹²,	90
	An eye-sore to our solemn festival.	
TRANIO	And tell us what occasion of import¹³	
	Hath all so long detained you from your wife	
	And sent you hither so unlike yourself.	

Petruchio brushes questions aside and insists on going to the church to be married dressed as he is. The rest of the family and guests follow. Tranio and Lucentio remain, discussing their plans to win Bianca.

 剧情简介：珀楚秋不理众人的质疑，坚持以他那身打扮去教堂完婚，其余亲友和宾客跟随去教堂。川纽和卢森修留下，商量计谋以赢得碧昂卡的芳心。

1 Why has Katherina left? (in pairs)

Petruchio seems surprised that Katherina is not there to greet him (line 100). A meeting between the two at this point might well cause sparks to fly.

- Improvise the conversation between Katherina and the person who comes to tell her that Petruchio has arrived (Bianca? Baptista? A servant?). How much would they reveal about the manner of Petruchio's arrival? What would Katherina's response be?

Themes 主题分析
Clothing, appearance and identity

Several directors have encouraged the actor playing Petruchio to emphasise line 107: 'To me she's married, not unto my clothes.' Petruchio will again state his view that appearance is not important in Act 4 Scene 3, lines 169–70.

- Script a conversation between two wedding guests who have overheard him say this. Do they agree with him or disagree?

2 What is Grumio doing? (by yourself)

Grumio does not speak from the time he arrives with Petruchio to his departure after line 113. Yet he must somehow be fully involved in the action.

- Put together a list of as many suggestions as you can to help the actor playing Grumio decide what to do during this scene.

Characters 人物分析
'He hath some meaning in his mad attire (服装)' (in pairs)

Once again, Tranio is the one who tries to explain what Petruchio is up to, although he does not elaborate on what Petruchio's reasons might be for wearing such 'mad attire' (line 114).

a Talk together about what meaning there might be in Petruchio's behaviour at this point. Try to produce an explanation that Tranio could offer, however implausible.

b What might Petruchio himself confide to the audience to explain his behaviour? Provide him with an aside as he leaves the stage.

---

1 Tedious 冗长
2 Sufficeth 简而言之
3 digress 改变计划
4 wears 正要过去
5 Good sooth 就是这样
6 wear 拥有；使……筋疲力尽
7 accoutrements 衣服
8 lovely = loving
9 put on better 穿好一点儿的衣服
10 event 结局
11 concerneth us 对我们很重要
12 skills 至关重要
13 fit him to our turn 利用他达到我们的目的

PETRUCHIO	Tedious[1] it were to tell, and harsh to hear.	95
	Sufficeth[2] I am come to keep my word	
	Though in some part enforcèd to digress[3],	
	Which at more leisure I will so excuse	
	As you shall well be satisfied with all.	
	But where is Kate? I stay too long from her.	100
	The morning wears[4], 'tis time we were at church.	
TRANIO	See not your bride in these unreverent robes;	
	Go to my chamber, put on clothes of mine.	
PETRUCHIO	Not I, believe me; thus I'll visit her.	
BAPTISTA	But thus, I trust, you will not marry her.	105
PETRUCHIO	Good sooth[5], even thus. Therefore ha' done with words;	
	To me she's married, not unto my clothes.	
	Could I repair what she will wear[6] in me	
	As I can change these poor accoutrements[7],	
	'Twere well for Kate and better for myself.	110
	But what a fool am I to chat with you	
	When I should bid good morrow to my bride	
	And seal the title with a lovely[8] kiss!	

Exit [with Grumio]

TRANIO	He hath some meaning in his mad attire.	
	We will persuade him, be it possible,	115
	To put on better[9] ere he go to church.	
BAPTISTA	I'll after him and see the event[10] of this.	

Exit [with Gremio, Biondello and Attendants]

TRANIO	[*To Lucentio*] But, sir, to love concerneth us[11] to add	
	Her father's liking, which to bring to pass,	
	As I before imparted to your worship,	120
	I am to get a man – whate'er he be	
	It skills[12] not much, we'll fit him to our turn[13] –	
	And he shall be Vincentio of Pisa	
	And make assurance here in Padua	
	Of greater sums than I have promisèd.	125
	So shall you quietly enjoy your hope	
	And marry sweet Bianca with consent.	

Lucentio and Tranio review their plot to win Bianca. Gremio returns and tells them about Petruchio's strange behaviour at the church – he has struck the priest!

 剧情简介：卢森修和川纽商议赢得碧昂卡的计策。葛莱缪赶回来，告诉他们珀楚秋在教堂的反常行为——他打了神父！

1 Staging the wedding (whole class)

Shakespeare chose not to stage the wedding itself, but movie directors have often been unable to resist the temptation to show this comic interlude (插曲).

a How would you direct the wedding scene for a new movie production set in your school? Think about the people you would cast, music for the film score, the set and props, the use of camera angles and special effects. Write out your ideas for filming this scene, or create a storyboard.

b The wedding could make for a very lively and entertaining scene on stage, so why do you think Shakespeare chose not to show it? Hold a class debate to explore the merits and drawbacks of including Petruchio and Katherina's wedding scene in a stage production of the play.

2 'The narrow-prying father' (in pairs)

a Look back through the play so far and decide whether line 136 is an accurate description of Baptista. Many modern productions feel they have to present him as a generally unlikeable figure. What do you think?

b In role as an actor who has been cast as Baptista in a new production, describe what you think of him and how you would want to portray him on stage.

> ### Language in the play 剧中语言
> #### The devil and the lamb
> In Act 1, Katherina was described as a devil, and now the word is applied to Petruchio. Katherina, however, is now a lamb, a dove and a harmless innocent (line 147).
>
> - Make a quick list of all the approving and disapproving words you would use to describe these two characters at this point in the play. Start with the words used in the script opposite, then add your own with reference to other parts of the play.
>
> | Katherina | | Petruchio | |
> | --- | --- | --- | --- |
> | Approving | Disapproving | Approving | Disapproving |
> | Lamb | Devil | | Devil |
> | Dove | | | |

1 **steal our marriage** 私奔
2 **watch our vantage** 我们寻找最佳时机
3 **narrow-prying** （因怀疑而）紧盯着
4 **quaint** 狡猾
5 **groom** 马夫，粗人
6 **grumbling** 脾气粗暴
7 **Curster** 脾气更暴
8 **fool** 小傻瓜
9 **gogs-wouns** = God's wounds （以上帝的伤口起誓）
10 **list** = pleases to

LUCENTIO	Were it not that my fellow schoolmaster
	Doth watch Bianca's steps so narrowly,
	'Twere good, methinks, to steal our marriage[1],	130
	Which once performed, let all the world say no,
	I'll keep mine own despite of all the world.
TRANIO	That by degrees we mean to look into
	And watch our vantage[2] in this business.
	We'll overreach the greybeard Gremio,	135
	The narrow-prying[3] father Minola,
	The quaint[4] musician, amorous Litio,
	All for my master's sake, Lucentio.

Enter Gremio.

	Signor Gremio! Came you from the church?
GREMIO	As willingly as e'er I came from school.	140
TRANIO	And is the bride and bridegroom coming home?
GREMIO	A bridegroom, say you? 'Tis a groom[5] indeed –
	A grumbling[6] groom, and that the girl shall find.
TRANIO	Curster[7] than she? Why, 'tis impossible.
GREMIO	Why, he's a devil, a devil, a very fiend!	145
TRANIO	Why, she's a devil, a devil, the devil's dam!
GREMIO	Tut, she's a lamb, a dove, a fool[8], to him.
	I'll tell you, Sir Lucentio: when the priest
	Should ask if Katherine should be his wife,
	'Ay, by gogs-wouns[9]!' quoth he, and swore so loud	150
	That, all-amazed, the priest let fall the book,
	And as he stooped again to take it up,
	This mad-brained bridegroom took him such a cuff
	That down fell priest and book, and book and priest!
	'Now take them up', quoth he, 'if any list[10].'	155
TRANIO	What said the wench when he rose again?

Gremio describes how, at the wedding, Petruchio raged, threw wine over the sexton, and kissed Katherina very enthusiastically. When the wedding party returns, Petruchio announces that he must leave immediately.

  剧情简介：葛莱缪描述珀楚秋在婚礼上大发雷霆，把葡萄酒泼在教堂司事身上，而且肆无忌惮地亲吻凯特芮娜。婚礼仪式结束，众人返回，珀楚秋宣布他必须马上离开。

1 The wedding description (in small groups)

Gremio's description of the wedding is very detailed (lines 148–72) and provides another set-piece (套路) dramatic narrative for the actor playing the part.

a In your groups, take it in turns to choose what you think is the funniest example of Petruchio's outrageous behaviour. Explain your choice to the others.

b Improvise a contemporary version of the wedding, but this time it is the bride who misbehaves. It is a 'society wedding', so spend some time preparing the right atmosphere in the church. Would a woman employ the same disruptive (颠覆性) style and techniques as Petruchio?

1 for why   因为
2 cozen   欺骗
3 aboard   在船上
4 carousing   开怀畅饮，互祝健康
5 quaffed off   喝光
6 muscadel   婚礼上喝的甜白葡萄酒
7 sops   浸酒的蛋糕
8 hungerly   如同营养不良
9 rout   人群（众宾客）
10 cheer   酒宴
11 hence   离开
12 take my leave   与你们告别
13 Make it no wonder   不要惊讶
14 beheld   见证

Characters 人物分析

The wedding party's arrival (in large groups)

Line 173 marks yet another dramatic entrance, with the potential for much comic business. Bands, paparazzi (狗仔队), curious hangers-on (看客) and journalists have all been used as the wedding party arrives.

- Gather everyone for a wedding photograph. Devise four to six photographs (tableaux) for the Minola family album. Make sure that future generations will be able to gain a fair idea of the personality of each person present.
- Accompany each 'photograph' with a witty or pithy caption (说明文字) from each character's perspective. You could make these up, or use a suitable quotation from the play to show what your guests were thinking when the photograph was taken.

The Taming of the Shrew Act 3 Scene 2
悍妇降服记

GREMIO	Trembled and shook, for why[1] he stamped and swore	
	As if the vicar meant to cozen[2] him.	
	But after many ceremonies done	
	He calls for wine. 'A health', quoth he, as if	160
	He had been aboard[3], carousing[4] to his mates	
	After a storm; quaffed off[5] the muscadel[6]	
	And threw the sops[7] all in the sexton's face,	
	Having no other reason	
	But that his beard grew thin and hungerly[8]	165
	And seemed to ask him sops as he was drinking.	
	This done, he took the bride about the neck	
	And kissed her lips with such a clamorous smack	
	That at the parting all the church did echo.	
	And I, seeing this, came thence for very shame,	170
	And after me, I know, the rout[9] is coming.	
	Such a mad marriage never was before!	

Music plays.

Hark, hark! I hear the minstrels play.

Enter Petruchio, Katherina, Bianca, Hortensio [as Litio], Baptista, [Grumio and others].

PETRUCHIO	Gentlemen and friends, I thank you for your pains.	
	I know you think to dine with me today	175
	And have prepared great store of wedding cheer[10],	
	But so it is, my haste doth call me hence[11],	
	And therefore here I mean to take my leave[12].	
BAPTISTA	Is't possible you will away tonight?	
PETRUCHIO	I must away today, before night come.	180
	Make it no wonder[13]; if you knew my business,	
	You would entreat me rather go than stay.	
	And, honest company, I thank you all	
	That have beheld[14] me give away myself	
	To this most patient, sweet and virtuous wife.	185
	Dine with my father, drink a health to me,	
	For I must hence, and farewell to you all.	

Petruchio ignores all pleas to stay. When Katherina refuses to go with him, he insists and orders the guests to go to the wedding breakfast.

 剧情简介：众人请他留下，珀楚秋概不理会。凯特芮娜拒绝跟他离开，珀楚秋坚持己见，命令众宾客去享用婚礼早餐。

1 Entreating Petruchio (in fours)

Petruchio insists that his new bride leaves with him before the wedding feast has begun, but Katherina shows 'a spirit to resist'. This is an important battle of wills between the newly married couple. Read aloud lines 188–97. Experiment with ways of saying the lines, especially those between Petruchio and Katherina. While doing so, consider the following:

- How would Katherina try to entreat her new husband? Would she use a sweet voice and flattering tone, or a commanding and demanding attitude? (Remember, line 194 is a crucial moment for Katherina.)
- How would Petruchio respond? Kind but firm or heartless and cruel?
- Do you want to create a comic atmosphere by focusing on the humour of the situation? Or do you think this scene requires a tense atmosphere full of conflict and antagonism (对抗)?

1 the … horses 燕麦吃了马（葛儒缪想说马吃了燕麦，也许葛儒缪不过是装傻？）
2 You … green 趁着你的靴子还新着赶紧走吧（源自一句对不受欢迎的宾客下逐客令的谚语）
3 jolly 傲慢，专横
4 take … roundly 刚一开始就要耍威风
5 What hast thou to do? 与你何干？
6 Father, be quiet 父亲，不必多言（不用管）
7 stay my leisure 等到我准备好
8 work 沸腾；发怒
9 domineer 大吃大喝
10 Carouse 玩乐，尽兴
11 maidenhead 处女之身

Themes 主题分析
Order and disorder

Grumio typically provides a comic moment as well as a shrewd observation when he says 'the oats have eaten the horses'. This is a ridiculous image of an upside-down world where horses are eaten by their food. There are other examples of disorder here, too, such as a daughter not listening to her father and a bride treating her groom like an unwelcome guest.

- Find and then write stage directions for these points in the script to advise the actor playing Katherina how to speak, act and use the stage space to show she is in control of the situation.

Write about it 写作练习
What would Baptista say?

- Katherina refuses to listen to Baptista in line 206. Compose four lines that he might have said if he was given the chance.
- Compose another four lines from one of the other characters present, giving advice to either Petruchio or Katherina about their behaviour or how their future looks at this point in the play.

TRANIO	Let us entreat you stay till after dinner.	
PETRUCHIO	It may not be.	
GREMIO	Let me entreat you.	
PETRUCHIO	It cannot be.	
KATHERINA	Let me entreat you.	190
PETRUCHIO	I am content.	
KATHERINA	Are you content to stay?	
PETRUCHIO	I am content you shall entreat me stay –	
	But yet not stay, entreat me how you can.	
KATHERINA	Now, if you love me, stay.	
PETRUCHIO	Grumio, my horse!	
GRUMIO	Ay, sir, they be ready – the oats have eaten the horses[1].	195
KATHERINA	Nay then,	
	Do what thou canst, I will not go today!	
	No, nor tomorrow – not till I please myself.	
	The door is open, sir, there lies your way;	
	You may be jogging whiles your boots are green[2].	200
	For me, I'll not be gone till I please myself.	
	'Tis like you'll prove a jolly[3] surly groom	
	That take it on you at the first so roundly[4].	
PETRUCHIO	O Kate, content thee; prithee be not angry.	
KATHERINA	I will be angry. What hast thou to do?[5]	205
	– Father, be quiet[6]. He shall stay my leisure[7].	
GREMIO	Ay, marry, sir, now it begins to work[8].	
KATHERINA	Gentlemen, forward to the bridal dinner.	
	I see a woman may be made a fool	
	If she had not a spirit to resist.	210
PETRUCHIO	They shall go forward, Kate, at thy command.	
	Obey the bride, you that attend on her.	
	Go to the feast, revel and domineer[9],	
	Carouse[10] full measure to her maidenhead[11],	
	Be mad and merry – or go hang yourselves.	215
	But for my bonny Kate, she must with me.	

Insisting that Katherina is his property, Petruchio 'defends' his wife against attack from the wedding party and rushes off with her. The guests are left confused and amused, and decide to go to the feast.

剧情简介：珀楚秋声称凯特芮娜是他的财产，他会"保护"妻子免受婚礼宾客的冒犯，于是拽着她匆匆离开。宾客们既不解又觉得好笑，决定去参加婚宴。

1 'I will be master of what is mine own'
(in large groups)

In lines 217–24, Petruchio gives a controversial speech that is often greeted with laughter, horror or scorn today. Discuss how you respond to this speech and then use the following activities to explore it in more detail.

a On the one hand, the speech is comic because Petruchio is exaggerating Katherina's response and the wedding guests' entreaties to stay for the wedding feast:

- 'Nay, look not big, nor stamp, nor stare, nor fret'. What actions might Katherina be doing here?
- 'Fear not, sweet wench, they shall not touch thee'. Are the wedding guests really attacking her?

b On the other hand, it is unpleasant and rather sinister (险恶) because Petruchio says he owns Katherina, now that he is married to her.

- In pairs, one person reads, pausing at each punctuation mark. At each pause, the other person says: 'Oh no, I'm not, because …' (give reasons).
- 'I will be master of what is mine own. / She is my goods, my chattels; she is my house'. What does Petruchio mean by this and how do you think Katherina responds?

> ### Characters 人物分析
> #### Playing the shrew
> According to Gremio, Petruchio is 'Kated' and has become as shrewish and irrational as her. Experiment by speaking Petruchio's lines in different styles – for example, as a formal lecture by a mad professor, as a rant (激昂演说) from a politician or as a routine by a comedian. Can you find a style to fit the language? How do you think Katherina feels, being on the receiving end of such shrewish behaviour?

2 'let them go' (in pairs)

Write a detailed stage direction to show how Petruchio and Katherina leave the stage. Does she leave quietly, resigned to her fate? Does he carry her out by force? Or does she storm out in frustration?

---

1 look not big 别凶巴巴的
2 chattels 动产
3 action on 控告
4 buckler （执小圆盾）保护
5 Went them not 假如他们不走
6 Kated 染上了凯特病
7 wants / For to supply 缺席
8 wants no junkets 不缺美味佳肴

Nay, look not big¹, nor stamp, nor stare, nor fret;
I will be master of what is mine own.
She is my goods, my chattels²; she is my house,
My household-stuff, my field, my barn, 220
My horse, my ox, my ass, my anything,
And here she stands. Touch her whoever dare,
I'll bring mine action on³ the proudest he
That stops my way in Padua. Grumio,
Draw forth thy weapon – We are beset with thieves! 225
Rescue thy mistress, if thou be a man.
– Fear not, sweet wench, they shall not touch thee, Kate;
I'll buckler⁴ thee against a million!

Exeunt Petruchio, Katherina [and Grumio]

BAPTISTA Nay, let them go – a couple of quiet ones!
GREMIO Went they not⁵ quickly, I should die with laughing. 230
TRANIO Of all mad matches never was the like.
LUCENTIO Mistress, what's your opinion of your sister?
BIANCA That being mad herself, she's madly mated.
GREMIO I warrant him, Petruchio is Kated⁶.
BAPTISTA Neighbours and friends, though bride and bridegroom wants 235
For to supply⁷ the places at the table,
You know there wants no junkets⁸ at the feast.
[*To Tranio*] Lucentio, you shall supply the bridegroom's place,
And let Bianca take her sister's room.
TRANIO Shall sweet Bianca practise how to bride it? 240
BAPTISTA She shall, Lucentio. Come, gentlemen, let's go.

Exeunt

The Taming of the Shrew
悍妇降服记

Looking back at Act 3 第3幕回顾
Activities for groups or individuals

1 Who wants what?

a List each character who appears in Act 3. For each character, write a single sentence that begins 'What I want is …'. How much agreement is there in the class about each character's motive?

b Add another layer of complexity to this activity by considering what one character might think about another. Character A says about Character B: 'What I think they want is …'.

2 Laughter and tears

Act 3 has enormous comic potential, with much physical action, some of which is described in great detail, and some of which the audience sees for itself. There are also moments when the action perhaps does not seem so funny to us, when the ways in which characters treat one another and the ideas they express seem to be problematic or to have a darker side.

All directors have to deal with both aspects of the play – and in Act 4, this becomes even more challenging. At this pivotal (关键) point, therefore, to what extent has the play prepared us for the sometimes disturbing elements that are to come?

- Script a conversation between a director who wants to highlight the troubling aspects of the play and an actor who wants to emphasise its comic elements. Concentrate particularly on the events and language of Act 3 as you develop your ideas about the play's broad comedy and darker side in this conversation.

3 Telling lies – what do they gain?

Many lies are told in the course of *The Taming of the Shrew* – a lot of them in Act 3. Most of the characters lie at some point, and several of them lie frequently!

- Bianca lies to Hortensio during her music lesson.
- Lucentio pretends to be Cambio.
- Hortensio pretends to be Litio.
- Tranio pretends to be Lucentio.
- Biondello lies when he tells Baptista about Petruchio's approach.
- Petruchio pretends that the wedding party threatens Katherina.

a Think about all these lies. Do the characters have good reasons for lying? What do they gain?

b How do we – the audience – respond to all the untruthfulness in the play? Write a couple of paragraphs outlining your thoughts on the effect of these lies on the audience.

4 Memorable moments

There are many memorable moments in Act 3. Identify some of them and assemble your own tableaux in the activities below.

a In groups, choose a key quotation from the scene you have selected and present a physical representation of it for the rest of your class to guess. Give the class five clues to help them.

b Choose another memorable moment and display it in a tableau. As a member of the class taps you on the shoulder, speak out what your character is thinking at that moment in time. Remember to use what you know of this character from the rest of the play, and try to use words or phrases they might use.

Grumio arrives at Petruchio's house, cold and tired. He orders Curtis to light a fire, threatening to complain to their new mistress. Curtis asks for news.

 剧情简介：葛儒缪回到珀楚秋府上，又冷又累。他命令柯提斯生火，还威胁要向新来的女主人打小报告。柯提斯向他打听消息。

Stagecraft 导演技巧

After the interval (in pairs)

Many productions place the interval between Acts 3 and 4, so that Grumio's arrival opens the second half. This allows for the change in the setting at this point in the play.

a How would you stage lines 1–8 to seize the audience's attention after the interval? Take turns to read the lines. Devise actions and gestures, with one of you in the role of director. Would you include music, scenery, sound effects, props?

b What the audience sees of Petruchio's house can reveal much about this character. Talk together about possible stage designs, then make a preliminary sketch for a set. What do you want your design to suggest about how Petruchio lives?

1 The journey (by yourself)

Petruchio's country house is four or five hours' ride from Padua, and the journey home after the wedding is an important feature of folktale versions of this story. Shakespeare also often uses a change in location to signify transformation or metamorphosis (变形).

- Try to decipher (解读) from the script what time of year it is. What do you think the journey was like for Katherina? Why do you think Petruchio made this difficult trip straight after the wedding? Write down your own ideas, as well as finding references in the script.

Write about it

Theories of the humours

The script opposite is full of references to the weather and allusions to the early modern theory of the humours (see p. 187). Grumio does not stop talking about how cold he is and how frozen his master and mistress are.

- Write a paragraph describing how the theories of the humours relate to Petruchio's plan to tame Katherina and rid her of her choleric (易怒) temper.

---

1 foul ways 泥泞的路
2 rayed 浑身烂泥
3 little pot and soon hot 壶小水易热（形容小人物急性子）
4 taller 更高大粗壮
5 coldly 瑟瑟发抖（也有"语气温和，不带怒气"的意思，表示讽刺）
6 run （指距离，根据上下文理解为"你可以从肩膀一直摸到我脚后跟，也不比从脑瓜摸到我脖子摸得更清楚"）
7 hot 容易发火
8 three-inch fool 三寸丁，矮矬子
9 horn 犄角（意同"绿帽子"）
10 hot office 生火的差使
11 have thy duty 赢得奖赏
12 wilt thou 你要多少（就有多少）
13 cony-catching 耍花招（cony 指家养的兔子，cony-catcher 指小偷）

Act 4 Scene 1
Petruchio's country house

Enter GRUMIO.

GRUMIO Fie, fie on all tired jades, on all mad masters, and all foul ways[1]! Was ever man so beaten? Was ever man so rayed[2]? Was ever man so weary? I am sent before to make a fire, and they are coming after to warm them. Now were not I a little pot and soon hot[3], my very lips might freeze to my teeth, my tongue to the roof of my mouth, my heart in my belly, ere I should come by a fire to thaw me. But I with blowing the fire shall warm myself, for, considering the weather, a taller[4] man than I will take cold. Holla, ho! Curtis!

Enter CURTIS.

CURTIS Who is that calls so coldly[5]?
GRUMIO A piece of ice. If thou doubt it, thou mayst slide from my shoulder to my heel with no greater a run[6] but my head and my neck. A fire, good Curtis.
CURTIS Is my master and his wife coming, Grumio?
GRUMIO O ay, Curtis, ay, and therefore fire, fire! Cast on no water.
CURTIS Is she so hot[7] a shrew as she's reported?
GRUMIO She was, good Curtis, before this frost. But thou know'st winter tames man, woman and beast; for it hath tamed my old master, and my new mistress, and myself, fellow Curtis.
CURTIS Away, you three-inch fool[8], I am no beast!
GRUMIO Am I but three inches? Why, thy horn[9] is a foot, and so long am I at the least. But wilt thou make a fire, or shall I complain on thee to our mistress, whose hand – she being now at hand – thou shalt soon feel, to thy cold comfort, for being slow in thy hot office[10].
CURTIS I prithee, good Grumio, tell me, how goes the world?
GRUMIO A cold world, Curtis, in every office but thine, and therefore, fire. Do thy duty, and have thy duty[11], for my master and mistress are almost frozen to death.
CURTIS There's fire ready, and therefore, good Grumio, the news.
GRUMIO Why, 'Jack boy, ho boy!' and as much news as wilt thou[12].
CURTIS Come, you are so full of cony-catching[13].

Grumio checks on the state of the house and servants. Curtis is anxious to hear the news, and Grumio eventually tells the story of the disastrous journey from the wedding.

 剧情简介：葛儒缪检查家里和仆人的准备情况。柯提斯急切地想听发生的事，葛儒缪最后讲述了婚礼后糟糕透顶的旅行。

1 Telling the tale (in small groups)

Once again Curtis asks Grumio for news (line 37). Grumio takes a long time to tell the story, and he certainly makes the most of it.

a Read lines 53–62. Talk together about how successful you think Grumio is as a story-teller.

b Go through Grumio's lines, identifying the words he might take particular delight in. Try ways of delivering these lines for the greatest comic effect.

c In a production at Shakespeare's Globe in 2012, Grumio used plates, cups and cutlery as 'puppets' for comic effect as he told the story. Assemble your own collection of 'puppets' and use them to tell Grumio's story as humorously as possible.

2 Film it (in fours)

Film directors frequently take advantage of the opportunities provided by Grumio's story in lines 53–62 to provide a great comic scene.

- Imagine you are making a movie of the play, and have decided to develop a major scene out of these ten lines. Use Grumio's words as a voice-over for a sequence of shots depicting this journey.
- With one of you acting as director, see how much fun you can get from Grumio's lines. You can add any amount of comic business as long as the scene follows Grumio's outline.
- Afterwards, either create a 3D storyboard of this sequence, or film it.

Characters 人物分析

Petruchio the shrew (by yourself)

Curtis says of Petruchio that 'he is more shrew than she'. How would an audience respond to this comment? Remember, we know about Petruchio's plan for 'taming' Katherina, whereas the other characters in the play do not.

- Write a brief description of Petruchio's shrewish behaviour. Then explain why you think he acts this way, writing firstly from the point of view of a character such as Curtis or Grumio, and then as a member of the audience. You might like to refer back to Act 2 Scene 1 as you do this.

---

1 **rushes strewed** 地上铺好了灯芯草
2 **fustian** 粗布工装
3 **officer** 仆人
4 **Jacks / Jills** 男仆女仆，酒杯酒碗
5 **carpets** 桌布
6 **feel** 感受
7 **sensible** 容易明白
8 *Imprimis* 开始（葛儒缪模仿公文用语）
9 **crossed** 打断，质问
10 **miry** 泥泞
11 **bemoiled** 满身烂泥
12 **die in oblivion** 彻底埋没
13 **By this reckoning** （仆人们从来没有见识过主人的这一面，这是因为珀楚秋故意演了这出戏）
14 **shrew** 泼辣凶悍（shrew可以形容男女，但更多用于形容女性）

The Taming of the Shrew Act 4 Scene 1
悍妇降服记

GRUMIO Why, therefore fire, for I have caught extreme cold. Where's the cook? Is supper ready, the house trimmed, rushes strewed[1], cobwebs swept, the servingmen in their new fustian[2], their white stockings, and every officer[3] his wedding garment on? Be the Jacks[4] fair within, the Jills[4] fair without, the carpets[5] laid, and everything in order?

CURTIS All ready, and therefore, I pray thee, news.

GRUMIO First know my horse is tired, my master and mistress fallen out.

CURTIS How?

GRUMIO Out of their saddles into the dirt, and thereby hangs a tale.

CURTIS Let's ha't, good Grumio.

GRUMIO Lend thine ear.

CURTIS Here.

GRUMIO There.

[*He boxes Curtis's ear.*]

CURTIS This 'tis to feel[6] a tale, not to hear a tale.

GRUMIO And therefore 'tis called a sensible[7] tale; and this cuff was but to knock at your ear and beseech listening. Now I begin. *Imprimis*[8] we came down a foul hill, my master riding behind my mistress.

CURTIS Both of one horse?

GRUMIO What's that to thee?

CURTIS Why, a horse.

GRUMIO Tell thou the tale. But hadst thou not crossed[9] me, thou shouldst have heard how her horse fell, and she under her horse; thou shouldst have heard in how miry[10] a place, how she was bemoiled[11], how he left her with the horse upon her, how he beat me because her horse stumbled, how she waded through the dirt to pluck him off me, how he swore, how she prayed that never prayed before, how I cried, how the horses ran away, how her bridle was burst, how I lost my crupper – with many things of worthy memory which now shall die in oblivion[12], and thou return unexperienced to thy grave.

CURTIS By this reckoning[13] he is more shrew[14] than she.

Grumio calls for the other servants to appear. He is anxious that their appearance and manners satisfy Petruchio. When Petruchio does arrive, he shouts at them angrily, accusing them of negligence.

 剧情简介：葛儒缪召集其他仆人都出来，急切希望他们的穿戴举止会让珀楚秋满意。珀楚秋到家，怒斥他们疏忽怠慢。

1 Servant gags (插科打诨) (in small groups)

Several servants enter at line 79. These 'spruce companions' say little but have much to do. Most productions provide slapstick (闹剧) comedy routines for Grumio, Curtis and the rest here.

a In your groups, take on the roles of these servants and devise your own stage business for lines 80–138. You should concentrate on your actions and movements rather than your few lines of dialogue. Are you all male? Would it make a difference if you weren't?

b Present a series of tableaux or movement pieces showing the servants as:
- incompetent and comic
- friendly and welcoming
- intimidating and cold.

Characters 人物分析

Arriving home

The painting of Petruchio below shows him arriving home with whip in hand and Katherina hiding behind him. This whip has become a popular stage prop for Petruchio, and appears in several productions.

- Describe what props you would want for Petruchio and for Katherina at this point in the play. Remember that they have just made a very difficult journey after their wedding.
- Explain what you hope each of your props would say to the audience about each character's personality and feelings.

1 blue　（仆人一般穿蓝色）
2 indifferent　规规矩矩（不引人注目）
3 curtsy　（男女通用的）屈膝礼
4 left legs　（通常认为屈左膝比屈右膝礼貌）
5 countenance　拜见（又有"脸、面容"之意）
6 credit　向……致敬
7 borrow　（上文的credit 也有"赊账、信用"的意思，葛儒缪显然取了此意）
8 How now　（一种友好愉快的问候语）
9 spruce　充满活力
10 Cock's passion　（感叹语）上帝啊，天啊（Cock's = God's）
11 knaves　男仆；靠不住的人
12 hold my stirrup　扶我下马
13 logger-headed　榆木脑袋

GRUMIO   Ay, and that thou and the proudest of you all shall find when he comes home. But what talk I of this? Call forth Nathaniel, Joseph, Nicholas, Philip, Walter, Sugarsop and the rest. Let their heads be slickly combed, their blue[1] coats brushed, and their garters of an indifferent[2] knit. Let them curtsy[3] with their left legs[4], and not presume to touch a hair of my master's horse-tail till they kiss their hands. Are they all ready?

CURTIS   They are.

GRUMIO   Call them forth.

CURTIS   Do you hear, ho? You must meet my master to countenance[5] my mistress.

GRUMIO   Why, she hath a face of her own.

CURTIS   Who knows not that?

GRUMIO   Thou, it seems, that calls for company to countenance her.

CURTIS   I call them forth to credit[6] her.

GRUMIO   Why, she comes to borrow[7] nothing of them.

Enter four or five SERVINGMEN.

NATHANIEL   Welcome home, Grumio.

PHILIP   How now[8], Grumio.

JOSEPH   What, Grumio.

NICHOLAS   Fellow Grumio.

NATHANIEL   How now, old lad.

GRUMIO   Welcome you; how now you; what you; fellow you; and thus much for greeting. Now, my spruce[9] companions, is all ready, and all things neat?

NATHANIEL   All things is ready. How near is our master?

GRUMIO   E'en at hand, alighted by this. And therefore be not – Cock's passion[10], silence! I hear my master.

Enter PETRUCHIO *and* KATHERINA.

PETRUCHIO   Where be these knaves[11]? What, no man at door
To hold my stirrup[12], nor to take my horse?
Where is Nathaniel, Gregory, Philip?

ALL SERVINGMEN   Here! Here sir, here sir!

PETRUCHIO   'Here sir, here sir, here sir, here sir'!
You logger-headed[13] and unpolished grooms!
What, no attendance? No regard? No duty?
Where is the foolish knave I sent before?

Petruchio accuses Grumio of failing to organise the servants. Grumio apologises for their poor state and appearance. Petruchio demands food, strikes the servants and accuses everyone of incompetence.

 剧情简介：珀楚秋指责葛儒缪管理仆人不当，葛儒缪为他们糟糕的状态和外表道歉。珀楚秋下令上饭，动手打了仆人，骂所有人无能。

1 Petruchio's 'performance' (in fives)

a Stand in a circle and read lines 100–26 aloud together. Identify the following examples of Petruchio's 'performance':

- orders to servants
- orders to Kate
- insults
- questions
- snatches of popular songs and ballads.

b Read the passage again, but this time a different person takes the lines relating to each of the examples you found above. What does this show you about the atmosphere of the scene? How does it shed light on how Katherina might feel about her new home?

Stagecraft 导演技巧

Incompetent servants?

Write notes in your Director's Journal describing how you would stage the script opposite. As you do so, consider the following points:

- Are the servants incompetent? Is it reasonable for Petruchio to expect better treatment from his employees?
- Are the servants innocent players in Petruchio's 'taming' scheme?
- Might Grumio be in league with Petruchio, inventing inadequacies where none exist (see line 126)?

2 'A married life is just a pain' (by yourself)

The original song Petruchio sings in line 111–12 is now lost. But Cole Porter reinvented it for the Broadway musical based on this play, *Kiss Me Kate*:

> *Where is the life that late I led?*
> *Where is it now? Totally dead.*
> *Where is the fun I used to find?*
> *Where has it gone? Gone with the wind.*
> *A married life is just a pain …*

Make up two more stanzas (诗节) of this song – one from Petruchio's perspective, the other from Katherina's. Try to use the same style and rhythm for your ballad, or if you prefer, write in prose as if giving the internal thoughts of both characters. What do they think of married life, of each other and of their future? Set your words to music if you can.

---

1 **whoreson** 婊子养的
2 **malthorse drudge** 驽马
3 **pumps** 便鞋
4 **all unpinked** 还没有装饰好（没有打好眼儿）
5 **link** 黑色涂料
6 **sheathing** 刀鞘，剑鞘
7 **When?** （表示不耐烦的感叹语）
8 **orders grey** 灰色长袍（一首失传的歌词的片段）
9 **spaniel Troilus** 猎犬特洛伊罗斯（一种腿短、耳垂、皮毛光滑的猎犬。有些民间版本的驯悍故事里丈夫经常找碴打狗来吓唬妻子）
10 **Will … fall?** 你是故意把盆掉在地上的吧？（很有可能是珀楚秋自己把盆打掉在地）

THE TAMING OF THE SHREW ACT 4 SCENE 1
悍妇降服记

GRUMIO   Here sir, as foolish as I was before.
PETRUCHIO   You peasant swain! You whoreson[1] malthorse drudge[2]!   100
            Did I not bid thee meet me in the park
            And bring along these rascal knaves with thee?
GRUMIO   Nathaniel's coat, sir, was not fully made,
            And Gabriel's pumps[3] were all unpinked[4] i'th'heel.
            There was no link[5] to colour Peter's hat   105
            And Walter's dagger was not come from sheathing[6].
            There were none fine but Adam, Rafe and Gregory;
            The rest were ragged, old and beggarly.
            Yet, as they are, here are they come to meet you.
PETRUCHIO   Go, rascals, go, and fetch my supper in.   110
                                            Exeunt Servingmen

            [*Sings*]   Where is the life that late I led?
                        Where are those –
            Sit down, Kate, and welcome. Food, food, food, food!

                        Enter Servants with supper.

            Why, when, I say? Nay, good sweet Kate, be merry.
            Off with my boots, you rogues, you villains! When?[7]   115
            [*Sings*]   It was the friar of orders grey[8]
                        As he forth walkèd on his way –
            Out, you rogue! You pluck my foot awry.
            Take that!
                        [*He strikes the Servant.*]
                        And mend the plucking off the other.
            Be merry, Kate. Some water here! What ho!   120

                        Enter one with water.

            Where's my spaniel Troilus[9]? Sirrah, get you hence
            And bid my cousin Ferdinand come hither –
                                            [*Exit a Servant*]
            One, Kate, that you must kiss and be acquainted with.
            Where are my slippers? Shall I have some water?
            Come, Kate, and wash, and welcome heartily.   125
            You whoreson villain! Will you let it fall?[10]
                        [*He strikes the Servant.*]

Katherina unsuccessfully tries to calm Petruchio. He invites her to eat, but finds fault with the food and throws it at the servants. He tells her they will fast instead and takes her off to the bridal chamber.

剧情简介：凯特芮娜没能让珀楚秋平静下来。珀楚秋请凯特芮娜用饭，但挑饭菜的毛病，还把吃的扔到仆人身上。他告诉凯特芮娜今晚禁食，接着带她去新房。

1 Kate's speeches (whole class)

a A volunteer reads Kate's lines in the script opposite in an aggressive and 'shrewish' manner. Afterwards, discuss as a class what other tones might be appropriate to her words. Other volunteers try reading them in these ways. Talk about how an audience might respond to these different readings.

b If you were directing the play, how would you show the differences and similarities between the two characters at this point? Who should be more shrewish – Katherina or Petruchio? Debate this as a class.

2 Insults (in pairs)

a List all the insulting words and phrases you can find in the first scene of Act 4. Choose three or four of them and write brief stage directions to show what is happening when these insults are used. Practise hurling the insults at each other.

b Talk together about whether you think Petruchio really means his insults. If he is not sincere, how might you show this on stage?

1 unwilling　不是故意的
2 beetle-headed　笨头笨脑
3 stomach　食欲；涵养
4 give thanks　就餐前感恩祷告
5 dresser　橱柜；上菜用的桌案
6 trenchers　木盘
7 heedless joltheads　马大哈
8 with you straight　这就找你算账
9 disquiet　生气；心烦
10 if you were so contented　只要您心平气和
11 dried away　烤干
12 mended　恢复正常，改正
13 for company　一起
14 in her own humour　以其人之道，还治其人之身

Themes 主题分析
'He kills her in her own humour' (in pairs)

According to some psychiatrists, mimicking (模仿) a problem child's unruly behaviour is an appropriate therapeutic (治疗性) treatment. Find examples of such mimicry of Katherina's anger, irrationality and bad temper in Petruchio's behaviour. Then, in role as a psychotherapist, write clinical notes on this episode.

Language in the play 剧中语言
Imagery of the humours

The servants exit when Petruchio throws the food back at them. When he and Katherina are left alone on stage, he explains why. His imagery comes from the theory of the humours (see p. 187).

- Which humour does Petruchio claim is dominating Katherina? Does his remedy seem sensible in the light of this theory of health and well-being?

THE TAMING OF THE SHREW ACT 4 SCENE 1
悍妇降服记

KATHERINA Patience, I pray you. 'Twas a fault unwilling[1].
PETRUCHIO A whoreson, beetle-headed[2], flap-eared knave!
Come, Kate, sit down, I know you have a stomach[3].
Will you give thanks[4], sweet Kate, or else shall I?   130
What's this? Mutton?
FIRST SERVINGMAN   Ay.
PETRUCHIO   Who brought it?
PETER   I.
PETRUCHIO 'Tis burnt, and so is all the meat.
What dogs are these! Where is the rascal cook?
How durst you villains bring it from the dresser[5]
And serve it thus to me that love it not?   135
There, take it to you, trenchers[6], cups and all!
[*He throws the food and dishes at them.*]
You heedless joltheads[7] and unmannered slaves!
What, do you grumble? I'll be with you straight[8].
                                        [*Exeunt Servants*]
KATHERINA I pray you, husband, be not so disquiet[9].
The meat was well, if you were so contented[10].   140
PETRUCHIO I tell thee, Kate, 'twas burnt and dried away[11],
And I expressly am forbid to touch it,
For it engenders choler, planteth anger;
And better 'twere that both of us did fast,
Since, of ourselves, ourselves are choleric,   145
Than feed it with such over-roasted flesh.
Be patient. Tomorrow't shall be mended[12],
And for this night we'll fast for company[13].
Come, I will bring thee to thy bridal chamber.
                                                              Exeunt

Enter Servants severally.

NATHANIEL Peter, didst ever see the like?   150
PETER He kills her in her own humour[14].

Grumio and Curtis talk about Katherina's confused state of mind. Petruchio tells the audience about his plan to tame Katherina by depriving her of food and sleep.

剧情简介：葛儒缪和柯提斯说起凯特芮娜的窘境。珀楚秋告诉观众他要通过禁食禁睡的方法驯服凯特芮娜。

1 Petruchio explains his plan (in small groups)

In lines 159–82, Petruchio makes his 'taming' plan absolutely clear.

a One person reads the whole soliloquy as if directly to the audience. Which words would you choose to stress and why? What tone of voice would you use?

b Work together to make a list of other statements by Petruchio in the play so far that fit with the views he expresses here.

c One person reads the lines again, but this time someone else enters in role as Katherina. How does she react to what she hears?

> ## Write about it 写作练习
> ### Falconry and hawking (驯鹰术)
> The imagery that gives depth to Petruchio's soliloquy derives from techniques for taming wild hawks. According to the novelist Tony White: '*The Taming of the Shrew* was pure hawk-mastery and must have been a play of enormous vividness to a generation which understood the falcon.'
>
> **a** Use the glossary on this page to help you identify all the terms that refer to falconry and hawking in the script opposite.
>
> **b** Read the information on falconry on pages 186–7 and then carry out some more research of your own. Write one or two paragraphs to explain how the imagery of falconry and hawking gives an audience a greater insight into Petruchio's plan to tame Katherina.

2 Petruchio's challenge (in small groups)

In the last two lines of his soliloquy, Petruchio challenges anyone in the audience to come up with a better idea to tame a shrew (lines 181–2).

a What do you think would be the most appropriate tone for these lines? Is it a boastful challenge, or an appeal for help from someone uncertain that he is doing the right thing? Do you admire his nerve or despise his approach?

b Reply to Petruchio's challenge by composing a rhyming couplet to either show your opinion of him and his taming methods, or to show what Katherina might say in response.

---

1 **continency** 自我约束
2 **rates** 责骂
3 **politicly** 蓄意
4 **falcon** 猎鹰（驯服凯特芮娜好比驯服一只鹰）
5 **sharp** 饥饿难耐
6 **stoop** 服从我（顺从地飞向诱饵）
7 **full-gorged** 喂饱
8 **lure** 做诱饵的死鸟（用来训练猎鹰不要急着吃猎物）
9 **man my haggard** 驯服我这只野鹰（要比训练一只家鹰难得多）
10 **watch her** 让她不能合眼
11 **kites** 鸢（这里也许是Kate的谐音）
12 **bate and beat** 狂扇翅膀飞离诱饵
13 **hurly** 胡闹
14 **intend** 假装
15 **watch** 不合眼
16 **nod** 睡着

THE TAMING OF THE SHREW ACT 4 SCENE 1

悍妇降服记

Enter Curtis.

GRUMIO   Where is he?
CURTIS   In her chamber,
Making a sermon of continency[1] to her,
And rails and swears and rates[2], that she, poor soul,   155
Knows not which way to stand, to look, to speak,
And sits as one new-risen from a dream.
Away, away, for he is coming hither.

[*Exeunt*]

Enter Petruchio.

PETRUCHIO   Thus have I politicly[3] begun my reign,
And 'tis my hope to end successfully.   160
My falcon[4] now is sharp[5] and passing empty,
And till she stoop[6] she must not be full-gorged[7],
For then she never looks upon her lure[8].
Another way I have to man my haggard[9],
To make her come and know her keeper's call,   165
That is, to watch her[10], as we watch these kites[11]
That bate and beat[12] and will not be obedient.
She ate no meat today, nor none shall eat;
Last night she slept not, nor tonight she shall not.
As with the meat, some undeservèd fault   170
I'll find about the making of the bed,
And here I'll fling the pillow, there the bolster,
This way the coverlet, another way the sheets.
Ay, and amid this hurly[13] I intend[14]
That all is done in reverend care of her.   175
And, in conclusion, she shall watch[15] all night,
And if she chance to nod[16] I'll rail and brawl
And with the clamour keep her still awake.
This is a way to kill a wife with kindness,
And thus I'll curb her mad and headstrong humour.   180
He that knows better how to tame a shrew,
Now let him speak – 'tis charity to show.   *Exit*

119

Tranio and Hortensio are watching Bianca and Lucentio courting. Hortensio throws off his disguise in disgust. Tranio suggests that they should both give up wooing Bianca.

 剧情简介：川纽和郝坦修看到碧昂卡和卢森修热恋。郝坦修厌恶地扯下伪装，川纽建议他俩都应该放弃追求碧昂卡。

1 Stage direction: '*They court*' (in pairs)

'Stand by, and mark the manner of his teaching' (line 5) is an internal stage direction to show that Hortensio and Tranio form an onstage audience to secretly watch the exchange between Lucentio and Bianca.

- Suggest what the lovers might be doing that so horrifies Hortensio in the script opposite. Write a detailed stage direction to the actors – remember, Hortensio is offended for two reasons: firstly, Bianca has spurned (冷拒) him; secondly, her new love is of a lower class than he is himself.

2 What is wonderful? (in pairs)

Tranio's words in line 15 can mean different things to different people. Finish the sentence 'I tell thee, Litio, this is wonderful because …' according to how it could be understood by:

- Hortensio
- Tranio himself
- you as a member of the audience.

1 **bears me fair in hand** 在耍手腕骗我
2 **satisfy** 使……相信
3 **mistress** 女士，小姐（或暗示碧昂卡是卢森修爱慕的对象）
4 **master** 男士，先生
5 **resolve** 回答
6 **profess** 承认；奉行
7 **The Art to Love** 《爱的艺术》（为奥维德 [Ovid] 所作，他认为爱情是一门学问）
8 **Quick proceeders** 进展迅速的学生
9 **marry** 以圣母马利亚起誓
10 **despiteful** 残酷
11 **wonderful** 令人惊讶
12 **cullion** 出身卑微的人
13 **entire** 毫无保留
14 **lightness** 轻浮
15 **Forswear** 放弃

▶ 'While you, sweet dear, prove mistress of my heart.' How would you have Bianca and Lucentio 'court' in your own production?

Act 4 Scene 2
Outside Baptista's house

Enter TRANIO [*disguised as Lucentio*] *and* HORTENSIO [*disguised as Litio*].

TRANIO	Is't possible, friend Litio, that mistress Bianca	
	Doth fancy any other but Lucentio?	
	I tell you, sir, she bears me fair in hand[1].	
HORTENSIO	Sir, to satisfy[2] you in what I have said,	
	Stand by, and mark the manner of his teaching.	5

[*They stand aside*].

Enter BIANCA [*and* LUCENTIO *disguised as Cambio*].

LUCENTIO	Now, mistress[3], profit you in what you read?	
BIANCA	What, master[4], read you? First resolve[5] me that.	
LUCENTIO	I read that I profess[6], *The Art to Love*[7].	
BIANCA	And may you prove, sir, master of your art.	
LUCENTIO	While you, sweet dear, prove mistress of my heart.	10

[*They court.*]

HORTENSIO	Quick proceeders[8], marry[9]! Now tell me, I pray,	
	You that durst swear that your mistress Bianca	
	Loved none in the world so well as Lucentio.	
TRANIO	O despiteful[10] love, unconstant womankind!	
	I tell thee, Litio, this is wonderful[11].	15
HORTENSIO	Mistake no more – I am not Litio,	
	Nor a musician as I seem to be,	
	But one that scorn to live in this disguise	
	For such a one as leaves a gentleman	
	And makes a god of such a cullion[12].	20
	Know, sir, that I am called Hortensio.	
TRANIO	Signor Hortensio, I have often heard	
	Of your entire[13] affection to Bianca,	
	And since mine eyes are witness of her lightness[14],	
	I will with you, if you be so contented,	25
	Forswear[15] Bianca and her love for ever.	

Hortensio vows to reject Bianca in favour of a wealthy widow whom he says he intends to marry in three days' time. Tranio, Lucentio and Bianca are delighted.

 剧情简介：郝坦修发誓放弃碧昂卡，他要找一个有钱的寡妇，并说打算三天后把她娶回家。川纽、卢森修、碧昂卡满心欢喜。

1 Unworthy of Hortensio? (in pairs)

a Decide which are the key words in Hortensio's speeches opposite. As one of you reads his lines aloud, the other echoes the key words.

b Identify the use of alliteration in these lines. What effect does this language device have? How does it add to our understanding of Hortensio's agitation (焦虑)?

c Write a diary entry for Hortensio, in which he explains his attitude towards Bianca, now that he knows she loves another man. Describe his plans to woo the 'wealthy widow' as quickly as possible.

Themes 主题分析

The 'taming-school'

Tranio says that Hortensio has gone to the 'taming-school', where husbands learn to tame their wives. Use your knowledge of the play so far to write a satirical prospectus for a 'taming-school', outlining some of the useful tricks that a man might learn there.

Language in the play 剧中语言

Falconry (in small groups)

Almost all of the imagery of falconry so far has related to Katherina, but now this imagery is applied to Bianca.

a In your groups, talk about how the language that links Bianca and Katherina could be seen to highlight other aspects of Bianca's character. Does making such a connection here suggest that she may not really be the modest and demure (端庄) young woman she has been portrayed as so far? Are there any ways in which Bianca could be seen as a 'proud disdainful haggard' or a 'shrew' like her sister?

b Refer to Lucentio's description of Bianca in Act 1 Scene 1 (lines 158–67), Baptista's description of her in Act 2 Scene 1 (lines 25–8) and Hortensio's description in Act 3 Scene 1 (lines 85–9). Then write a paragraph in which you explore how your view of Bianca may have changed as the play progresses. Include information on the language that the other characters use to describe her.

1 fondly 愚蠢地
2 unfeignèd 真诚
3 beastly 像动物一样
4 Kindness 善良；真情
5 In resolution 下了决心
6 'longeth = belongs
7 tane you napping 在您不备时抓住您（看见你们亲热）
8 lusty 性欲旺盛，饥渴难耐（考虑到她情愿被求婚并要马上结婚）
9 eleven and twenty long 恰好对症下药（原为打牌术语）

The Taming of the Shrew Act 4 Scene 2
悍妇降服记

HORTENSIO See how they kiss and court! Signor Lucentio,
Here is my hand, and here I firmly vow
Never to woo her more, but do forswear her
As one unworthy all the former favours   30
That I have fondly[1] flattered her withal.

TRANIO And here I take the like unfeignèd[2] oath
Never to marry with her though she would entreat.
Fie on her! See how beastly[3] she doth court him.

HORTENSIO Would all the world but he had quite forsworn!   35
For me, that I may surely keep mine oath,
I will be married to a wealthy widow
Ere three days pass, which hath as long loved me
As I have loved this proud disdainful haggard.
And so farewell, Signor Lucentio.   40
Kindness[4] in women, not their beauteous looks,
Shall win my love; and so I take my leave,
In resolution[5] as I swore before.   [*Exit*]

[*Tranio joins Lucentio and Bianca.*]

TRANIO Mistress Bianca, bless you with such grace
As 'longeth[6] to a lover's blessèd case!   45
Nay, I have tane you napping[7], gentle love,
And have forsworn you with Hortensio.

BIANCA Tranio, you jest – but have you both forsworn me?

TRANIO Mistress, we have.

LUCENTIO   Then we are rid of Litio.

TRANIO I'faith, he'll have a lusty[8] widow now   50
That shall be wooed and wedded in a day.

BIANCA God give him joy!

TRANIO Ay, and he'll tame her.

BIANCA   He says so, Tranio?

TRANIO Faith, he is gone unto the taming-school.

BIANCA The taming-school? What, is there such a place?   55

TRANIO Ay, mistress, and Petruchio is the master,
That teacheth tricks eleven and twenty long[9]
To tame a shrew and charm her chattering tongue.

剧情简介：卞代娄找到一个可以假扮卢森修父亲的商人。川纽编故事唬住这位商人，说由于政乱，凡是从曼图亚到帕多瓦来的人都会被处死。

1 A con man (骗子) at work (in small groups)

The encounter between Tranio and the Merchant (lines 72–120) shows how one clever (disguised) character can pull the wool over the eyes of a less clever – often older – character. This is a common type of 'con trick' in Shakespeare's comedies.

a In your groups, talk about how the various 'clever' characters in the play manage to con the others. Who are these characters and why do they find this trickery so easy?

b Imagine that the Merchant is not so easily conned by Tranio. Improvise his questions and Tranio's replies. How might he voice his suspicions? How would Tranio convince him?

▼ Many productions have sought to highlight the Merchant's fear. One Tranio hinted that there was a Mafia-style (黑手党式) plot to kill the Merchant, while another employed a passing soldier to add credibility to his story. What would you choose?

1 ancient angel 老先生（说angel可能是因为祈祷有回应，angel也可能指一种金币，所以卞代娄也许想说这是一个出身上层社会的人）
2 serve the turn 能实现我们的目的
3 What 什么样的人
4 marcantant 商人
5 trust 相信
6 let me alone 交给我吧
7 farre on 继续赶路
8 at the farthest 走到头
9 goes hard 重要的事
10 stayed 被扣留
11 For 因为
12 'Tis marvel 这就奇怪了
13 than so 比你刚才所说
14 bills 汇票（从佛罗伦萨汇来的钱凭汇票在这里取现）

THE TAMING OF THE SHREW ACT 4 SCENE 2

悍妇降服记

Enter BIONDELLO.

BIONDELLO	O master, master, I have watched so long	
	That I am dog-weary, but at last I spied	60
	An ancient angel¹ coming down the hill	
	Will serve the turn².	
TRANIO	What³ is he, Biondello?	
BIONDELLO	Master, a marcantant⁴, or a pedant,	
	I know not what, but formal in apparel,	
	In gait and countenance surely like a father.	65
LUCENTIO	And what of him, Tranio?	
TRANIO	If he be credulous and trust⁵ my tale,	
	I'll make him glad to seem Vincentio	
	And give assurance to Baptista Minola	
	As if he were the right Vincentio.	70
	Take in your love, and then let me alone⁶.	

[*Exeunt Lucentio and Bianca*]

Enter a MERCHANT.

MERCHANT	God save you, sir.	
TRANIO	And you, sir. You are welcome.	
	Travel you farre on⁷ or are you at the farthest⁸?	
MERCHANT	Sir, at the farthest for a week or two,	
	But then up farther, and as far as Rome,	75
	And so to Tripoli, if God lend me life.	
TRANIO	What countryman, I pray?	
MERCHANT	Of Mantua.	
TRANIO	Of Mantua, sir? Marry, God forbid!	
	And come to Padua careless of your life?	
MERCHANT	My life, sir? How, I pray? For that goes hard⁹.	80
TRANIO	'Tis death for anyone in Mantua	
	To come to Padua. Know you not the cause?	
	Your ships are stayed¹⁰ at Venice, and the Duke,	
	For¹¹ private quarrel 'twixt your Duke and him,	
	Hath published and proclaimed it openly.	85
	'Tis marvel¹² – but that you are but newly come,	
	You might have heard it else proclaimed about.	
MERCHANT	Alas, sir, it is worse for me than so¹³.	
	For I have bills¹⁴ for money by exchange	
	From Florence, and must here deliver them.	90

125

Tranio claims that the wealthy Vincentio is his father. The Merchant accepts this and agrees to impersonate Vincentio to avoid arrest. Tranio explains that his father is coming to Padua to complete the marriage arrangements.

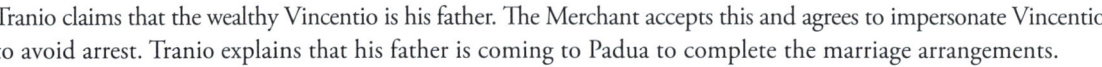剧情简介：川纽声称富有的文森修是他父亲，商人信了他的话，同意假扮文森修以免被捕。川纽解释说他的父亲要来帕多瓦给儿子办婚礼。

1 'incomparable wealth' (in pairs)

Once again we are reminded of how important wealth is in this play. The Merchant is impressed by the mention of Vincentio (supposedly Tranio's father) because he knows him to be a very rich man.

- Make a list of all the ways in which money has been shown to be important in the play, and the manner in which it is viewed by the main characters.

2 Further disguises (in small groups)

Now someone else is about to put on a disguise – the Merchant agrees to disguise himself as Vincentio.

- Make sure everyone knows what's going on: work out which characters are in disguise, who they are pretending to be, and why. Present your findings as a diagram.
- Identify which characters know the most about what is going on, and which are most in the dark. Is this because of their personality or simply circumstances?

1	apple doth an oyster	就像苹果和牡蛎那样长得像（是一句俗语，反讽）
2	all one	简直一模一样
3	credit	社会地位
4	undertake	顶替；假装
5	take upon you	扮演好您的角色
6	repute you	把您当作
7	patron	庇护者
8	make the matter good	按计划行事
9	by the way	路上
10	let you understand	让您明白
11	pass assurance	做担保

Themes 主题分析

'clothe you as becomes you' (in small groups)

Clothing is very important in this play, especially clothes that turn a person into someone else. We have seen characters dress both above and below their normal station in life, and have considered clothing in relation to the theme of appearance and reality. Now compile a list of references to clothing, and in writing describe how this adds depth to the language and links different thematic ideas. Start with the following references:

- 'What think you, if he were conveyed to bed, / Wrapped in sweet clothes, rings put upon his fingers, / … Would not the beggar then forget himself?' (Induction 1, lines 33–7)
- 'Master, has my fellow Tranio stolen your clothes or you stolen his, or both?' (Act 1 Scene 1, lines 214–15)
- 'To me she's married, not unto my clothes' (Act 3 Scene 2, line 107)

TRANIO	Well, sir, to do you courtesy,	
	This will I do, and this I will advise you –	
	First tell me, have you ever been at Pisa?	
MERCHANT	Ay, sir, in Pisa have I often been,	
	Pisa renownèd for grave citizens.	95
TRANIO	Among them know you one Vincentio?	
MERCHANT	I know him not, but I have heard of him,	
	A merchant of incomparable wealth.	
TRANIO	He is my father, sir, and sooth to say,	
	In count'nance somewhat doth resemble you.	100
BIONDELLO	[*Aside*] As much as an apple doth an oyster[1], and all one[2]!	
TRANIO	To save your life in this extremity,	
	This favour will I do you for his sake –	
	And think it not the worst of all your fortunes	
	That you are like to Sir Vincentio –	105
	His name and credit[3] shall you undertake[4],	
	And in my house you shall be friendly lodged.	
	Look that you take upon you[5] as you should –	
	You understand me, sir? So shall you stay	
	Till you have done your business in the city.	110
	If this be court'sy, sir, accept of it.	
MERCHANT	O sir, I do, and will repute you[6] ever	
	The patron[7] of my life and liberty.	
TRANIO	Then go with me to make the matter good[8].	
	This, by the way[9], I let you understand[10]:	115
	My father is here looked for every day	
	To pass assurance[11] of a dower in marriage	
	'Twixt me and one Baptista's daughter here.	
	In all these circumstances I'll instruct you.	
	Go with me to clothe you as becomes you.	120
	Exeunt	

Katherina, starving and exhausted, pleads with Grumio to fetch her some food. Grumio teases her, offering tempting delicacies and then finding reasons to deny her.

 剧情简介：凯特芮娜又饿又累，求葛儒缪给她拿点儿吃的。葛儒缪故意逗凯特芮娜，说出几样美食，却找借口拒绝给她。

Stagecraft 导演技巧

Katherina's state (in pairs)

Katherina's opening speech in Scene 3 has often been delivered as a virtual soliloquy, to provide a dramatic balance with Petruchio's soliloquy at the end of Scene 1.

a Read lines 2–16 aloud together and devise suitable gestures each time Katherina's physical state is mentioned. What props would you give her for this scene to make her situation clear?

b Draw costume designs or find images in magazines that show how you want to portray her physical appearance.

1 Poor little rich girl (in pairs)

Katherina comes from a wealthy home and has never had to 'entreat' for anything. Now she must either beg or starve.

a Read lines 15–30 in the following ways:
- as someone with low status: head hanging, feet close together, lowered eyes, using as little stage space as possible
- as someone with equal status: open and friendly manner, taking up as much stage space as others, with equality of movement
- as someone with high status: upright and confident manner, eyes lifted and chin up, takes up more stage space than others, possibly more movement or less movement at centre stage.

Now talk about how skilled Katherina is at begging food from Grumio.

b Create two tableaux that represent Katherina and Grumio at line 18 and at line 31.

Characters 人物分析

Master and servant

How closely do Grumio's tactics with Katherina parallel Petruchio's in Act 4 Scene 1? Improvise an aside in which Petruchio has been listening and comments on what he has seen and heard in lines 17–30. Remember that Petruchio himself suffers the same deprivations he imposes on Katherina, while Grumio is often portrayed on stage as deliberately taunting (羞辱) her and eating in front of her.

1 my wrong 让我受的委屈
2 spite 折磨
3 famish 使挨饿
4 Upon entreaty 只要他们开口乞讨
5 a present alms 立马就得到的施舍
6 meat 食物
7 spites 惹怒
8 repast 饭菜
9 neat 小牛，公牛
10 choleric 容易引发怒火
11 very name 光说名字

Act 4 Scene 3
Petruchio's house

Enter KATHERINA *and* GRUMIO.

GRUMIO	No, no, forsooth, I dare not for my life!	
KATHERINA	The more my wrong[1], the more his spite[2] appears.	
	What, did he marry me to famish[3] me?	
	Beggars that come unto my father's door	
	Upon entreaty[4] have a present alms[5];	5
	If not, elsewhere they meet with charity.	
	But I, who never knew how to entreat,	
	Nor never needed that I should entreat,	
	Am starved for meat[6], giddy for lack of sleep,	
	With oaths kept waking, and with brawling fed.	10
	And that which spites[7] me more than all these wants,	
	He does it under name of perfect love,	
	As who should say, if I should sleep or eat	
	'Twere deadly sickness or else present death.	
	I prithee go and get me some repast[8] –	15
	I care not what, so it be wholesome food.	
GRUMIO	What say you to a neat's[9] foot?	
KATHERINA	'Tis passing good. I prithee let me have it.	
GRUMIO	I fear it is too choleric[10] a meat.	
	How say you to a fat tripe finely broiled?	20
KATHERINA	I like it well. Good Grumio, fetch it me.	
GRUMIO	I cannot tell, I fear 'tis choleric.	
	What say you to a piece of beef and mustard?	
KATHERINA	A dish that I do love to feed upon.	
GRUMIO	Ay, but the mustard is too hot a little.	25
KATHERINA	Why then, the beef, and let the mustard rest.	
GRUMIO	Nay then, I will not. You shall have the mustard,	
	Or else you get no beef of Grumio.	
KATHERINA	Then both, or one, or anything thou wilt.	
GRUMIO	Why then, the mustard without the beef.	30
KATHERINA	Go, get thee gone, thou false deluding slave	
	Beats him.	
	That feed'st me with the very name[11] of meat.	

Petruchio and Hortensio arrive with food for Katherina. They sit down to dine, but Hortensio has strict orders to eat all the food. Petruchio talks about fine clothes, and a tailor is announced.

 剧情简介：珀楚秋和郝坦修给凯特芮娜带来食物。他们坐下来用餐，但郝坦修奉命吃光所有食物。珀楚秋说起华服盛装，随即传唤裁缝。

1 Thanks (in pairs)

In your pairs, come up with as many different ways as possible to stage the key lines for each character in the script opposite. You might like to start with lines 36, 41, 44 and 47.

- Experiment with speaking the lines angrily, lovingly, jokingly, impatiently and ironically.
- Try emphasising different words. How does this change the meaning of what is said? What gestures would you use to accompany your chosen emphasis?
- Which version best portrays how you want the audience to understand the characters at this point?

2 Eating and talking (in threes)

After Petruchio has told Hortensio to eat all the food, he talks to Katherina at some length, describing a long list of fashion accessories. What is happening at the table during this speech?

- One person reads lines 51–8, while the other two mime what might be going on between Hortensio and Katherina.

3 Silent Kate – again (in pairs)

In this scene, Katherina is thwarted (挫败) by three men working together. Once again, she is silent during a long sequence of Petruchio's outrageous behaviour.

a Why do you think Katherina has no lines to speak here? Is she too weak and hungry, too angry, too distracted by the idea of clothes? Or is she just trying to remain composed in front of their guest, Hortensio?

b One person reads Petruchio's lines 50–60 in as provocative a way as possible, pausing at the end of each line. The other person, in role as Katherina, provides appropriate interjections at each pause. Try to encapsulate her feelings each time. Is she frustrated? Exhausted? Sulky (生闷气)? Furious? Desperate?

---

1 amort 无精打采
2 what cheer? 您好哇！
3 cold 冷静（这句的幽默在于凯特芮娜没了往日的火暴脾气反而变得冷静甚至忧郁了）
4 merits 有理由得到
5 pains … proof 辛苦全白费了
6 you are to blame 这就是您的不对了
7 bravely 着装华丽
8 ruffs and cuffs 褶皱领子和花边袖口
9 farthingales 里面用裙架撑起来的大圆裙
10 double change 备两套替换
11 brav'ry 华丽精致的饰品
12 knav'ry 杂七杂八的小玩意儿
13 stays 等候
14 ruffling 华丽精美

THE TAMING OF THE SHREW ACT 4 SCENE 3

悍妇降服记

                Sorrow on thee and all the pack of you
                That triumph thus upon my misery!
                Go, get thee gone, I say.   35

                    Enter PETRUCHIO *and* HORTENSIO *with meat.*

PETRUCHIO How fares my Kate? What, sweeting, all amort[1]?
HORTENSIO Mistress, what cheer?[2]
KATHERINA   Faith, as cold[3] as can be.
PETRUCHIO Pluck up thy spirits; look cheerfully upon me.
             Here, love, thou seest how diligent I am
             To dress thy meat myself, and bring it thee.   40
             I am sure, sweet Kate, this kindness merits[4] thanks.
             What, not a word? Nay then, thou lov'st it not,
             And all my pains is sorted to no proof[5].
             Here, take away this dish.
KATHERINA   I pray you, let it stand.
PETRUCHIO The poorest service is repaid with thanks,   45
             And so shall mine before you touch the meat.
KATHERINA I thank you, sir.
HORTENSIO Signor Petruchio, fie, you are to blame[6].
             Come, Mistress Kate, I'll bear you company.
PETRUCHIO [*Aside*] Eat it up all, Hortensio, if thou lov'st me –   50
             [*To Katherina*] Much good do it unto thy gentle heart.
             Kate, eat apace. And now, my honey love,
             Will we return unto thy father's house
             And revel it as bravely[7] as the best,
             With silken coats and caps, and golden rings,   55
             With ruffs and cuffs[8] and farthingales[9] and things,
             With scarves and fans and double change[10] of brav'ry[11],
             With amber bracelets, beads and all this knav'ry[12].
             What, hast thou dined? The tailor stays[13] thy leisure,
             To deck thy body with his ruffling[14] treasure.   60

                    Enter TAILOR.

             Come, tailor, let us see these ornaments.
             Lay forth the gown.

The Haberdasher brings in a hat, but Petruchio dismisses it in spite of Katherina's protests that she likes it. The gown brought on by the Tailor is also rejected by Petruchio.

 剧情简介：帽子商带来一顶帽子，但是珀楚秋把它退了，不理会凯特芮娜对帽子的喜爱和抗议。裁缝带来的礼服也被珀楚秋拒绝。

1 How can you make men listen? (in pairs)

In lines 73–80, Katherina states her right to be angry and to express her anger in words.

a What tone would you advise an actor to adopt as she speaks these words. Angry? Whining? Pleading? Rational? Demanding? Co-operative? Condescending (居高临下)? Bitter?

b Imagine that Katherina has made an appointment to visit a family counsellor and has repeated these words to them. In role as this counsellor, write out the advice you would give her about her need to speak her mind and be heard, and about the problems she is having with her husband in general.

Themes 主题分析

Taming techniques

Petruchio continues to use his 'taming techniques' in this scene. Identify the techniques below in the script opposite:

- deliberately misunderstanding the situation
- ignoring what Katherina is saying
- pretending she means something different
- telling someone else off instead of her.

Write about it 写作练习

A woman's voice

a Some critics regard the power struggle between the two social 'rebels' Katherina and Petruchio as being unfairly weighted in favour of the man. What reasons can you give to support this view?

b Imagine the play was set in a country where a woman's freedom was restricted and she was seen as inferior to men. Write out a presentation of the ideas contained within Katherina's speech as a radio broadcast. The words are all the audience has to go on. Your task is to present the speech in such a way that men will really hear what is being said, and to give a voice to women who are denied one in their own lives.

1 bespeak 定做
2 porringer 小盆
3 lewd 俗气
4 cockle 鸟蛤
5 knack 不值钱的小物件
6 toy 毫无价值的东西
7 trick 荒唐可笑的东西
8 doth fit the time 时髦
9 paltry 低劣
10 custard-coffin 蛋挞棺材（即蛋挞的酥皮）
11 bauble 不值钱的东西
12 Thy gown? （珀楚秋假装将凯特芮娜说的none听成gown，这时帽子商离开，裁缝上场）
13 masking stuff 上台穿的艳俗戏袍
14 demi-cannon 加农炮
15 up … apple-tart 像苹果挞的油酥壳那样裂开
16 censer 香炉（上端有孔）

Enter HABERDASHER.

What news with you, sir?

HABERDASHER　Here is the cap your worship did bespeak.¹
PETRUCHIO　Why, this was moulded on a porringer² –
　　　　　　A velvet dish! Fie, fie, 'tis lewd³ and filthy.　　　　　　　　　　65
　　　　　　Why, 'tis a cockle⁴ or a walnut-shell,
　　　　　　A knack⁵, a toy⁶, a trick⁷, a baby's cap.
　　　　　　Away with it! Come, let me have a bigger.
KATHERINA　I'll have no bigger. This doth fit the time⁸,
　　　　　　And gentlewomen wear such caps as these.　　　　　　　　　　　70
PETRUCHIO　When you are gentle you shall have one too,
　　　　　　And not till then.
HORTENSIO　[*Aside*]　　　That will not be in haste.
KATHERINA　Why, sir, I trust I may have leave to speak,
　　　　　　And speak I will. I am no child, no babe.
　　　　　　Your betters have endured me say my mind,　　　　　　　　　　　75
　　　　　　And if you cannot, best you stop your ears.
　　　　　　My tongue will tell the anger of my heart,
　　　　　　Or else my heart concealing it will break,
　　　　　　And, rather than it shall, I will be free
　　　　　　Even to the uttermost, as I please, in words.　　　　　　　　　　80
PETRUCHIO　Why, thou say'st true – it is a paltry⁹ cap.
　　　　　　A custard-coffin¹⁰, a bauble¹¹, a silken pie!
　　　　　　I love thee well in that thou lik'st it not.
KATHERINA　Love me or love me not, I like the cap,
　　　　　　And it I will have, or I will have none.　　　　　　　　　　　　85
PETRUCHIO　Thy gown?¹² Why, ay. Come, tailor, let us see't.

　　　　　　　　　　　　　　　　　　　　　　　　　[*Exit Haberdasher*]

　　　　　　O mercy God! What masking stuff¹³ is here?
　　　　　　What's this – a sleeve? 'Tis like a demi-cannon¹⁴.
　　　　　　What, up and down carved like an apple-tart¹⁵?
　　　　　　Here's snip and nip and cut and slish and slash,　　　　　　　　90
　　　　　　Like to a censer¹⁶ in a barber's shop.
　　　　　　Why, what a devil's name, tailor, call'st thou this?
HORTENSIO　[*Aside*] I see she's like to have neither cap nor gown.
TAILOR　　　You bid me make it orderly and well,
　　　　　　According to the fashion and the time.　　　　　　　　　　　　95

Petruchio and Katherina disagree about the gown, and Petruchio turns on the Tailor with a string of insults. Grumio quarrels with the Tailor over the order for the gown.

 剧情简介：珀楚秋和凯特芮娜对礼服的看法不一致，珀楚秋大骂裁缝，说了一连串侮辱他的话。葛儒缪和裁缝就礼服订单争吵起来。

Stagecraft 导演技巧

Puppet on a string (in small groups)

a Read lines 103–5 aloud several times in as many different ways as you can. Then talk together about the effect of these three lines when they are spoken in quick succession. How would you advise the actors to say the lines to achieve the greatest comic effect at this point? How would you want the audience to react?

b Read out lines 106–10. What do you think the effect on Katherina might be when Petruchio suddenly turns on the Tailor and starts insulting him? Work together on advice a director could give the actor about her behaviour throughout the dialogue in the script opposite. Write up your decisions in your Director's Journal. Come to a conclusion about what Katherina must be feeling here.

1 **Marry, and did** 是啊，我的确这么说了
2 **mar it to the time** 按流行的款式反而把它毁了
3 **kennel** 排水沟，阴沟
4 **quaint** 设计精巧
5 **puppet** 木偶
6 **nail** 纳尔（当时量布的长度单位，相当于5.7厘米或1/16码）
7 **Braved** 放肆
8 **quantity** 布条，布片
9 **bemete** 用尺子量（这里是"打"的意思）
10 **yard** 裁缝专用的木制板尺
11 **As … liv'st** 让你下次再撒这样的谎时掂量掂量
12 **stuff** 原材料
13 **faced** 修剪（也有"大胆面对"之意）
14 *Ergo* 因此（法庭术语，接下来葛儒缪和裁缝都用法律术语当堂对质）
15 **note** 书面订单
16 **lies in's throat** 完全是说谎
17 **he = it** （指订单，把订单比喻成目击证人）

▼ In this production, Petruchio is teasing Katherina about the hat. The Haberdasher is played by a woman here. Do you think this would make any difference to the impact of the scene?

PETRUCHIO Marry, and did¹. But if you be remembered,
I did not bid you mar it to the time².
Go, hop me over every kennel³ home,
For you shall hop without my custom, sir.
I'll none of it. Hence, make your best of it. 100
KATHERINA I never saw a better-fashioned gown,
More quaint⁴, more pleasing, nor more commendable.
Belike you mean to make a puppet⁵ of me.
PETRUCHIO Why, true, he means to make a puppet of thee.
TAILOR She says your worship means to make a puppet of her. 105
PETRUCHIO O monstrous arrogance! Thou liest, thou thread, thou thimble,
Thou yard, three-quarters, half-yard, quarter, nail⁶!
Thou flea, thou nit, thou winter-cricket thou!
Braved⁷ in mine own house with a skein of thread?
Away, thou rag, thou quantity⁸, thou remnant! 110
Or I shall so bemete⁹ thee with thy yard¹⁰
As thou shalt think on prating whilst thou liv'st¹¹.
I tell thee, I, that thou hast marred her gown.
TAILOR Your worship is deceived. The gown is made
Just as my master had direction. 115
Grumio gave order how it should be done.
GRUMIO I gave him no order; I gave him the stuff¹².
TAILOR But how did you desire it should be made?
GRUMIO Marry, sir, with needle and thread.
TAILOR But did you not request to have it cut? 120
GRUMIO Thou hast faced¹³ many things.
TAILOR I have.
GRUMIO Face not me. Thou hast braved many men; brave not me. I will neither be faced nor braved. I say unto thee, I bid thy master cut out the gown, but I did not bid him cut it to pieces. *Ergo*¹⁴, thou liest. 125
TAILOR Why, here is the note¹⁵ of the fashion to testify.
PETRUCHIO Read it.
GRUMIO The note lies in's throat¹⁶ if he¹⁷ say I said so.

Grumio and the Tailor continue to argue about the details of the order. The gown is rejected by Petruchio. He secretly asks Hortensio to pay the Tailor later.

剧情简介：葛儒缪和裁缝继续争论订单的细节。礼服被珀楚秋拒绝，他偷偷让郝坦修稍后付钱给裁缝。

1 Challenge: taming Petruchio (in pairs)

Does Petruchio need a taste of his own medicine? It is clear that he is sometimes just as shrewish as Katherina, and that he could benefit from the same kind of training. But how should he be tamed?

- Write your own prescription for Petruchio. You might like to use medical terminology, such as 'two drops of … and a shot of … to be administered thrice daily'.

2 'Take no unkindness'

In his aside to Hortensio (line 158), Petruchio comes back down to Earth, to the real world in which the Tailor must be paid. This clearly contradicts what has been said earlier about the man's poor workmanship with the dress, and it reminds the audience that Petruchio is creating an unreal world – a fantasy that he is manipulating for his own purposes.

a How do you think the Tailor might react to what Petruchio and Hortensio say to him in lines 159–62?

b Improvise a dialogue that takes place the following day between Hortensio and the Tailor when he arrives to pay the bill. Imagine that the Tailor is still angry at his treatment.

Characters

Interpreting Kate's silence

One of the most surprising elements of this play is how little Katherina actually says. Every director has to decide how to interpret her silences. In the script opposite, she is once again silenced by Petruchio – he makes sure she does not get a word in. However, actions can sometimes speak louder than words.

a How could Katherina's actions show her shrewish behaviour or her intense frustration? Would you want to portray this as comic or cruel? What is she actually thinking?

b Write a diary entry for Katherina, explaining how she is feeling and, in particular, what she thinks of her husband's treatment of the Tailor and the Haberdasher.

---

1 **loose-bodied** 宽松式样（葛儒缪理解为适合风流女子或妓女）
2 **bottom** 线轴
3 **compassed** 裁剪成圆形
4 **trunk** 全长
5 **curiously** 细心巧妙
6 **bill** 订单
7 **prove upon thee** 和你决一雌雄来证明
8 **and … where** 如果我把你安置在合适的地方（裁缝理解为法庭，葛儒缪指的是适合打架的地方）
9 **for thee straight** 随时可以和你较量
10 **odds** 优势
11 **unto thy master's use** 让你老板看着办
12 **conceit** 意义
13 **deeper** 更不正当

THE TAMING OF THE SHREW ACT 4 SCENE 3
悍妇降服记

TAILOR	[*Reads*] '*Imprimis*, a loose-bodied[1] gown –'	130
GRUMIO	Master, if ever I said 'loose-bodied gown', sew me in the skirts of it and beat me to death with a bottom[2] of brown thread. I said 'a gown'.	
PETRUCHIO	Proceed.	
TAILOR	'With a small compassed[3] cape.'	135
GRUMIO	I confess the cape.	
TAILOR	'With a trunk[4] sleeve.'	
GRUMIO	I confess two sleeves.	
TAILOR	'The sleeves curiously[5] cut.'	
PETRUCHIO	Ay, there's the villainy.	140
GRUMIO	Error i'th'bill[6], sir, error i'th'bill! I commanded the sleeves should be cut out and sewed up again – and that I'll prove upon thee[7], though thy little finger be armed in a thimble.	
TAILOR	This is true that I say, and I had thee in place where[8] thou should'st know it.	145
GRUMIO	I am for thee straight[9]. Take thou the bill, give me thy mete-yard and spare not me.	
HORTENSIO	God-a-mercy, Grumio, then he shall have no odds[10].	
PETRUCHIO	Well, sir, in brief, the gown is not for me.	
GRUMIO	You are i'th'right sir, 'tis for my mistress.	150
PETRUCHIO	Go, take it up unto thy master's use[11].	
GRUMIO	Villain, not for thy life! Take up my mistress' gown for thy master's use?	
PETRUCHIO	Why, sir, what's your conceit[12] in that?	
GRUMIO	O sir, the conceit is deeper[13] than you think for. Take up my mistress' gown to his master's use? O fie, fie, fie!	155
PETRUCHIO	[*Aside*] Hortensio, say thou wilt see the tailor paid. [*To Tailor*] Go, take it hence; be gone and say no more.	
HORTENSIO	[*Aside*] Tailor, I'll pay thee for thy gown tomorrow, Take no unkindness of his hasty words. Away I say, commend me to thy master.	160

Exit Tailor

Petruchio lectures Katherina on the unimportance of clothes. He tells her they are about to leave for Baptista's, making a deliberate mistake about the time of day. Katherina corrects him and the trip is cancelled.

 剧情简介：珀楚秋教训凯特芮娜说穿戴并不重要，还说他们要去巴普提斯塔家，却故意说错时间。凯特芮娜纠正他，结果行程被取消。

1 What's the lesson? (in pairs)

Read lines 163–74 aloud, then talk together about Petruchio's moral lesson. Do you think he really means it, or is he being ironic? There are many ways in which this speech could be delivered. Some productions have suggested a softening of Petruchio's attitude here: that he attempts a rational explanation for his behaviour (which some Katherinas show that they understand), or holds Katherina's hand. Think about how gestures like this could make a difference to an audience's response. Then write a detailed stage direction for the actors at this point.

1 mean habiliments 朴素的家常便服
2 peereth 透过……显露
3 habit 装束
4 What 从哪方面来说
5 painted 颜色鲜亮
6 furniture 穿戴，打扮
7 lay it on 责怪
8 frolic 高兴起来
9 dinner-time 午餐时间
10 supper-time 晚餐时间（大约晚上7点）
11 Look what 无论怎样
12 crossing 唱反调

* apostrophe 转叹，一种修辞手法，指剧中人中断对观众说话，借助一声叹息转而对不在场的某一第三者说话，这第三者多是虚拟或抽象的人或事物（如上帝、爱情等）。

Language in the play 剧中语言
Verse and prose

Use the following activities to help you distinguish between Shakespearean verse and prose.

a Petruchio uses an iambic rhythm and a range of rhetorical devices. Identify the following:
  - rhetorical questions
  - apostrophes* (an address to someone who is not there, or to an inanimate object)
  - contrasts
  - similes/comparisons
  - logical arguments ('if … then … therefore').

b What is Petruchio actually saying? Write out the key lines in modern English to show how they might sound in prose. What difference does it make to the impact of the speech?

Characters 人物分析
Game-playing or controlling?

Are lines 185–9 an example of Petruchio inviting Katherina to play a new game that others will never understand? Or is he putting his foot down and demanding absolute obedience from her?

- Compose a short reply from Katherina, written in the same moralising style.

The Taming of the Shrew Act 4 Scene 3
悍妇降服记

PETRUCHIO	Well, come, my Kate, we will unto your father's
	Even in these honest mean habiliments¹.
	Our purses shall be proud, our garments poor, 165
	For 'tis the mind that makes the body rich,
	And as the sun breaks through the darkest clouds,
	So honour peereth² in the meanest habit³.
	What⁴, is the jay more precious than the lark
	Because his feathers are more beautiful? 170
	Or is the adder better than the eel
	Because his painted⁵ skin contents the eye?
	O no, good Kate; neither art thou the worse
	For this poor furniture⁶ and mean array.
	If thou account'st it shame, lay it on⁷ me, 175
	And therefore frolic⁸! We will hence forthwith
	To feast and sport us at thy father's house.
	[*To Grumio*] Go call my men, and let us straight to him,
	And bring our horses unto Long-lane end,
	There will we mount, and thither walk on foot. 180
	Let's see, I think 'tis now some seven o'clock,
	And well we may come there by dinner-time⁹.
KATHERINA	I dare assure you, sir, 'tis almost two,
	And 'twill be supper-time¹⁰ ere you come there.
PETRUCHIO	It shall be seven ere I go to horse. 185
	Look what¹¹ I speak, or do, or think to do,
	You are still crossing¹² it. Sirs, let't alone.
	I will not go today, and, ere I do,
	It shall be what o'clock I say it is.
HORTENSIO	[*Aside*] Why so this gallant will command the sun. 190
	[*Exeunt*]

139

Tranio completes the preparations to turn the Merchant into Vincentio. Biondello confirms that he will play his part in the deception. Tranio introduces his 'father' to Baptista.

剧情简介：为把商人扮成文森修，川纽做好一切准备。卞代娄确认他会在这场骗局中演好他的角色。川纽把他的"父亲"介绍给巴普提斯塔。

1 'Set your countenance' (in pairs)

Tranio warns the Merchant to put on the right expression as Baptista approaches (line 18).

- Imagine the Merchant has a panic attack just at this moment. Script a brief scene in which Tranio calms him down and gives him advice. Remember to include stage directions to indicate tone and gesture.

Stagecraft 导演技巧

Hidden clues (in small groups)

Shakespeare's stage was quite bare and the actors did not have time to rehearse the play in detail. Read the script opposite for clues that Shakespeare gives the actors for internal stage directions. Look out also for lines that give the audience more information about what is happening on the stage. Copy the table below and fill it in, adding further examples.

Quotation	Action for actor	Imagination for audience
'dressed like Vincentio'		How convincing should he be? Remember, the Merchant might not really look like him at all.
'Where we were lodgers at the Pegasus' (line 5)		The Merchant is afraid Baptista might remember him from when they met twenty years ago.
'But, sir, here comes your boy' (line 8)	A third actor walks on stage	
''Twere good he were schooled' (line 9)		
'Set your countenance, sir' (line 18)		

1 **but I be deceived** 除非我受骗了
2 **Pegasus** 飞马旅馆（pegasus 是神话中一种长翅膀的马，当时伦敦有很多以此命名的旅馆）
3 **hold your own** 保持您现在的身份
4 **case** 情况
5 **austerity** 庄重
6 **schooled** 被交代清楚
7 **tall** 能干
8 **hold thee that to drink** 拿着这个去买酒喝
9 **Set your countenance** 摆出应有的神态表情
10 **stand** （对我来说）您本人就是
11 **patrimony** 继承的遗产

Act 4 Scene 4
Outside Baptista's house

Enter TRANIO [*disguised as Lucentio*] *and the* MERCHANT, *booted and bare headed, dressed like Vincentio.*

TRANIO	Sir, this is the house. Please it you that I call?
MERCHANT	Ay, what else? And, but I be deceived[1],
	Signor Baptista may remember me
	Near twenty years ago in Genoa
	Where we were lodgers at the Pegasus[2]. 5
TRANIO	'Tis well. And hold your own[3], in any case[4],
	With such austerity[5] as 'longeth to a father.
MERCHANT	I warrant you.

Enter BIONDELLO.

	But, sir, here comes your boy;
	'Twere good he were schooled[6].
TRANIO	Fear you not him. Sirrah Biondello, 10
	Now do your duty throughly, I advise you:
	Imagine 'twere the right Vincentio.
BIONDELLO	Tut, fear not me.
TRANIO	But hast thou done thy errand to Baptista?
BIONDELLO	I told him that your father was at Venice, 15
	And that you looked for him this day in Padua.
TRANIO	Th'art a tall[7] fellow; hold thee that to drink[8].

[*He gives him money.*]

Enter BAPTISTA *and* LUCENTIO [*disguised as Cambio*].

	Here comes Baptista. Set your countenance[9], sir.
	Signor Baptista, you are happily met.
	Sir, this is the gentleman I told you of. 20
	I pray you stand[10] good father to me now:
	Give me Bianca for my patrimony[11].

The Merchant plays his part convincingly and agrees to the marriage. Baptista therefore gives it his blessing. It is decided that detailed arrangements should be made at Tranio's lodgings.

 剧情简介：商人演得让人信以为真，他表示同意儿子的婚事，于是巴普提斯塔祝福了他们。众人决定在川纽的住处商定婚礼的具体安排。

1 Getting it right (in small groups)

The Merchant has only one chance to impress Baptista, and there is much riding on his performance. Although it could potentially be a comic scene, everybody on stage (and also Bianca off stage) has a great deal to lose if the Merchant fails.

a Would Tranio, Lucentio and Biondello sit back and enjoy the Merchant's performance (as in the image below) or would the Merchant forget his lines and need some prompts?

b Read through his speech (lines 24–37) and identify the places where the Merchant seems to pause and forget what to say next.

c Prepare a reading of these lines, with the other characters miming prompts for the Merchant behind Baptista's back. Look especially at the pauses and the repetition of 'and' in his speech. Think what gestures you could use to remind the Merchant of what he needs to say.

1	Soft	等一等
2	weighty cause	重要的问题
3	for	由于
4	to stay him not	为了不让他（久）等
5	to like	满意
6	curious	斤斤计较
7	pass	保证；授予
8	affied	正式订婚
9	assurance tane	完成法律手续
10	As … stand	令双方都满意
11	Pitchers	水罐（手柄似人耳，谚语：small pitchers have wide ears，这里是"隔墙有耳"的意思）
12	heark'ning	（暗地）等待
13	happily	也许
14	and it like you	如果您愿意
15	lie	暂住

2 'Pitchers have ears' (in sixes)

In lines 48–57, Baptista is concerned about where he and the Merchant (pretending to be Vincentio) will meet to discuss the marriage plans further.

- Why is this? Take turns to read line 52, with each person giving it a different tone and emphasis. Afterwards, create a tableau that illustrates this line and reflects Baptista's state of mind.

142

THE TAMING OF THE SHREW ACT 4 SCENE 4

悍妇降服记

MERCHANT Soft[1], son.
Sir, by your leave, having come to Padua
To gather in some debts, my son Lucentio   25
Made me acquainted with a weighty cause[2]
Of love between your daughter and himself.
And – for[3] the good report I hear of you,
And for the love he beareth to your daughter,
And she to him – to stay him not[4] too long,   30
I am content, in a good father's care,
To have him matched. And if you please to like[5]
No worse than I, upon some agreement
Me shall you find ready and willing
With one consent to have her so bestowed,   35
For curious[6] I cannot be with you,
Signor Baptista, of whom I hear so well.

BAPTISTA Sir, pardon me in what I have to say.
Your plainness and your shortness please me well.
Right true it is your son Lucentio here   40
Doth love my daughter, and she loveth him –
Or both dissemble deeply their affections –
And therefore, if you say no more than this,
That like a father you will deal with him,
And pass[7] my daughter a sufficient dower,   45
The match is made and all is done:
Your son shall have my daughter with consent.

TRANIO I thank you, sir. Where, then, do you know best
We be affied[8] and such assurance tane[9]
As shall with either part's agreement stand[10]?   50

BAPTISTA Not in my house, Lucentio, for you know
Pitchers[11] have ears, and I have many servants.
Besides, old Gremio is heark'ning[12] still,
And happily[13] we might be interrupted.

TRANIO Then at my lodging, and it like you[14].   55
There doth my father lie[15], and there this night
We'll pass the business privately and well.

Baptista arranges for Cambio (Lucentio) to tell Bianca what has happened. Tranio leads Baptista off to his lodgings. Biondello explains to Lucentio that Baptista was deceived, and Bianca is almost won.

 剧情简介：巴普提斯塔安排坎毕欧（卢森修）告诉碧昂卡事情的进展。川纽带巴普提斯塔到他的住处。卞代娄告诉卢森修他们骗过了巴普提斯塔，碧昂卡几乎已经到手了。

1 Clever servants (in pairs)

Resourceful servants feature in a number of Shakespeare's plays, as well as in Roman comedies and in the Italian *commedia dell'arte* tradition. Two such clever, enterprising servants take part in this scene: Biondello and Tranio.

- Take on their roles and improvise some gossip between yourselves about the moments when you think you have been clever (and got away with things) during the action of the play so far.

2 'to expound the meaning' (in pairs)

Biondello certainly seems a quick-witted servant at the end of this scene, where he tries to explain what is happening to a rather slow-on-the-uptake Lucentio.

a Take parts and read through lines 73–103. Then discuss what would be lost if the whole passage was cut, as it sometimes is in performance.

b Use the Internet to research other literary examples where a servant is cleverer than his or her master. These do not necessarily have to be from Shakespeare.

> ## Themes
> ### Food and celebration (in small groups)
>
> Food plays a very important part in *The Taming of the Shrew* – and indeed in many of Shakespeare's plays. In the script opposite, Tranio seems concerned that the food will be insufficient. He says 'One mess is like to be your cheer' (line 70) and warns Baptista of 'a thin and slender pittance' (line 61).
>
> - Think back to other moments in the play when food and drink are offered as part of a welcome or a celebration, or when they are not offered at all or denied to someone.
> - Then talk together about why each of these occasions is important in the play. Refer particularly to Act 3 Scene 2 (lines 186–97), Act 4 Scene 1 (lines 159–70) and Act 4 Scene 3 (lines 2–47).

1 **scrivener** 公证人（起草法律协议等文书的人）
2 **thin and slender pittance** 粗茶淡饭
3 **hie** 赶快
4 **Dally not with the gods** 不要说天道地浪费时间
5 **mess** 菜肴
6 **cheer** 招待
7 **moralise** 解释
8 **safe** 没问题

	Send for your daughter by your servant here.	
	[*He indicates Lucentio and winks at him.*]	
	My boy shall fetch the scrivener¹ presently.	
	The worst is this, that at so slender warning	60
	You are like to have a thin and slender pittance².	
BAPTISTA	It likes me well. Cambio, hie³ you home,	
	And bid Bianca make her ready straight,	
	And, if you will, tell what hath happenèd:	
	Lucentio's father is arrived in Padua,	65
	And how she's like to be Lucentio's wife.	

[*Exit Lucentio*]

BIONDELLO	I pray the gods she may, with all my heart!
TRANIO	Dally not with the gods⁴, but get thee gone.

Exit Biondello

	– Signor Baptista, shall I lead the way?	
	Welcome. One mess⁵ is like to be your cheer⁶.	70
	Come sir, we will better it in Pisa.	
BAPTISTA	I follow you.	

Exeunt

Enter Lucentio [disguised as Cambio] and Biondello.

BIONDELLO	Cambio!	
LUCENTIO	What say'st thou, Biondello?	
BIONDELLO	You saw my master wink and laugh upon you?	75
LUCENTIO	Biondello, what of that?	
BIONDELLO	Faith, nothing – but 'has left me here behind to expound the meaning or moral of his signs and tokens.	
LUCENTIO	I pray thee, moralise⁷ them.	
BIONDELLO	Then thus: Baptista is safe⁸, talking with the deceiving father of a deceitful son.	80
LUCENTIO	And what of him?	
BIONDELLO	His daughter is to be brought by you to the supper.	
LUCENTIO	And then?	
BIONDELLO	The old priest at Saint Luke's church is at your command at all hours.	85

Biondello urges Lucentio to organise his secret wedding quickly. On the way to Baptista's, Petruchio insists that it is night, not day. When Katherina contradicts him, he orders everyone home.

剧情简介：卞代娄催促卢森修赶紧举行秘密婚礼。在去巴普提斯塔家的路上，珀楚秋硬把白天说成黑夜，凯特芮娜纠正他，他下令全体打道回府。

1 Lucentio's soliloquy (in small groups)

a Experiment with reading lines 100–3 in different ways. Use tones that are confident, confused, romantic, nervous, heroic, etc. Which do you think makes for the most effective conclusion to the scene? Would it make a difference if these lines were cut?

b Write out a similar four-line soliloquy for Bianca when she hears that Lucentio is coming with a priest to marry her.

Characters 人物分析

Has Katherina made progress? (in threes)

a Look at the image below, from a production that staged Katherina and Petruchio's entrance on a bicycle made for four. What line from the script opposite do you think Katherina has just said to provoke Petruchio's reaction here? What do you imagine Hortensio and Grumio (the two in the middle) are thinking, given their body language?

b Read Act 4 Scene 5, lines 1–25, at least three times. Take turns to be Katherina and experiment with different ways of delivering her lines. Has she genuinely given in to her new husband's will or not? Discuss how you think these opening lines should be played.

1	**Take you assurance** 您要确保
2	***cum ... solum*** （原义为"版权所有"，这里指结婚生养的专有权）
3	**that you look for** 您所盼望
4	**against you come** 以备您随时到
5	**appendix** 另一半（这里指碧昂卡）
6	**Hap what hap may** 无论发生什么
7	**roundly go about her** 直截了当跟她说
8	**list** 愿意
9	**Or e'er** 在……之前
10	**crossed** 唱反调

THE TAMING OF THE SHREW ACT 4 SCENE 5
悍妇降服记

LUCENTIO   And what of all this?
BIONDELLO   I cannot tell, except they are busied about a counterfeit assurance. Take you assurance¹ of her *cum privilegio ad imprimendum solum*². To the church! Take the priest, clerk and some sufficient honest witnesses.
    If this be not that you look for³, I have no more to say,
    But bid Bianca farewell for ever and a day.
LUCENTIO   Hear'st thou, Biondello?
BIONDELLO   I cannot tarry. I knew a wench married in an afternoon as she went to the garden for parsley to stuff a rabbit. And so may you, sir; and so adieu, sir. My master hath appointed me to go to Saint Luke's to bid the priest be ready to come against you come⁴ with your appendix⁵.   *Exit*
LUCENTIO   I may and will, if she be so contented.
    She will be pleased – then wherefore should I doubt?
    Hap what hap may⁶, I'll roundly go about her⁷.
    It shall go hard if Cambio go without her.   *Exit*

90

95

100

Act 4 Scene 5
On the road to Padua

Enter PETRUCHIO, KATHERINA, HORTENSIO [*and* SERVANTS].

PETRUCHIO   Come on, a God's name! Once more toward our father's.
    Good Lord, how bright and goodly shines the moon!
KATHERINA   The moon? The sun! It is not moonlight now.
PETRUCHIO   I say it is the moon that shines so bright.
KATHERINA   I know it is the sun that shines so bright.
PETRUCHIO   Now, by my mother's son – and that's myself –
    It shall be moon or star or what I list⁸
    Or e'er⁹ I journey to your father's house.
    [*To Servants*] Go on and fetch our horses back again.
    Evermore crossed¹⁰ and crossed, nothing but crossed!
HORTENSIO   Say as he says, or we shall never go.

5

10

Katherina accepts what Petruchio says – she will see the world as he instructs. Petruchio tests her by asking her to greet Vincentio as if he were a young girl.

 剧情简介：凯特芮娜同意接受珀楚秋的说法，珀楚秋要她怎么看世界，她就怎么看。为了考验她，珀楚秋让她把文森修当成小姑娘去问候。

1 Different interpretations (in small groups)

A number of Petruchio's and Katherina's lines in this scene can be spoken in different ways to evoke different audience responses:

- 'It shall be moon or star or what I list' (line 7)
- 'And be it moon or sun or what you please' (line 13)
- 'I know it is the moon' (line 16b)
- 'And the moon changes even as your mind' (line 20)
- 'And so it shall be so for Katherine' (line 22)

Choose some of the lines above (and any others you think are important) and complete the following activities.

a Speak each in turn round the group, but each person changes the emphasis and the tone in which the words are spoken. Someone acts as chairperson and stops the proceedings occasionally to ask the person speaking to explain and justify their interpretations.

b When you have been through all the lines, talk together about the ways in which these different interpretations can change an audience's attitude to the characters and to the scene as a whole.

Themes 主题分析
Game-playing and supposing

Several people play games in this act (Tranio, Hortensio, Lucentio, the Merchant) but none of them is as thought-provoking as the game Petruchio plays to break Katherina's resistance and contrariness. According to the actor Paola Dionisotti, there comes a point when Katherina 'has finally discovered that it is a game, and that they can play it together.'

a Do you think Katherina enjoys the fun of entering into Petruchio's game? Or do you think she is simply agreeing with everything Petruchio says in order to get on with the journey home? Like Hortensio, perhaps she thinks it is best to just 'say what he says', but she is secretly afraid of him and angry with him?

b Prepare a list of ten questions to ask Katherina, then take turns to sit in the hot-seat and answer those questions, to explore what might be going through her mind at this crucial point in the play.

1 rush-candle 昏暗的蜡烛
2 moon ... mind 月亮和你的心思一样变化不定（凯特芮娜暗示珀楚秋变化无常甚至疯癫）
3 go thy ways 再接再厉
4 bowl （地滚球游戏中所用的偏心球，可沿曲线滚动）
5 bias 地滚球滚动的偏斜路线（比喻凯特芮娜不会迷失自己的本性了）
6 soft 嘘
7 where away 您这是去哪儿
8 fresher 更年轻
9 war of white and red 白里透红
10 A = He
11 sun （凯特芮娜故意提及太阳，联系刚才珀楚秋的太阳月亮之争，说明她已掌握游戏规则和技巧）
12 green 鲜嫩，富有朝气

KATHERINA	Forward, I pray, since we have come so far.
	And be it moon or sun or what you please;
	And if you please to call it a rush-candle[1],
	Henceforth I vow it shall be so for me. 15
PETRUCHIO	I say it is the moon.
KATHERINA	I know it is the moon.
PETRUCHIO	Nay then you lie, it is the blessèd sun.
KATHERINA	Then God be blessed, it is the blessèd sun.
	But sun it is not, when you say it is not,
	And the moon changes even as your mind[2]. 20
	What you will have it named, even that it is,
	And so it shall be so for Katherine.
HORTENSIO	[*Aside*] Petruchio, go thy ways[3]. The field is won.
PETRUCHIO	Well, forward, forward! Thus the bowl[4] should run
	And not unluckily against the bias[5]. 25

Enter VINCENTIO.

But soft[6], company is coming here.
[*To Vincentio*] Good morrow, gentle mistress, where away[7]?
Tell me, sweet Kate, and tell me truly too,
Hast thou beheld a fresher[8] gentlewoman?
Such war of white and red[9] within her cheeks! 30
What stars do spangle heaven with such beauty
As those two eyes become that heavenly face?
Fair lovely maid, once more good day to thee.
Sweet Kate, embrace her for her beauty's sake.

HORTENSIO	[*Aside*] A[10] will make the man mad, to make the woman of 35
	him.
KATHERINA	Young budding virgin, fair and fresh and sweet,
	Whither away, or where is thy abode?
	Happy the parents of so fair a child!
	Happier the man whom favourable stars 40
	Allots thee for his lovely bedfellow.
PETRUCHIO	Why, how now, Kate! I hope thou art not mad.
	This is a man – old, wrinkled, faded, withered –
	And not a maiden, as thou say'st he is.
KATHERINA	Pardon, old father, my mistaking eyes 45
	That have been so bedazzled with the sun[11]
	That everything I look on seemeth green[12].

Vincentio introduces himself as Lucentio's father. Petruchio tells him that his son is married to Katherina's sister. Hortensio vows to tame the Widow in the same way as Petruchio has tamed Katherina.

 剧情简介：文森修介绍自己是卢森修的父亲，珀楚秋告诉他说他儿子已和凯特芮娜的妹妹结婚。郝坦修发誓要像珀楚秋那样把他娶的寡妇驯服。

1 Petruchio's sixth sense (in pairs)

Is Petruchio clairvoyant (有洞察力，未卜先知), or has Shakespeare slipped up? In lines 59–63, Petruchio reveals that Lucentio has married Bianca, although he can hardly know this yet. A similar problem arises when Hortensio confirms the marriage.

- Do you think these inconsistencies matter? Would an audience notice such things during a performance? Some productions find ways to explain these problems – for example, by organising the arrival of a telegram or a phone call. What would you do? Write notes in your Director's Journal.

1 encounter　（相遇时的）问候方式
2 by this　到现在
3 so qualified as　有（相配的）容貌才德
4 beseem　与……相配
5 pleasant　幽默风趣
6 break a jest　耍个把戏寻开心
7 jealous　起疑心
8 Have to　现在我要去对付
9 untoward　倔强，顽强

Stagecraft 导演技巧

'Wonder not, / Nor be not grieved'

a How does Vincentio react when Petruchio calls him 'my loving father' and he realises that his son has married Katherina's sister? Remember that it is possible he thinks Petruchio and Katherina are crazy because of the practical joke they have just been playing.

b Petruchio describes Bianca in glowing terms to Vincentio, to emphasise what a good catch she is: wealthy and high-class. How would you portray this on stage for greatest comic effect?

Characters 人物分析

What has Hortensio learnt? (in pairs)

This scene ends with a brief monologue. Hortensio thanks Petruchio for teaching him how to tame the Widow if she proves 'froward'. He thinks he has learnt a great deal from observing Petruchio's taming methods, but has he learnt the right lessons?

a As Hortensio, try speaking lines 77–9 in different styles: cruelly, hopefully, determinedly, joyfully.

b Write his diary entry or a letter to a close friend, showing what he has really learnt about love and women. Describe how he intends to use this knowledge when he courts and marries the rich Widow.

	Now I perceive thou art a reverend father.	
	Pardon, I pray thee, for my mad mistaking.	
PETRUCHIO	Do, good old grandsire, and withal make known	50
	Which way thou travellest – if along with us	
	We shall be joyful of thy company.	
VINCENTIO	Fair sir, and you, my merry mistress,	
	That with your strange encounter[1] much amazed me,	
	My name is called Vincentio, my dwelling Pisa,	55
	And bound I am to Padua, there to visit	
	A son of mine which long I have not seen.	
PETRUCHIO	What is his name?	
VINCENTIO	Lucentio, gentle sir.	
PETRUCHIO	Happily met – the happier for thy son.	
	And now by law as well as reverend age	60
	I may entitle thee my loving father.	
	The sister to my wife, this gentlewoman,	
	Thy son by this[2] hath married. Wonder not,	
	Nor be not grieved. She is of good esteem,	
	Her dowry wealthy, and of worthy birth;	65
	Beside, so qualified as[3] may beseem[4]	
	The spouse of any noble gentleman.	
	Let me embrace with old Vincentio,	
	And wander we to see thy honest son,	
	Who will of thy arrival be full joyous.	70
VINCENTIO	But is this true, or is it else your pleasure,	
	Like pleasant[5] travellers, to break a jest[6]	
	Upon the company you overtake?	
HORTENSIO	I do assure thee, father, so it is.	
PETRUCHIO	Come, go along and see the truth hereof,	75
	For our first merriment hath made thee jealous[7].	

Exeunt [all but Hortensio]

HORTENSIO	Well, Petruchio, this has put me in heart!
	Have to[8] my widow, and if she be froward,
	Then hast thou taught Hortensio to be untoward[9]. *Exit*

Looking back at Act 4 第4幕回顾
Activities for groups or individuals

1 Headlines

A lot has happened in this act, so you should now try to summarise the action. One half of the class tells the story in the form of tabloid newspaper (小报) headlines. Use five or six headlines, making sure you include everything significant that has occurred. The other half of the class does the same thing for a broadsheet newspaper (大报). Remember, alliteration will make for striking headlines in both types of newspaper!

2 Hortensio's monologue

Throughout Act 4, the two major plots continue to compete for our attention. The only person who links the two stories in this act is Hortensio. What does he think of Petruchio's battle with Katherina and the odd assortment (各种) of suitors scrambling (争夺) for Bianca's favour?

- Write a brief monologue in which Hortensio describes the events of Act 4 and comments on the various characters involved in them.

3 Masters and servants

Many servants appear in Act 4. What are their stories?

- Working in groups, each person chooses a particular servant. Include those who say very little (or nothing at all), as well as Grumio, Curtis and Biondello. Sit in a circle and relate their stories. Keep to the plot in broad terms, but think about how events looked from their point of view. What about their lives off stage? What do they think about their masters? What do they know and what are they completely unaware of?

Looking back at Act 4

4 Expressing Katherina's thoughts

Katherina is perhaps the only one of Shakespeare's comic heroines who has no female friend with whom to share her thoughts.

- Find four points in the play where Katherina is silent but where she might have preferred to express her thoughts. Why is she quiet? If she had spoken, what might she have said? Compose an alternative script for these parts of the play.

5 What happens next?

What do you think might happen next in the play? Imagine you have witnessed how events unfold, and write the beginning of the next act. If you prefer, you can write an imagined first-person account instead.

6 What's the story?

There is surely a fascinating story behind Biondello's memory of 'a wench married in an afternoon / as she went to the garden for parsley to stuff a rabbit.' (Act 4 Scene 4, lines 95–6).

- Tell the story in no more than a page, and try to include some of the stock characters you have encountered in this play, as well as some of the ideas about the battle for control between the sexes.
- Alternatively, play 'consequences' in groups. Pass a piece of paper around so each member of the group can contribute to the story. Fold the paper down after each addition, and wait until everyone has written their bit before reading it out.

153

Lucentio and Bianca set off to be married. Petruchio directs Vincentio to his son's lodgings. The Merchant, still pretending to be Vincentio, turns them away.

 剧情简介： 卢森修和碧昂卡出发去完婚。珀楚秋指引文森修来到他儿子的住处，依旧假扮文森修的商人把他们拒之门外。

1 The father's arrival

Vincentio, Lucentio's father, arrives at his son's house to find a large party in full swing (劲头) and no welcome for him. There is a dramatic irony here, as the audience knows what is happening and what his son has been up to.

a Imagine that Lucentio lists each of the deceptions that he has been involved in throughout the sub-plot of the play. In role as Lucentio, copy and complete the list below:

- First, I disguised myself as Cambio, a teacher.
- Second, Tranio disguised himself as me.
- Third …

b Predict what might happen in the rest of this act, when his father finds out what has been going on. Remember, Lucentio's marriage to Bianca is about to happen and could easily be disrupted.

1	**I'll … back** 我要看你们进教堂结婚
2	**marvel** 奇怪
3	**bears** 在……方向
4	**some cheer is toward** 应该能得到某种款待
5	**withal** = with
6	**frivolous circumstances** 琐碎的细节

Use this image to contrast Lucentio's plans for marriage to Bianca with his father's anger at being deceived.

2 Gremio's ignorance

Gremio's line 'I marvel Cambio comes not all this while' is full of dramatic irony and comic potential. Somehow the old, rich lover is on stage at the same time, but he does not observe the hurried conversation between Biondello and Lucentio, who quickly leaves with Bianca.

- Talk together about how you would stage lines 1–15 for greatest comic effect.

Act 5 Scene 1
Outside Lucentio's lodgings

Enter BIONDELLO, LUCENTIO [*as himself*] *and* BIANCA. GREMIO *is out before.*

BIONDELLO Softly and swiftly, sir, for the priest is ready.

LUCENTIO I fly, Biondello. But they may chance to need thee at home; therefore leave us.

Exit Lucentio [*with Bianca*]

BIONDELLO Nay, faith, I'll see the church a'your back[1], and then come back to my master's as soon as I can. *Exit*

GREMIO I marvel[2] Cambio comes not all this while.

Enter PETRUCHIO, KATHERINA, VINCENTIO, GRUMIO, *with* ATTENDANTS.

PETRUCHIO Sir, here's the door, this is Lucentio's house.
My father's bears[3] more toward the market-place;
Thither must I, and here I leave you, sir.

VINCENTIO You shall not choose but drink before you go.
I think I shall command your welcome here,
And by all likelihood some cheer is toward[4].

He knocks.

GREMIO They're busy within. You were best knock louder.

MERCHANT *looks out of the window.*

MERCHANT What's he that knocks as he would beat down the gate?

VINCENTIO Is Signor Lucentio within, sir?

MERCHANT He's within, sir, but not to be spoken withal[5].

VINCENTIO What if a man bring him a hundred pound or two to make merry withal?

MERCHANT Keep your hundred pounds to yourself. He shall need none so long as I live.

PETRUCHIO Nay, I told you your son was well beloved in Padua. Do you hear, sir? To leave frivolous circumstances[6], I pray you tell Signor Lucentio that his father is come from Pisa and is here at the door to speak with him.

The Merchant and Vincentio both claim to be Lucentio's father. Vincentio recognises Biondello, who denies knowing him. Vincentio beats him angrily.

剧情简介：商人和文森修都声称是卢森修的父亲。文森修认出卞代娄，卞代娄却说不认识他，文森修一怒之下打了他。

1 'I never saw you before' (in pairs)

a Read lines 33–46 and then choose what you think is:
- the most comic moment
- the wittiest retort from Biondello
- the best opportunity for action.

b Why does Biondello pretend not to know Vincentio? Do you think the age difference will affect the exchange? Talk together about how successfully Biondello scores points off Vincentio. Rehearse this sequence between the two men, making the scene as lively as possible.

2 Who is telling the truth? (in small groups)

Compile a list of questions that the characters might ask in order to ascertain who is Lucentio's real father. Two of the group take on the roles of Vincentio and the Merchant. The rest ask the questions as if they were members of a crowd trying to decide who is telling the truth. Don't let the students playing Vincentio and the Merchant know these questions beforehand!

1 **Thou liest** 你撒谎
2 **flat knavery** 不要脸的丑恶行为
3 **a means to cozen** 他想诈骗
4 **countenance** 名字；身份
5 **good shipping** 一路顺风
6 **undone** 完蛋
7 **crack-hemp** 吊死鬼，该被绞死的坏蛋（hemp指麻绳，可做绞刑的套索）
8 **choose** （选择是否过去或谁是主子）

Stagecraft 导演技巧

Another 'show' (in pairs)

a There have been several onstage audiences in this play, but this is the first time that Petruchio and Katherina watch others. Suggest different positions from which these two characters could view the action (line 48).

b In your Director's Journal, write notes on the difference their presence and reactions might make to an audience's response to the events unfolding on stage. Remember that layers of illusion are built up when a real audience watches a stage audience (first Sly and his 'wife' watching the players, and in this case Petruchio and Katherina). Members of a real audience may also feel self-conscious as they see their own reactions mirrored or mimicked on stage.

The Taming of the Shrew Act 5 Scene 1
悍妇降服记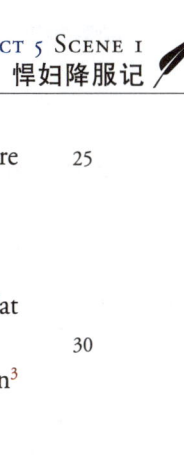

MERCHANT Thou liest[1]. His father is come from Mantua and here looking out at the window. 25

VINCENTIO Art thou his father?

MERCHANT Ay, sir, so his mother says, if I may believe her.

PETRUCHIO [*To Vincentio*] Why, how now, gentleman! Why, this is flat knavery[2], to take upon you another man's name. 30

MERCHANT Lay hands on the villain. I believe a means to cozen[3] somebody in this city under my countenance[4].

Enter Biondello.

BIONDELLO [*Aside*] I have seen them in the church together – God send 'em good shipping[5]! But who is here? Mine old master, Vincentio! Now we are undone[6] and brought to nothing! 35

VINCENTIO Come hither, crack-hemp[7].

BIONDELLO I hope I may choose[8], sir.

VINCENTIO Come hither, you rogue! What, have you forgot me?

BIONDELLO Forgot you? No, sir. I could not forget you, for I never saw you before in all my life. 40

VINCENTIO What, you notorious villain! Didst thou never see thy master's father, Vincentio?

BIONDELLO What, my old worshipful old master? Yes, marry, sir, see where he looks out of the window.

VINCENTIO Is't so indeed? 45

He beats Biondello.

BIONDELLO Help! Help! Help! Here's a madman will murder me!
[*Exit*]

MERCHANT Help, son! Help, Signor Baptista!   [*Exit from the window*]

PETRUCHIO Prithee, Kate, let's stand aside and see the end of this controversy.

[*They stand aside.*]

Vincentio is astonished to see Tranio pretending to be Lucentio. He fears for his son's life. Despite Gremio's suspicions, Vincentio is on the point of being arrested.

 剧情简介：文森修惊讶地发现川纽假扮卢森修，他担心儿子遭遇不测。尽管葛莱缪开始怀疑这件事，文森修险些被捕。

1 Tranio caught red-handed (in pairs)

Tranio, dressed as his master Lucentio, pretends not to know Vincentio.

a Compare how Tranio deals with the shock of Vincentio's arrival with Biondello's reaction (lines 34–46). In your pairs, find three differences and consider them in depth, in relation to the characters of Tranio and Biondello.

b Vincentio begins to think that the servants have murdered his son and stolen his money. What verbal cues suggest a comic response here? Are there any elements of cruelty or humiliation? How would you choose to stage this moment – to highlight the comedy or with increasing pity for Vincentio's distress?

1 offer　胆敢
2 fine　衣着华丽
3 hose　紧身裤
4 copatain　穹顶
5 husband　管家
6 what 'cerns it you　与您何干
7 maintain　负担得起
8 forthcoming　随时前来接受审判
9 dotard　傻老头儿
10 haled　（粗鲁地）拖拽

Themes 主题分析

What are you wearing?

Vincentio appears to be angry that Tranio is wearing grand clothes and assuming an identity that does not fit his status as a servant. Tranio rather impertinently (无礼地) comments on how Vincentio's 'sober' (respectable) style of clothing is an attempt to disguise the madman underneath.

- How is Tranio's understanding of clothing and social status similar to Petruchio's ideas about clothing and identity?
- Find three quotations that relate to clothing. Use these to formulate your own ideas about the themes of appearance and reality and social class relations in the play.

2 Suspicious Gremio (in threes)

What is it that makes Gremio suspicious (lines 74–81)? One of you take his part, and the other two ask him why he suspects a trick and yet is afraid to swear to it on oath.

3 What would Sly say?

In some performances of the play in Shakespeare's day, Christopher Sly attempts to intervene when Vincentio is about to be sent to jail at lines 74–9. He interrupts the action with: 'I say we'll have no sending to prison.'

- Choose three other moments in this scene and add further comments from Sly.

THE TAMING OF THE SHREW ACT 5 SCENE 1
悍妇降服记

Enter Merchant [below] with SERVANTS, BAPTISTA *and* TRANIO
[disguised as Lucentio].

TRANIO   Sir, what are you that offer[1] to beat my servant?   50

VINCENTIO   What am I, sir? Nay, what are you, sir? O immortal gods! O fine[2] villain! A silken doublet, a velvet hose[3], a scarlet cloak, and a copatain[4] hat! O I am undone, I am undone! While I play the good husband[5] at home my son and my servant spend all at the university.

TRANIO   How now, what's the matter?   55

BAPTISTA   What, is the man lunatic?

TRANIO   Sir, you seem a sober ancient gentleman by your habit, but your words show you a madman. Why, sir, what 'cerns it you[6] if I wear pearl and gold? I thank my good father, I am able to maintain[7] it.

VINCENTIO   Thy father? O villain! He is a sail-maker in Bergamo.   60

BAPTISTA   You mistake, sir; you mistake, sir. Pray, what do you think is his name?

VINCENTIO   His name? As if I knew not his name! I have brought him up ever since he was three years old, and his name is Tranio.

MERCHANT   Away, away, mad ass! His name is Lucentio and he is mine only son, and heir to the lands of me, Signor Vincentio.   65

VINCENTIO   Lucentio? O, he hath murdered his master! Lay hold on him, I charge you in the Duke's name. O my son, my son! Tell me, thou villain, where is my son Lucentio?

TRANIO   Call forth an officer.   70

[Enter an OFFICER.*]*

Carry this mad knave to the jail. Father Baptista, I charge you see that he be forthcoming[8].

VINCENTIO   Carry me to the jail?

GREMIO   Stay, officer. He shall not go to prison.

BAPTISTA   Talk not, Signor Gremio. I say he shall go to prison.   75

GREMIO   Take heed, Signor Baptista, lest you be cony-catched in this business. I dare swear this is the right Vincentio.

MERCHANT   Swear, if thou dar'st.

GREMIO   Nay, I dare not swear it.

TRANIO   Then thou wert best say that I am not Lucentio.   80

GREMIO   Yes, I know thee to be Signor Lucentio.

BAPTISTA   Away with the dotard[9], to the jail with him!

VINCENTIO   Thus strangers may be haled[10] and abused. O monstrous villain!

Lucentio begs Vincentio to forgive him. He then explains to Baptista that he is now Bianca's husband. Both fathers are far from happy.

 剧情简介：卢森修乞求文森修的宽恕，接着向巴普提斯塔解释他已经是碧昂卡的丈夫。两位父亲都大为恼火。

1 Discovery!

Lines 87–93 make an intensely dramatic and funny episode. Suddenly all is revealed.

a In role as the director of a new production, write about how you would stage these lines to make the action as entertaining as possible, while also ensuring that the audience understands what is going on.

b Look at Vincentio's response when Lucentio asks him to pardon Tranio (line 105) and Baptista's response to the secret marriage (105–11). Do you think it likely that their fathers will forgive them any time soon? How would you show this in the expressions, gestures, tone and atmosphere on stage?

2 Fathers (in pairs)

The two fathers, Vincentio and Baptista, are far from delighted by the revelations made in Act 5 Scene 1. Look at their final words in the scene, then improvise a conversation between them as they leave the stage. Include their opinions about Lucentio's and Bianca's disregard for their fathers' blessing.

1 **spoiled** 完蛋了
2 **counterfeit supposes** 假象；误信
3 **bleared thine eyne** 骗过了您的双眼
4 **packing** 骗局
5 **faced and braved me** 当面藐视顶撞我（拿我不当回事）
6 **wrought** 创造
7 **do you hear** 您听我说
8 **Go to** 冷静；别担心
9 **My cake is dough** 我的蛋糕成了面团子（指希望破灭）

Language in the play 剧中语言

'Love wrought these miracles' (in pairs)

a One person reads lines 98–104 aloud several times. Talk together about the language Lucentio uses here. Then the other person reads the lines again, this time exaggerating both language and gesture. Remember that Lucentio and Bianca are on their knees, asking for forgiveness.

b Lucentio uses high-flown (浮夸；言之凿凿) language and blames his wrongdoings on the strength of his love for Bianca. Could Shakespeare be presenting an alternative view of these lovers? If so, what view is he presenting?

c Write a paragraph or two exploring how the idea of romantic love is subject to parody (戏仿作品) and satire.

The Taming of the Shrew Act 5 Scene 1
悍妇降服记

Enter Biondello, Lucentio and Bianca.

BIONDELLO O, we are spoiled¹, and yonder he is! Deny him, forswear him, or else we are all undone.   85

Exeunt Biondello, Tranio and Merchant, as fast as may be

LUCENTIO Pardon, sweet father.

Lucentio and Bianca kneel.

VINCENTIO Lives my sweet son?

BIANCA Pardon, dear father.

BAPISTA How hast thou offended?
Where is Lucentio?

LUCENTIO Here's Lucentio,
Right son to the right Vincentio,   90
That have by marriage made thy daughter mine
While counterfeit supposes² bleared thine eyne³.

GREMIO Here's packing⁴, with a witness, to deceive us all!

VINCENTIO Where is that damnèd villain, Tranio,
That faced and braved me⁵ in this matter so?   95

BAPTISTA Why, tell me, is not this my Cambio?

BIANCA Cambio is changed into Lucentio.

LUCENTIO Love wrought⁶ these miracles. Bianca's love
Made me exchange my state with Tranio
While he did bear my countenance in the town,   100
And happily I have arrived at the last
Unto the wishèd haven of my bliss.
What Tranio did, myself enforced him to;
Then pardon him, sweet father, for my sake.

VINCENTIO I'll slit the villain's nose that would have sent me to the jail!   105

BAPTISTA But do you hear⁷, sir? Have you married my daughter without asking my good will?

VINCENTIO Fear not, Baptista, we will content you. Go to⁸. But I will in to be revenged for this villainy.   *Exit*   110

BAPTISTA And I, to sound the depth of this knavery.   *Exit*

LUCENTIO Look not pale, Bianca, thy father will not frown.

Exeunt [Lucentio and Bianca]

GREMIO My cake is dough⁹, but I'll in among the rest,
Out of hope of all but my share of the feast.   *[Exit]*

161

Katherina reluctantly kisses Petruchio. He feels very pleased with the way things have turned out. Lucentio welcomes everyone to the banquet held to celebrate the three weddings.

剧情简介：凯特芮娜不情愿地吻了珀楚秋。珀楚秋很满意事态的发展。卢森修请众人参加宴会，庆祝三桩婚事。

1 'kiss me, Kate' (in pairs)

The stage has cleared and Petruchio and Katherina are left alone. For the first time, Katherina calls Petruchio 'love' (line 123) and completes his rhyme (away/stay).

a How should she kiss him: willingly, reluctantly, tenderly, coldly, resignedly, passionately?

b As Katherina and Petruchio kiss, imagine two passers-by commenting on what they see and hear. Improvise their conversation and give their views about this couple showing such affection in a public place.

1 ado 麻烦事
2 Better … late 一次总比没有强，迟来总比不来强（此处糅合两个谚语：better late than never和it is never too late to mend）
3 scapes = escapes（危险时刻）
4 overblown 消失；过去
5 close our stomachs up 吃到嗓子眼了（也指结束争吵）
6 affords 提供
7 this kindness 如此热情的款待
8 nothing but what is kind 天生的热情好客

2 If music be the food of love (in small groups)

The scene opens with a musical image, perhaps suggesting that harmony has finally been achieved. But there are also many references to conflict in the script opposite. Find as many as you can.

- What music would you use in a modern production, to accompany Lucentio's speech and echo this tension between harmony and conflict?

KATHERINA	Husband, let's follow, to see the end of this ado¹.	115
PETRUCHIO	First kiss me, Kate, and we will.	
KATHERINA	What, in the midst of the street?	
PETRUCHIO	What, art thou ashamed of me?	
KATHERINA	No sir, God forbid – but ashamed to kiss.	
PETRUCHIO	Why then, let's home again.	120
	[*To Grumio*] Come, sirrah, let's away.	
KATHERINA	Nay, I will give thee a kiss.	
	[*She kisses him.*]	
	Now pray thee, love, stay.	
PETRUCHIO	Is not this well? Come, my sweet Kate,	
	Better once than never, for never too late².	125

Exeunt

Act 5 Scene 2
Lucentio's lodgings

Enter BAPTISTA, VINCENTIO, GREMIO, *the* MERCHANT, LUCENTIO *and* BIANCA, [HORTENSIO] *and the* WIDOW, [PETRUCHIO *and* KATHERINA], TRANIO, BIONDELLO *and* GRUMIO *with* SERVINGMEN *bringing in a banquet.*

LUCENTIO	At last, though long, our jarring notes agree,	
	And time it is when raging war is done	
	To smile at scapes³ and perils overblown⁴.	
	My fair Bianca, bid my father welcome,	
	While I with selfsame kindness welcome thine.	5
	Brother Petruchio, sister Katherina,	
	And thou Hortensio, with thy loving widow,	
	Feast with the best, and welcome to my house.	
	My banquet is to close our stomachs up⁵	
	After our great good cheer. Pray you, sit down,	10
	For now we sit to chat as well as eat.	
PETRUCHIO	Nothing but sit and sit, and eat and eat!	
BAPTISTA	Padua affords⁶ this kindness⁷, son Petruchio.	
PETRUCHIO	Padua affords nothing but what is kind⁸.	

The guests exchange witty banter, especially the Widow and Katherina, encouraged by the men. Bianca leads the women from the room.

剧情简介： 宾客们耍嘴皮子，相互逗乐子，尤其是受了男人鼓励的寡妇和凯特芮娜。碧昂卡带众女宾离席。

1 Proverbs (in small groups)

Widows in the Elizabethan period were often stereotyped as assertive and independent women, and Hortensio's new wife has been described as a 'wealthy' and 'lusty' widow (Act 4 Scene 2, lines 37 and 50). Her remark at line 20 is insulting to Katherina, who demands to know what she means by it (lines 26–7).

a Explain in your own words what the meaning is in this context (the Widow explains in lines 28–30).

b Create a tableau or short mime to express this meaning. Compare your version with those of other groups.

Stagecraft 导演技巧

Swapping witticisms (俏皮话) (in pairs)

a At first, the guests seem to indulge in good-natured banter, and traditionally this scene is played with a number of the characters drunk. Discuss whether you would stress the festive atmosphere, the underlying tension – or both.

b At what point do you think the atmosphere might alter, and why? Remember, there are a number of sexual puns opposite, which might change the atmosphere. Here are a few:

- *conceive* become pregnant (or understand)
- *tale* sexual organ (or story)
- *bush* pubic hair (or place).

c Talk together about how appropriate this language is to the characters who use it.

Language in the play 剧中语言

'To her … ' (in small groups)

In lines 16–37, Petruchio and Hortensio champion their wives in a battle of wits.

a Identify the puns and work out how the Widow, Petruchio and Katherina change the meaning of words to fling insults around.

b Set up a mock arm-wrestling contest. As the battle of words is fought, respond physically so that you can show success or failure. Is there a clear winner?

---

1 **fears his widow** （既可指郝坦修怕妻子又可指他使妻子害怕）
2 **sensible** 敏感
3 **Roundly** 坦率，直言不讳
4 **conceive** 了解（又有"怀孕"之意）
5 **mean meaning** 卑劣的意思
6 **I … you** 比起您来，我的所作所为还过得去
7 **put her down** 压过她，赢了她
8 **an officer** 公差
9 **Ha'** = Here's
10 **butt** 用头撞
11 **butt** 尾巴，臀部
12 **bitter** 犀利敏锐
13 **bird** 靶子

THE TAMING OF THE SHREW ACT 5 SCENE 2
悍妇降服记

HORTENSIO   For both our sakes I would that word were true.   15
PETRUCHIO   Now, for my life, Hortensio fears his widow¹!
WIDOW   Then never trust me if I be afeard.
PETRUCHIO   You are very sensible², and yet you miss my sense:
             I mean Hortensio is afeard of you.
WIDOW   He that is giddy thinks the world turns round.   20
PETRUCHIO   Roundly³ replied.
KATHERINA   Mistress, how mean you that?
WIDOW   Thus I conceive⁴ by him.
PETRUCHIO   Conceives by me! How likes Hortensio that?
HORTENSIO   My widow says, thus she conceives her tale.
PETRUCHIO   Very well mended. Kiss him for that, good widow.   25
KATHERINA   'He that is giddy thinks the world turns round.'
             I pray you tell me what you meant by that.
WIDOW   Your husband, being troubled with a shrew,
             Measures my husband's sorrow by his woe –
             And now you know my meaning.   30
KATHERINA   A very mean meaning⁵.
WIDOW   Right, I mean you.
KATHERINA   And I am mean indeed, respecting you⁶.
PETRUCHIO   To her, Kate!
HORTENSIO   To her, widow!
PETRUCHIO   A hundred marks my Kate does put her down⁷.   35
HORTENSIO   That's my office.
PETRUCHIO   Spoke like an officer⁸. Ha'⁹ to thee, lad.
                          He drinks to Hortensio.
BAPTISTA   How likes Gremio these quick-witted folks?
GREMIO   Believe me, sir, they butt¹⁰ together well.
BIANCA   Head and butt¹¹! An hasty-witted body   40
             Would say your head and butt were head and horn.
VINCENTIO   Ay, mistress bride, hath that awakened you?
BIANCA   Ay, but not frighted me; therefore I'll sleep again.
PETRUCHIO   Nay, that you shall not. Since you have begun,
             Have at you for a bitter¹² jest or two.   45
BIANCA   Am I your bird¹³? I mean to shift my bush,
             And then pursue me as you draw your bow.
             You are welcome all.
                          Exeunt Bianca, [Katherina and Widow]

165

The men joke about whose wife is least obedient. Petruchio proposes a wager – each husband will send for his wife to see which one obeys most promptly. Lucentio begins the contest.

 剧情简介：男人们调侃谁的妻子最不温顺。珀楚秋提议打个赌，每位丈夫都派人去请自己的妻子，看谁的妻子最听话来得最快。卢森修开始了这场比赛。

1 Sporting images

a The script opposite contains a number of images taken from blood-sports (狩猎运动), which were extremely popular in Elizabethan times. Identify as many as you can. How does this imagery reflect the relationship between the men in this scene?

b In your Director's Journal, make notes on how you would want the script opposite to be staged. Consider whether this is all good-humoured banter, or whether there might be a sense of threat and violence just beneath the surface. Remember – Vincentio and Baptista may not have forgiven Lucentio, and all the newly married men are probably anxious to show that they have made the best match.

2 A confident father (in pairs)

Baptista seems to be pretty sure that Bianca will do as she's told. Do you think his confidence in line 78 is well placed? Think back to earlier scenes where she has behaved in a way that defies expectations, especially Act 3 Scene 1 and Act 4 Scene 2. Write a paragraph explaining your thoughts on this, giving reasons for your decision.

Characters 人物分析

The wager (in pairs)

a Talk together about the way in which Petruchio initiates the wager in the script opposite. Is he bold and confident or reckless and competitive?

b How much of a risk do you think Petruchio is taking and does his challenge suggest he still thinks of Katherina as he would a hawk, a hound or a horse. Or is he returning control to her?

c One actor who played Petruchio claimed that he was driven by money to begin with and he only later developed feelings for Katherina. Do you agree? Write a paragraph explaining how far you think Petruchio is motivated by money.

1	slipped	放开（狗绳）
2	swift	迅速；恰当
3	currish	恶狗一般暴躁
4	does … bay	让您陷入困境
5	gird	打赌时挖苦人的笑话
6	here	（郝坦修指着头继续刚才那个头撞角 [horn指绿帽子] 的笑话）
7	A … me	他的讽刺确实惹我生气
8	good sadness	一本正经，十分严肃
9	veriest	最彪悍，最厉害
10	Sir Assurance	（对过于自信的巴普提斯塔或卢森修的称呼，表示挖苦）
11	be your half	替您出一半赌注

The Taming of the Shrew Act 5 Scene 2
悍妇降服记

PETRUCHIO She hath prevented me. Here, Signor Tranio,
This bird you aimed at, though you hit her not –
Therefore a health to all that shot and missed.

TRANIO O sir, Lucentio slipped[1] me like his greyhound,
Which runs himself and catches for his master.

PETRUCHIO A good swift[2] simile, but something currish[3].

TRANIO 'Tis well, sir, that you hunted for yourself –
'Tis thought your deer does hold you at a bay[4].

BAPTISTA O, O, Petruchio! Tranio hits you now.

LUCENTIO I thank thee for that gird[5], good Tranio.

HORTENSIO Confess! Confess! Hath he not hit you here[6]?

PETRUCHIO A has a little galled me[7], I confess,
And as the jest did glance away from me,
'Tis ten to one it maimed you two outright.

BAPTISTA Now in good sadness[8], son Petruchio,
I think thou hast the veriest[9] shrew of all.

PETRUCHIO Well, I say no, and therefore, Sir Assurance[10],
Let's each one send unto his wife,
And he whose wife is most obedient
To come at first when he doth send for her
Shall win the wager which we will propose.

HORTENSIO Content. What's the wager?

LUCENTIO   Twenty crowns.

PETRUCHIO Twenty crowns?
I'll venture so much of my hawk or hound,
But twenty times so much upon my wife.

LUCENTIO A hundred then.

HORTENSIO   Content.

PETRUCHIO   A match! 'Tis done.

HORTENSIO Who shall begin?

LUCENTIO   That will I.
Go Biondello, bid your mistress come to me.

BIONDELLO I go.   *Exit*

BAPTISTA Son, I'll be your half[11] Bianca comes.

LUCENTIO I'll have no halves; I'll bear it all myself.

Biondello returns with the news that neither Bianca nor the Widow will come. Katherina, however, answers the summons. Petruchio sends her back to fetch the other two wives.

 剧情简介： 卞代娄回禀说碧昂卡和寡妇都不会来。而凯特芮娜却应召而来，珀楚秋让她回去把另外两位妻子叫来。

1 'Let's each one send' (in small groups)

a Read through lines 80–98, then talk together about ways of raising the tension as the men wait for each successive answer from their wives, and the outcome of their wager. What stage business would you use: what facial expressions, gestures, pauses, music, lighting, sound, movement?

b What answer do the first two wives give? Describe how you would advise the actors playing the men to react to these reponses. Would they be surprised, angry, amazed, embarrassed, sad?

1 **goodly jest in hand** 准备好好听的玩笑（说反话）
2 **The fouler** 更糟
3 **my holidame** = my holy dame （我的圣母；惊讶的感叹）
4 **conferring** 商量事情；聊天
5 **Swinge me them soundly** 好好地替我打她们一顿直到她们肯来

Characters 人物分析

What are they doing?

The audience sees what is happening between the men, but what is taking place off stage?

- Improvise and then script the scene with the three women, showing what happens when Biondello and Grumio arrive to summon them to their new husbands. Make sure you reveal their true character and motivations in the way they treat these messengers.

2 'What is your will, sir?' (in small groups)

Katherina's entrance should be a very striking theatrical moment. Take turns to read line 100 in as many ways as possible. Try saying it charmingly, with biting sarcasm, sincerely, insincerely, in an over-the-top manner or resentfully. Talk about the effect you want it to have on an audience and on the other characters on the stage.

Write about it 写作练习

Comment on Katherina (in pairs)

Choose a character who is on stage at line 100 and, in role, compose an aside to the audience, telling them what you think about Katherina at this point. Remember – what a character thinks will be influenced by the way in which the line is spoken, so write an aside that responds to all the different ways this line has been spoken in the activity above.

The Taming of the Shrew Act 5 Scene 2
悍妇降服记

Enter Biondello.

How now, what news?

BIONDELLO Sir, my mistress sends you word 80
That she is busy, and she cannot come.

PETRUCHIO How? 'She's busy and she cannot come'!
Is that an answer?

GREMIO Ay, and a kind one too.
Pray God, sir, your wife send you not a worse.

PETRUCHIO I hope better. 85

HORTENSIO Sirrah Biondello, go and entreat my wife
To come to me forthwith.

Exit Biondello

PETRUCHIO O ho, 'entreat' her!
Nay then, she must needs come.

HORTENSIO I am afraid, sir,
Do what you can, yours will not be entreated.

Enter Biondello.

Now, where's my wife? 90

BIONDELLO She says you have some goodly jest in hand[1].
She will not come. She bids you come to her.

PETRUCHIO Worse and worse! 'She will not come'! O vile,
Intolerable, not to be endured!
Sirrah Grumio, go to your mistress. 95
Say I command her come to me.

Exit [Grumio]

HORTENSIO I know her answer.

PETRUCHIO What?

HORTENSIO She will not.

PETRUCHIO The fouler[2] fortune mine, and there an end.

Enter Katherina.

BAPTISTA Now, by my holidame[3], here comes Katherina!

KATHERINA What is your will, sir, that you send for me? 100

PETRUCHIO Where is your sister, and Hortensio's wife?

KATHERINA They sit conferring[4] by the parlour fire.

PETRUCHIO Go fetch them hither. If they deny to come,
Swinge me them soundly[5] forth unto their husbands.
Away, I say, and bring them hither straight. 105

[Exit Katherina]

Baptista congratulates Petruchio and awards him a second dowry. On Katherina's return with Bianca and the Widow, Petruchio instructs her to tell the other women the duty they owe their husbands.

剧情简介：巴普提斯塔祝贺珀楚秋，又给了他一笔陪嫁。凯特芮娜领着碧昂卡和寡妇回来，珀楚秋让她给两位讲讲为人妻之道。

Themes 主题分析

Petruchio's view of marriage (in small groups)

a   While one person speaks lines 108–10, the others echo the key words. Talk together about what these words suggest about Petruchio's idea of marriage.

b   Write a paragraph, using embedded quotations, to describe what Petruchio thinks makes a good marriage. Consider the following suggestions and then add your own:

- He can trust her and she won't embarrass him.
- He can boss her about and make her a slave.
- He can feel good about himself and so can she.
- He can be cruel and heartless and she will obey him.

1   **bodes** 预示
2   **awful** 要求尊重
3   **what not** 一切
4   **fair befall thee** 好运降临到你身上
5   **as she had never been** 好像她之前从未出现过
6   **that cap** （凯特芮娜在台上总戴着那顶饱受嘲讽的帽子，穿着那件礼服 [参见第4幕第3场]）
7   **laying** 下赌注

1 She obeys (in pairs)

Just how does Katherina throw down her cap? A huge range of options is open to the actor. It is sometimes the cap from Act 4 Scene 3, and Katherina might take great care not to damage it. Others hurl it aside, their enthusiasm suggesting she will obey any order he cares to give.

- Discuss what you think is most appropriate, then script an interview that takes place later between Katherina and Bianca or the Widow. They demand to know why she behaved as she did. Compose at least three questions, along with Katherina's responses.

2 Lucentio and Bianca (in pairs)

Read lines 125–9 aloud, then swap roles and read them again. Improvise a brief discussion between Lucentio and Bianca about what each expects from their marriage.

LUCENTIO	Here is a wonder, if you talk of a wonder.	
HORTENSIO	And so it is. I wonder what it bodes[1].	
PETRUCHIO	Marry, peace it bodes, and love, and quiet life,	
	An awful[2] rule and right supremacy	
	And, to be short, what not[3] that's sweet and happy.	110
BAPTISTA	Now fair befall thee[4], good Petruchio!	
	The wager thou hast won, and I will add	
	Unto their losses twenty thousand crowns,	
	Another dowry to another daughter,	
	For she is changed, as she had never been[5].	115
PETRUCHIO	Nay, I will win my wager better yet,	
	And show more sign of her obedience –	
	Her new-built virtue and obedience.	

Enter Katherina, Bianca and Widow.

	See where she comes, and brings your froward wives	
	As prisoners to her womanly persuasion.	120
	Katherine, that cap[6] of yours becomes you not:	
	Off with that bauble – throw it underfoot!	

[She obeys.]

WIDOW	Lord, let me never have a cause to sigh	
	Till I be brought to such a silly pass!	
BIANCA	Fie, what a foolish duty call you this?	125
LUCENTIO	I would your duty were as foolish too.	
	The wisdom of your duty, fair Bianca,	
	Hath cost me a hundred crowns since supper-time.	
BIANCA	The more fool you for laying[7] on my duty.	
PETRUCHIO	Katherine, I charge thee, tell these headstrong women	130
	What duty they do owe their lords and husbands.	
WIDOW	Come, come, you're mocking. We will have no telling.	
PETRUCHIO	Come on, I say, and first begin with her.	
WIDOW	She shall not.	
PETRUCHIO	I say she shall. And first begin with her.	135

Katherina rebukes Bianca and the Widow for their aggression and for failing to recognise their husbands' superior status. She compares women to a prince's subjects, saying they should likewise serve and obey.

 剧情简介：凯特芮娜斥责碧昂卡和寡妇的霸道，没有认识到丈夫至高无上的地位。她把女人比作国君的臣民，说她们应该同样地服侍、顺从丈夫。

1 A wife's duty (in small groups)

a Katherina's final speech about a wife's duty of obedience to her husband presents a challenge to the actor, director and audience. Petruchio has already won his bet, preserved his pride and gained a second dowry, so what is the purpose of this controversial speech? How would you advise the actor cast as Katherina to speak and behave on stage?

- As insane, literally driven mad by Petruchio's tormenting, speaking in the monotone of a broken victim and obeying Petruchio's every command in a servile way? If so, the play could be seen as a commentary on domestic violence and emotional abuse – the cruel subjection of one person's will to another's.
- As humorously ironic and tactical, taking Hortensio's earlier advice to 'say as he says or we shall never go …' and showing that she will, in fact, be the one in charge? If so, the play is not about absolute obedience, but willing obedience for her own purposes.
- As expressing mutuality, a shared understanding of what love means, and revealing that she and Petruchio are playing an elaborate game? If so, this could be a play about social rebels who work together to bring each other wealth and respect.

b In your groups, choose one of the suggestions above to explore in more detail. Find evidence from the script to either agree or disagree with it. Then create a tableau to give a visual interpretation of your response to this speech.

1 unkind 不自然，不友善
2 blots 有损于
3 meads 田地
4 Confounds thy fame 毁了你的名声
5 moved 发怒；难相处
6 ill-seeming 丑；令人不快
7 thick 被污物堵塞
8 watch 不合眼，挑灯夜战
9 tribute 回报
10 honest 高尚，尊贵
11 graceless 罪恶
12 simple 愚蠢
13 conditions 品性

Language in the play
Katherina's big moment

a While one person reads Katherina's speech, others choose particular aspects to concentrate on: men, women, love, weakness, strength and rank. Throughout the speech, echo the words that reflect your chosen aspect. Don't worry if more than one of you claims the same words!

b Write a paragraph, using embedded quotations, describing the picture you get of the relationship between the sexes in this scene. You might like to print out or photocopy the speech so you can colour-code and annotate it as you formulate your thoughts and begin to write.

The Taming of the Shrew Act 5 Scene 2
悍妇降服记

KATHERINA Fie, fie, unknit that threatening unkind[1] brow,
And dart not scornful glances from those eyes
To wound thy lord, thy king, thy governor.
It blots[2] thy beauty as frosts do bite the meads[3],
Confounds thy fame[4] as whirlwinds shake fair buds,   140
And in no sense is meet or amiable.
A woman moved[5] is like a fountain troubled,
Muddy, ill-seeming[6], thick[7], bereft of beauty,
And while it is so, none so dry or thirsty
Will deign to sip, or touch one drop of it.   145
Thy husband is thy lord, thy life, thy keeper,
Thy head, thy sovereign; one that cares for thee
And for thy maintenance; commits his body
To painful labour both by sea and land,
To watch[8] the night in storms, the day in cold,   150
Whilst thou li'st warm at home, secure and safe,
And craves no other tribute[9] at thy hands
But love, fair looks and true obedience –
Too little payment for so great a debt.
Such duty as the subject owes the prince,   155
Even such a woman oweth to her husband.
And when she is froward, peevish, sullen, sour,
And not obedient to his honest[10] will,
What is she but a foul contending rebel
And graceless[11] traitor to her loving lord?   160
I am ashamed that women are so simple[12]
To offer war where they should kneel for peace,
Or seek for rule, supremacy and sway,
When they are bound to serve, love and obey.
Why are our bodies soft, and weak, and smooth,   165
Unapt to toil and trouble in the world,
But that our soft conditions[13] and our hearts
Should well agree with our external parts?

Katherina concludes her speech by stressing the physical weakness of women. She says she will place her hand beneath Petruchio's foot as a token of submission. He is delighted, and they go off to bed.

剧情简介：凯特芮娜结束演讲，强调女人天性柔弱。她说愿意把手放在丈夫的脚下以示顺从。珀楚秋很高兴，二人离席就寝。

Themes 主题分析

A husband's duty (in pairs)

Katherina's humble expression of wifely obedience may be more radical than it appears. In line 158, she talks of obedience to a husband's 'honest will' (honourable and fair wishes).

- Do you think Katherina would be obedient to someone who was not honourable or fair? Find examples elsewhere in her speech of the duties a husband owes his wife, and fill out a table with two columns headed 'Husband's duties' and 'Wife's duties'.

1 Bianca and the Widow (in pairs)

Neither Bianca nor the Widow speaks again in the play. Is this because they have already left the stage? Or are they still on stage and contributing to the scene on another way (perhaps laughing because they feel uncomfortable, or by using impatient gestures because they think what Katherina is saying is ridiculous)? Write detailed stage directions to advise the actors playing these two women of what to do as the play comes to an end here.

2 'My hand is ready' (in threes)

Does Katherina literally kneel to put her hand under Petruchio's foot at line 179? If so, how does Petruchio react? Or is Katherina speaking metaphorically and referring to the idea of giving him a helping hand over obstacles? She may simply be referring to a medieval marriage ritual, but today the gesture may seem strange.

- One of you plays Katherina and one Petruchio. The third directs the others to interpret the moment in different ways.

3 The end (in large groups)

a How do Katherina and Petruchio leave the stage? Are they heading off to consummate their marriage (圆房) or is there a more ambiguous resolution? How do those who remain respond?

b Compose final comments for all characters in the style of Hortensio and Lucentio in the last two lines of the play.

c Create a tableau for the final image the audience sees in your production of the play, just before the lights are cut.

1 unable worms 可怜虫
2 big 高傲
3 heart 勇气；脾气
4 bandy 交换；(像打网球般)打来打去
5 That ... are 把我们的缺点当优点
6 vail your stomachs 收收你们的傲气
7 no boot 没用；没好处
8 go thy ways 干得漂亮
9 old lad 老兄（对珀楚秋亲昵的称呼）
10 good hearing 听了大有益处
11 toward 顺从
12 sped 被打败；完了
13 hit the white 正中靶心（即娶了心上人碧昂卡；Bianca在意大利语里是"白"的意思）
14 being a winner 趁我还是个赢家

THE TAMING OF THE SHREW ACT 5 SCENE 2
悍妇降服记

	Come, come, you froward and unable worms¹,	
	My mind hath been as big² as one of yours,	170
	My heart³ as great, my reason haply more,	
	To bandy⁴ word for word and frown for frown.	
	But now I see our lances are but straws,	
	Our strength as weak, our weakness past compare,	
	That seeming to be most which we indeed least are⁵.	175
	Then vail your stomachs⁶, for it is no boot⁷,	
	And place your hands below your husband's foot.	
	In token of which duty, if he please,	
	My hand is ready, may it do him ease.	
PETRUCHIO	Why, there's a wench! Come on and kiss me, Kate.	180
LUCENTIO	Well, go thy ways⁸, old lad⁹, for thou shall ha't.	
VINCENTIO	'Tis a good hearing¹⁰ when children are toward¹¹.	
LUCENTIO	But a harsh hearing when women are froward.	
PETRUCHIO	Come, Kate, we'll to bed.	
	We three are married, but you two are sped¹².	185
	[*To Lucentio*] 'Twas I won the wager, though you hit the white¹³,	
	And being a winner¹⁴, God give you good night.	
	Exeunt Petruchio [and Katherina]	
HORTENSIO	Now, go thy ways; thou hast tamed a curst shrew.	
LUCENTIO	'Tis a wonder, by your leave, she will be tamed so.	
	[*Exeunt*]	

The Taming of the Shrew
悍妇降服记

Looking back at the play 本剧回顾
Activities for groups or individuals

1 Happily ever after?

a Petruchio says, 'you two are sped' to Hortensio and Lucentio at the end of the play, meaning their marriages are doomed before they start. What do you think? Will Hortensio's and Lucentio's marriages last? Will Petruchio and Katherina's?

b In groups, present wedding photographs for all the weddings that have taken place. Choose one couple and create the wedding photo as a tableau; then create a tableau for a photo taken a year after the wedding. Stay in role as the character you have chosen for these tableaux and explain to the rest of the class what will happen to this couple.

2 A sequel (续集) – the tamer tamed

In Shakespeare's own time the play provoked a theatrical 'reply'. John Fletcher, a young playwright who worked closely with Shakespeare, wrote a play called *The Woman's Prize, or The Tamer Tamed*. It was performed about seventeen years after the first performance of *The Taming of the Shrew*. In it, Katherina has died and Petruchio remarries, but this time it is his new wife, Maria, who is determined to tame him.

- Either write a synopsis (故事梗概) of this play, or write the first scene, showing how Petruchio fares in his second marriage. Describe how Maria might tame Petruchio.

3 Closing the Induction

Productions in earlier centuries often cut the first two scenes, because they thought it was strange that Sly did not reappear at the end of the play. However, the 'Sly story' is certainly highly theatrical and in modern times it has received much attention from both critics and directors.

a You are in a group about to put on the play. Half want to cut the Induction; half want to keep it. Argue together about what will be gained and what will be lost.

b Compose the 'frame' for the play by writing an epilogue, either in verse or in narrative form that explains or enacts what happens to Sly after the conclusion of the play-within-the-play.

4 What is the play about?

Consider the following descriptions of *The Taming of the Shrew*:

- A heart-warming tale of two lonely people who find a relationship that is probably deeper and more meaningful than others in the play.
- A dark comedy about female obedience, submission and domination, and male supremacy.
- A jolly farce (滑稽戏) about two people on a journey of self-discovery.
- A play that is demeaning (贬低) to women and outrageously chauvinistic (大男子主义), showing physical and mental abuse.
- A romantic comedy in which two social outcasts find a soulmate and reject the social values of their time.
- A disturbing battle of the sexes where women lose out and are continually repressed, while men resort to using bullying, torture and abuse.

In groups, choose one description, then find quotations from the play and images from magazines to create a poster to illustrate it. After you have viewed the posters made by all the other groups, script a conversation between two people who have contrasting views of the play.

The Taming of the Shrew 悍妇降服记

Perspectives and themes 视角与主题

What is the play about?

One way of answering this question is to identify the themes of the play. Themes are ideas or concepts of fundamental importance that recur throughout a text, linking together plot, characters and language. Themes echo, reinforce and comment upon each other and the whole play in interesting ways. For example, it is difficult to write about marriage in the play without referring to issues of money and social status. It is equally difficult to write about marriage without addressing the power struggles that can exist between the sexes, or the possibilities for personal transformation that can occur through love.

Themes are not individual categories but a 'tangle' of ideas and concerns that are interrelated in complex ways. In your writing, you should aim to explore the way these themes cross over and illuminate each other, rather than simply listing each one. You might also like to think about the way the themes work at different levels: the individual level (psychological or personal); the social level (linked to society and nation); and the natural level (the natural or supernatural world). For example, in *The Taming of the Shrew* you can clearly see how the theme of appearance and reality works across all three of these levels.

Power and desire in relationships

Different ideas of love are put forward in the Induction, the main plot and the sub-plot, and all three strands of *The Taming of the Shrew* explore the nature of relationships between men and women. This relates to issues of gender equality, power and desire, as well as masculinity, femininity and the battle between the sexes.

Money, marriage and social status

Padua is an acquisitive (物欲横流) society, concerned with money and possessions, ways of showing off, or gaining status over others. Women are often the pawns (棋子) in such status games. Baptista is a member of the newly prosperous merchant class, anxious to find suitably rich partners for his daughters to secure his family's social status. Petruchio announces on his arrival that he has come to 'wive it wealthily in Padua; / If wealthily, then happily in Padua' (Act 1 Scene 2, lines 72–3) – bluntly equating wealth, happiness and marriage.

The balance between order and disorder

The struggle to maintain or destroy social and natural bonds is explored at the level of the home (through family relationships) and society (through social norms and conventions). Ideas of obedience and rebellion relate to this theme, as does the idea of a 'natural' social order that places a man in authority over a woman and a father over his children.

Perspectives and themes

Education, training and personal development
From Lucentio's arrival in Padua, the 'nursery of the arts' and home of a famous university in Shakespeare's day, to Petruchio's infamous 'taming school', education and training are important themes in the play. In Shakespeare's Padua one could be educated into new knowledge, behaviour and social status. This is most obvious in Petruchio's elaborate education of Katherina, modelled on the taming of a falcon. Whether Petruchio is a benign educator and whether Katherina benefits from his lessons is worth exploring further, with reference to other themes and perspectives.

Personal transformation, disguise and assumed identity
In the play, transformation occurs through trickery (Christopher Sly), through disguise (Hortensio and Lucentio) and through 'taming'/love/education (Katherina). Such transformation is closely linked with identity – how each person sees themselves and is seen by others around them. In many cases, a character's behaviour, clothing and relationships shape their identity. Changes in these external attributes can reflect an internal transformation.

Appearance and reality
Rebellion and discord may lurk (潛藏) behind fair looks, and appearances can be deceitful. The theme occurs throughout in the many costume changes and disguises that abound in the sub-plot, as well as in Petruchio's moralising on the difference between what is seen externally and what is real in the main plot.

Game-playing
'Supposing' is imagining one thing to be another for the purpose of trickery or transformation. The play portrays and invites supposition on many levels: in the Induction, Sly is imagined to be a lord suffering from amnesia (健忘症); Petruchio's plan for taming Katherina involves treating her as a mild-mannered and caring woman. The play also has lots of game-playing, performances and wagers. Katherina learns the rules of Petruchio's game and together they win wealth and social respect through the wager.

- ◆ Working in small groups, devise a tableau that shows some of the themes of the play. Present your tableau, frozen for one minute, for other groups to guess which themes are being portrayed. Discuss why you have chosen to portray these particular themes and what links there are between them.

- ◆ What do you think *The Taming of the Shrew* is about? Imagine you are asked to explain the play to an eight-year-old child, and then afterwards to your teacher or a lecturer. Write your explanations to each of them, using these two pages and the activities throughout the book to help you.

The Taming of the Shrew
悍妇降服记

Perspectives

Another way of thinking about *The Taming of the Shrew* is to explore the possibilities for a range of interpretations that are presented throughout the play, particularly at the end. There are many perspectives on the play, some of which are outlined below:

> *One cannot help thinking a little wistfully that Petruchian discipline had something to say for itself.*
>
> Sir Arthur Quiller-Couch, 1928

> *This Shrew was being played as Sly's dream, a male supremacist's (男人至上主义者) fantasy of revenge upon women.*
>
> RSC programme note, 1978

> *By comparison with the husband who binds his erring spouse, beats her, bleeds her into a state of debility (病态的虚弱) or incarcerates (监禁) her inside the salted skin of a dead horse … Petruchio – although no Romeo – is almost a model of intelligence and humanity.*
>
> Anne Barton, 1974

> *A play that seems totally offensive to our age and society. My own feeling is that it should be put back firmly and squarely on the shelf.*
>
> Michael Billington, 1978

> *The Taming of the Shrew is not a knockabout farce of wife-battering, but the cunning adaptation of a folk-motif (民俗主题) to show the forging of a partnership between equals.*
>
> Germaine Greer, 2002

> *Kate is less powerful, less wealthy, less cheerful, less in the playwright's confidence – less everything than Petruchio. When the conflict with women is stressed but unequal, as it is here, we are surely justified in levelling the charge of sexism.*
>
> Linda Bamber, 1984

> *I think it's an irresponsible and silly thing to make that play into a feminist tract. It [is] not simply the high jinks (狂欢作乐) of an intolerably selfish man who was simply destroying a woman to satisfy his own vanity, but a sacramental (关乎圣礼) view of the nature of marriage.*
>
> Jonathan Miller, 1988

> *The Taming of the Shrew is about 'a couple hell-bent (不顾一切) on confusing and outwitting each other right up to the play's equivocal and controversial conclusion … Only the gold-digging Petruchio, a man as maddeningly strong-willed and perverse as Katherina herself, is equal to the task of bullying her to the altar'.*
>
> Shakespeare's Globe, 2012

◆ Choose two or three of these views and discuss in small groups whether you agree or disagree with them.

◆ Make notes about each view by finding examples and direct quotations to support your opinion.
Use your notes to write a response presenting your perspective on the play. Structure your response with an introduction, paragraphs giving your perspective on each view you chose (one view per paragraph) and a conclusion.

The contexts of *The Taming of the Shrew*
《悍妇降服记》的创作背景

As with all Shakespeare's plays, it is important to set *The Taming of the Shrew* in the context of its time – the world that Shakespeare knew. His imagination was influenced by many features of that world. Layers of dramatic possibilities within the script are built on other performances (such as the English mystery plays) and contemporary events or topical concerns (such as the nature of education, the public punishments for scolds and rebellious women, and domestic harmony as a reflection of social order). This layering of stories and traditions within the three main plot strands gives Shakespeare's play great depth, without limiting it to any single or specific social, religious or political meaning.

Shakespeare's focus on marriage and the relationship between a husband and wife in the main plot echoes other familiar stories and tales he would have been familiar with. In England, the shrewish wife had a colourful presence in earlier literature and dramatic traditions. This figure was present in the English mystery plays, where Noah's wife repeatedly refused to obey Noah and get into the ark, and in Chaucer's *Canterbury Tales*, in which the Wife of Bath told a humorous story about marriage, with a shrewish wife and a husband who would be master. It was also believed that Socrates had a jealous, shrewish wife by the name of Xanthippe.

The brutal, domineering (专横跋扈) husband also had a presence in folklore and in ballads. One example of such ballads is 'Here Begynneth a Merry Jest of a Shrewde and Curste Wyfe, Lapped in Morrelles Skin, for Her Good Behavyour', in which the man beats his wife and kills his horse so that he can wrap her in its salted skin until she learns obedience.

In Shakespeare's day, bad-tempered women or aggressive wives who refused to listen to their husbands were called 'shrews' or 'scolds.' Interesting depictions of shrews can be found carved into some of the seats at Holy Trinity Church, which Shakespeare attended when in Stratford-upon-Avon. A scold mocking, making faces and finally wearing a bridle is shown, as is a woman beating a man with a pan. The punishments for such unruly women included public shaming – parading them through the streets on a cart, forcing them to wear a 'scold's bridle' with a metal bit to keep the tongue in place, and repeatedly dunking (浸一下) them in the river on a special 'ducking stool'.

Shakespeare would also have been familiar with sermons and pamphlets that were based on the Bible. These encouraged men and women to live together in mutual support of one another and with respect for authority. 'The Anglican Homily on Marriage' was one such sermon ordered by the monarch to be read in churches from 1562 onwards. Sermons like this included preaching against disobedience and rebellion in the home, and reinforced the idea – as Katherina does in her last speech – that a woman's duty was to honour and obey the man, as the man's was to honour and obey the king or queen.

◆ Script an imaginary conversation between Bianca and Katherina, as they meet again for the first time a year after the play ends. They reflect on the events that are recorded in the play. What would this conversation reveal about their characters and about some aspects of their culture and context? Do they agree with the message Shakespeare seems to present about mutual respect and harmony between a husband and wife? Or does one of them seem to be more shrewish than the other?

The Taming of the Shrew
悍妇降服记

Characters 人物分析

Petruchio and Katherina

Most critics – and indeed actors and audiences – focus above all else on the relationship between Petruchio and Katherina. Is this because they dominate the action? Think back on the play and consider how often and for how long they are on stage together. Unlike many of the characters in the sub-plot involving Bianca, Petruchio and Katherina are not stock characters and we really don't know how they are going to behave. They are not stereotypes and they keep surprising us.

Social rebels

From the start of the play, Katherina's 'mad' and 'froward' behaviour marks her out as a rebellious and violent woman. She is contrasted with her sister Bianca, who behaves with mildness and gentleness for most of the play. But if Katherina makes a point of rebelling against the way her society expects her to behave, then Petruchio is equally prepared to flout (公然蔑视) social norms – for example, in his dress and behaviour at the wedding. Some critics believe it is possible to see both Petruchio and Katherina as outsiders or misfits in Paduan society. These commentators suggest that Petruchio's main role in the play is to show Katherina how to survive in a society that they both despise.

Victim and bully

It is easy to see Petruchio as a sexist bully, because he often seems to revel in presenting himself as exactly that (although one wonders how much of this is just macho [大男子气] posturing in front of other men). Shakespeare often gives Katherina very few lines, or even keeps her totally silent when we would expect her to respond to events taking place around her. Many actors find this difficult and are relieved when Katherina does finally speak at length – as for example in Act 4 Scene 3, lines 73–80.

Petruchio often provides a direct comment on the gender politics of Shakespeare's day. To what extent can his attitudes and behaviour still be observed in the relationships between men and women today?

Worthy opponents

It is also possible to see Petruchio and Katherina as worthy opponents who have met their match in each other. Most modern productions find a way to suggest that they are in love – either by highlighting the chemistry between them when they meet or by making it clear at the end of the play. Nonetheless, this does seem to be an odd relationship. Lovers in other Shakespearean comedies have many obstacles to overcome, but with Petruchio and Katherina there is uncertainty right to the end – and it seems that the battle of wits will continue.

Understanding Katherina and Petruchio

Katherina has no mother, she is alienated from her father, who makes a laughing-stock of her; she also has a turbulent relationship with her sister Bianca. She has no close female friend to confide in. Katherina can be seen in several different ways, as:

- a troubled and unhappy woman at the beginning of the play, who changes into somebody who is able to find and give love in the end
- a rebel – wild, ungovernable and 'stark mad' – who is forced to become a compliant wife
- a broken and damaged woman who is bullied into submission by the end of the play
- a woman desperately in love with Petruchio, who wants to make her husband feel good.

Petruchio is also alienated from the rest of the male characters and is an outsider in Padua. He has been seen as:

- a selfish, mercenary (唯利是图) man who is a fortune-hunter at heart and a gold-digger by nature
- a match for Katherina – someone as strong-willed and obstinate (执拗) as she is, who will take no nonsense
- a sensitive and intelligent man with charisma and charm beneath a rough exterior
- a cruel and loud-mouthed bully who only cares about himself and the power he can exert over others

CHARACTERS

- a man grieving for his dead father, taking his anger out on others, but who is interested by Katherina and her ability to outwit him.

◆ Choose one or two of the views above, and in pairs prepare a short speech to either agree or disagree with them. Remember to refer to the play in detail as you put forward your reasons for agreeing or disagreeing. Take turns to read out your speeches to the rest of the class.

According to Lisa Dillon, who played Katherina at the Royal Shakespeare Company (RSC) in 2012, Katherina is labelled as a shrew and this becomes a self-fulfilling prophecy, similar to a cycle of addiction:

You've got to remove something and almost go into detox (戒瘾) in order to be a better human being. And that's what Petruchio does: he gives her the detox of her life.

David Caves, who played Petruchio, described him as a man who is put out by a woman who outwits him:

If he dishes something out to her, she dishes it back to him twice as bad. He's constantly having to improvise.

According to Nichola McAuliffe, who has played Katherina twice, Petruchio is often misunderstood because of his references to falconry. However:

If you know anything about falconry, you would know that you have to go through this with the bird: if it's cruel, it's cruel to yourself, too.

◆ Try to find comments from other actors who have performed in *The Taming of the Shrew*. Choose one comment that relates to Katherina and one that relates to Petruchio, then gather evidence to display in a mind map or in notes in your book as you decide if you agree or disagree with the comments.

◆ Compose an imaginary conversation with the actor from your chosen quotation, in which you discuss his or her interpretation of the characters.

The Taming of the Shrew
悍妇降服记

Bianca and Lucentio

It is interesting to trace the development of the romance between Bianca and Lucentio because, although it has many elements of romantic love, it also reveals more about their characters. They are outwardly respectable young people who end up flouting the rules. It seems that the 'well-behaved' Lucentio and Bianca do not mind subverting (颠覆) accepted standards of behaviour to obtain what they want.

Bianca and Katherina move in opposite directions throughout the play. Katherina starts off as rebellious and shrewish, but it is Bianca who is more likely to wear these labels at the end. The demure younger sister is not so sweet, and her modest obedience to her father does not translate into support of her husband.

Similarly, Lucentio's romantic love and courtly ideals – characterised by poetic idealisation of Bianca and culminating in an elopement (私奔) – are contrasted unfavourably with Petruchio. Petruchio is forthright, brash and pragmatic; he willingly marries Katherina knowing all her faults. Lucentio falls head over heels (完全) in love with Bianca and plays romantic games, yet he fails to fully understand the woman he is going to marry.

◆ Choose a character from the play and think of an actor (real or imagined) who you would like to play them. Draft a letter asking this person to take on the role in your next production. Write in role as the director, and explain why you think they would be good for this part. Give the actor a clear impression of how you see the character and how you want them to be played.

Characters

Tranio, Biondello and Grumio

These servants play significant roles, and each one contributes to the plot development as well as providing comic episodes and witty observations from the sidelines. Grumio's witticisms and his role as a sidekick (左膀右臂) to Petruchio mark him out as similar to the stock clown character from the Italian *commedia dell'arte*. Like the comic *zanni*, the canny (精明) trickster and witty servant Grumio is an astute (机敏) observer of what happens around him. He is also involved in many of the slapstick routines and verbal misunderstandings.

Biondello is involved in much of the comic confusion, and he comments on the action of the other characters. It is Biondello's willingness to be part of the deceptions of the sub-plot that cause them to succeed, but he is not trusted by his master to the same extent as Tranio is, nor is he as close to his master as Grumio is to his.

Tranio, Lucentio's servant, is elevated to the status of his social superiors when he takes on his master's identity. The situation that provided the Lord and his Servingmen with such amusement in the Induction actually happens in the sub-plot. Furthermore, Tranio seems to have more sense and cunning than the love-sick Lucentio – and this could be some sort of joke directed back at the Lord who plays tricks on the hopelessly drunk Sly in the Induction. Lucentio is portrayed as an inexperienced youth who is led astray by romantic notions and Tranio's ultimately impractical deceptions.

- Improvise a scene in which each of you, in role, tells the story of the play from the point of view of one of these servants or the stereotypical lovers. Be clear about what your chosen character knows and doesn't know.

Hortensio and Gremio

Hortensio and Gremio are stereotypical suitors who rehearse well-known jokes about the battle between the sexes. Gremio shares many characteristics of the old, rich 'pantaloon' from the Italian *commedia dell'arte*. This stock figure was an old man who pursues young women and is the subject of many jokes that refer to his age and his wealth. When he realises he has been out-manoeuvred by 'Lucentio' (Tranio in disguise as his master) and his wealth and dowry are surpassed, he decides to hang around and enjoy his 'share of the feast'!

Hortensio is a lover who, like Lucentio, adopts a disguise in order to win Bianca's affections. He is mistreated both by Katherina, who breaks a lute over his head, and Bianca, who spurns (冷落) him for Lucentio. He then decides to take lessons in love from Petruchio, picking up the same terminology from falconry, and wanting to learn how to tame his wife-to-be. By the end of the play it is not clear what lessons he has learned, but it is obvious that the rich widow he has married is in charge!

- Draw a prop that you feel would give the audience important information about one of the characters in the play, and which would also help the actor to step into role. It must be something that the character will use in at least one scene. Pass your drawing around the class so that others can guess which character the prop is for.

The Taming of the Shrew
悍妇降服记

The language of *The Taming of the Shrew*
《悍妇降服记》的语言

Creative language

Shakespeare's creativity with language was extraordinary. He used English slang, mock Latinisms and newly invented compound words. He also freely transformed nouns into verbs, relied on **puns** and in general enjoyed the verbal and visual games he could play with language on the stage.

The Taming of the Shrew is a game of language – it revolves around the use and abuse of language, witty banter based on puns, the language of power, and the ability of language to confuse and disorientate. The play is full of action, deception, confusion and confrontation (both physical and psychological), and the language Shakespeare uses here is equally vigorous – and sometimes aggressive – in its witty verbal deceptions and game-playing.

Recurring imagery (意象)

Imagery is the use of words and phrases that conjure up vivid mental pictures. It is a kind of verbal painting that stirs the imagination, deepens dramatic impact and gives insight into character. *The Taming of the Shrew* is rich in imagery, and certain images recur throughout the play, helping to create its distinctive atmosphere.

Clothing

Shakespeare's stage had minimal scenic and mechanical aids, but it did make use of lavish costumes – hence his interest in clothing as both a metaphor and a dramatic device. In earlier medieval drama (dominated by morality plays – allegories of virtue triumphing over sin – and mystery plays, which dramatised the stories of the Bible) clothing had a specific meaning. Shakespeare references this in the play: the difference between outward appearances and inner realities. The idea of clothes as concealing (or revealing) the real person beneath is another preoccupation of the play, shown in Petruchio's response to criticism of his appearance at his wedding: 'To me she's married, not unto my clothes' (Act 3 Scene 2, line 107).

Theatre

Shakespeare's fascination with his own profession provided him with another recurring theme: the world as a stage. On this stage, humans make brief appearances to play their parts and take on different roles in different contexts. This is reflected in the many audiences that are formed on stage during *The Taming of the Shrew*, as well as in the asides from characters like Grumio, who comment on the action and do not let the audience forget that they are watching a play.

Sports and games

There are many references to sports and games, ranging from playing cards to archery and hunting with greyhounds and falcons. There are also many references to games of 'supposing' and 'imagining', and these ideas play on the theatricality of the various plots and the themes that emerge. The Lord makes a game of supposing that Sly is also a lord – one who has lost his mind. Petruchio plays a similar game in supposing Katherina is not bad-tempered or shrewish, but fair and gentle.

Falconry

Falconry is a key image used by Shakespeare, and the taming of a wild hawk is not only a major theme reflected in the main plot, but is also part of the recurring imagery.

A wild falcon or hawk is put through a severe training regime in order to make it an obedient bird in the field. One aspect of this training is to carefully monitor its food so that its appetite is regulated. Another aspect involves 'waking' – keeping the hawk awake until it is exhausted. Still another is to use a hood (or, at the time, to sew up the hawk's eyelids) so that it is blind for a time and totally dependent on the falconer. All these steps force the hawk to attend to the falconer and be readily obedient when out hunting.

The language of The Taming of the Shrew

A contemporary account of the training of falcons is given in George Tuberville's *Booke of Falconrie* (1575). In this, he makes it clear that the purpose of training a falcon is not to break the bird's spirit, but to harness its wildness for successful hunting in the field. To tame the bird for future use, a trusting relationship has to be created between master and hawk. Once tamed, however, the hawk needs to be released to have its obedience tested.

Cattle and markets

There are references to cattle-market negotiations when Baptista talks about his daughters' marriages. There are also references to the many types of diseases horses could catch. Petruchio treats Katherina like a horse in Act 2 Scene 1 (lines 242–6):

> Why does the world report that Kate doth limp?
> O sland'rous world! Kate like the hazel twig
> Is straight and slender, and as brown in hue
> As hazel-nuts and sweeter than the kernels.

His reference to her gait and her colouring is couched in terms that would be used to describe a horse and this, of course, was intended to infuriate (激怒) her.

The humours

In Shakespeare's day, it was thought that the human body had natural fluids that were linked to the four elements of the natural world: fire, water, air and earth. These fluids were responsible for a person's emotional and physical health. If they were in balance a person was completely healthy, but if they were out of balance a person could suffer from emotional disorder, mental instability or physical diseases. The four humours were:

Choleric (胆汁质): having hot and dry qualities and linked to fire. People who were choleric were short-tempered, fiery and argumentative.

Phlegmatic (黏液质): having cold and moist qualities and linked to water. People who were phlegmatic were sluggish, lazy and apathetic (冷漠).

Sanguine (多血质): having hot and moist qualities and linked to air. People who were sanguine were optimistic, cheerful and carefree, though often irresponsible.

Melancholic (抑郁质): having cold, dry qualities and linked to the earth. People who were melancholy were preoccupied with themselves and often incapable of decisive action.

Love and romance

The Bianca–Lucentio and Katherina–Petruchio plots are both, of course, about love and marriage, although surprisingly this play has comparatively few scenes in which the language of love is straightforwardly presented. Lucentio confesses his love of Bianca in traditionally exaggerated language: 'Tranio, I burn! I pine, I perish, Tranio, / If I achieve not this young modest girl' (Act 1 Scene 1, lines 146–7). Do we ever hear Bianca and Lucentio speaking 'the language of love' together?

The Taming of the Shrew
悍妇降服记

No one is allowed to stay entranced by love for long in this play. Tranio tries to bring Lucentio down to earth, urging: 'I pray, awake, sir … / Bend thoughts and wits to achieve her' (lines 169–70). In other words, the world of disguise is just about to kick in.

Yet, there is some of the traditional language of love in the Katherina–Petruchio plot. At the end of Act 5 Scene 1, Katherina and Petruchio kiss and he then makes a comment that is often heavily stressed in productions: 'Is not this well?' (line 124).

- Choose one example of recurring imagery in the play and collect as many pictures from magazines or the Internet as you can that represent this. Find quotations from the play that link to the images you have chosen and think of an appropriate way to display them, such as in a collage.

- In role as a movie director, write out your ideas for how the imagery in certain passages might be visualised in a film production. Prepare a screenplay or script for one or two of these passages to illustrate your ideas.

Metaphor, simile and personification

Shakespeare's imagery uses metaphor, simile and personification. All are comparisons.

A **simile** compares one thing to another using 'like' or 'as'. Petruchio facetiously uses a simile when he says 'Kate like the hazel twig / Is straight and slender', and the Lord's Servingmen describe the grief of Sly's 'wife' with a simile: 'And till the tears that she hath shed for thee / Like envious floods o'er-run her lovely face'.

A **metaphor** is also a comparison, suggesting that two dissimilar things are actually the same. Katherina says about her sister: 'She is your treasure.'

Personification is a special kind of imagery that turns all kinds of things into persons, giving them human feelings or attributes. It is used when Petruchio describes how he expects to get on with Katherina in Act 2 Scene 1, lines 128–31:

And where two raging fires meet together
They do consume the thing that feeds their fury.
Though little fire grows great with little wind,
Yet extreme gusts will blow out fire and all.

- Compile lists of metaphors, similes and examples of personification from the play. Use these lists to create a visual representation of the characters and situations they refer to. You might like to use images from magazines, newspapers or the Internet. Or, if you prefer, you could describe the effect in writing and sketch the visual images that are prompted by the language.

- How does this kind of imagery add to your understanding of the play and its characters?

Verse and prose

Shakespeare almost always mixes poetry and verse in his plays. Some characters, such as Katherina, Petruchio, Baptista and Bianca, speak mostly in verse, while some, such as Curtis, speak only in prose. A few characters, including Sly, Grumio and Biondello, speak in verse and prose at different times.

Blank verse

The characters who speak in verse use **blank verse**, which consists of unrhymed lines that have carefully placed stressed and unstressed syllables. Each line has five feet (groups of syllables) called iambs, which are an unstressed (×) and stressed (/) syllable that sounds like a heartbeat (da DUM, da DUM, da DUM, da DUM, da DUM):

× / × / × / × / × /
I see a woman may be made a fool.

Shakespeare uses a varied rhythmic pattern throughout the play. He sometimes wrote lines of more or fewer than ten syllables, sometimes changed the pattern of stresses in a line, and sometimes used rhyming couplets for effect. He ensured that the rhythm of the verse was appropriate to the meaning and mood of the speech: reflective, fearful, apprehensive, anguished or confused. This rhythmic pattern is what distinguishes verse from prose, not whether or not it rhymes.

The language of The Taming of the Shrew

Caesura ([诗行中的]切分处；停顿处) and enjambement*

Shakespeare also used the **caesura** and **enjambement** to add to the rhythm of his blank verse. A caesura is where the phrasing of the line is broken to create a pause or a break in the dialogue or action. With enjambement, the end of one sentence carries over into the next line of poetry, giving the impression that the phrases are spilling over and building up from one line to the next.

- The human heartbeat has an iambic rhythm. Put your hand on your heart to hear the basic rhythm of weak and strong stresses. Then choose a verse speech and explore ways of speaking it to emphasise the metre. For example, you could clap hands, tap the desk or walk five paces to accompany each line.

- Compose eight or more lines of your own in the same style.

Prose

Prose is different from blank verse: it is everyday language with no specific rhythm, metric scheme or rhyme. Shakespeare uses prose to break up the verse in his plays, to signify characters' madness or low status, or to draw attention to changes in plot or character.

It is easy to tell the difference between verse and prose: verse passages begin with a capital letter and the lines do not reach the other side of the page, whereas prose passages have lines that reach both sides of the pages and only use capital letters at the beginning of sentences.

Other language devices

Puns

A **pun** is a play on words where a word has more than one meaning. *The Taming of the Shrew* is full of such wordplay. In the outrageous wooing scene between Petruchio and Katherina, puns are the main weapon of choice in their battle of wits. The servants Tranio, Biondello and Grumio revel in puns, and in the final scene characters hurl their words back and forth across the banquet table, the men at one point taking wagers on who will win the battle of wits.

- Look back through the play and find examples of puns. How do they add to the humour of the play?

- What do they reveal to an audience about the wit and intelligence of the characters who use them? Is there a difference in the type of puns used by high-status characters and those of lower status in the play?

Repetition of words

Sometimes the same word is repeated in a short space of time in order to increase pace and tension. Petruchio uses repetition as he attempts to tame Katherina:

> *For I am he am born to tame you, Kate,*
> *And bring you from a wild Kate to a Kate*
> *Conformable as other household Kates.*

At other times a word is repeated throughout a passage so that the idea can be developed or extended for comic or dramatic effect:

> GREMIO *Why, he's a devil, a devil, a very fiend!*
> TRANIO *Why, she's a devil, a devil, the devil's dam!*

Repetition of sounds

Sometimes sounds are repeated. When they are placed at the end of a line, they form **rhyming couplets** or a rhyming scheme that commonly has an ABAB pattern. Rhyming couplets are often used by Shakespeare at the conclusion of an act or scene.

> PETRUCHIO *Why, there's a wench! Come on and kiss me, Kate.*
> LUCENTIO *Well, go thy ways, old lad, for thou shalt ha't.*
> VINCENTIO *'Tis a good hearing, when children are toward.*
> LUCENTIO *But a harsh hearing when women are froward.*
> PETRUCHIO *Come, Kate, we'll to bed.*
> *We three are married, but you two are sped.*

---

* enjambement　跨行，指一行诗在印刷排版中因过长而无法排成一整行而不得不将长出来的部分排到下一行的情况。

The Taming of the Shrew
悍妇降服记

Other repetitions of sound can be provided by **alliteration**, which is the repetition of consonants (at the beginning of words): 'But will you woo this wildcat?' and by **assonance**, which is the repetition of vowel sounds (in the middle of words): 'And will you, nill you, I will marry you.' These repetitions are opportunities for actors to intensify the emotional impact of what they are saying and to create echoes of sound and meaning throughout the play.

Repetition of patterns

Anaphora is the repetition of the same word at the beginning of successive sentences:

> KATHERINA   What, in the midst of the street?
> PETRUCHIO   What, art thou ashamed of me?

Epistrophe is the repetition of a word or phrase at the end of a series of sentences or clauses:

> PETRUCHIO   I say it is the moon that shines so bright
> KATHERINA   I know it is the sun that shines so bright.

Polyptoton (一词多形法) is repetition of words derived from the same root word, but with different endings or forms:

> But now I see our lances are but straws,
> Our strength as weak, our weakness past compare…

◆ Turn randomly to any two or three pages of *The Taming of the Shrew* and identify all the ways in which Shakespeare uses repetition on those pages. Try out different ways of speaking the lines to discover how emphasising or playing down the repetition can contribute to dramatic effect.

Soliloquies and asides

A **soliloquy** is a monologue, a kind of internal debate spoken by a character who is alone (or assumes he or she is alone) on stage. It gives the audience direct access to the character's mind, revealing their inner thoughts and motives. You will have noticed that Petruchio is given opportunities to share his thoughts with the audience, while Katherina is often silent.

An **aside** is a brief comment or address to the audience that shows the character's unspoken thought, unheard by other characters on stage. The audience is taken into this character's confidence or can see deeper into their motivations and experiences. Asides can also be used for characters to comment on the action as it unfolds.

◆ Identify some of the play's soliloquies and asides. Choose one and write notes on how you would speak it on stage to maximise its dramatic effect.

The Taming of the Shrew in performance
《悍妇降服记》的演出

Performance on Shakespeare's stage

The first record of a production of *The Taming of the Shrew* was written by Simon Forman, who described a performance he saw at the Globe Theatre on Bankside in 1611. Many of Shakespeare's plays were performed at the Globe – one of the many specially designed outdoor playhouses built at the end of the sixteenth century. They were modelled on the public amphitheatres*, like the bear-baiting (斗熊) rings that existed in the seedier (肮脏) location outside the city walls (and the city's jurisdiction [管辖范围]).

During Shakespeare's lifetime, plays in outdoor amphitheatres like the Globe were performed in broad daylight during the summer months. So, at 2:00 p.m. people would assemble with food and drink to watch a play – with no lighting and no rule of silence for the audience. There were high levels of background noise and interaction during performances and audience members were free to walk in and out of the theatre.

In the Globe, the audience was positioned on three sides of the stage: the 'groundlings' (站票观众) stood in the pit (无座观众池) around the stage while those who paid more were seated in three levels around the pit. Actors would see around three thousand faces staring up or down at them.

The positioning of the audience made it difficult for everyone to hear all that was going on. Inevitably, the actors would have their backs to sections of the audience at times. The best place for an actor to stand, especially for a soliloquy or an aside, was at the front of the stage so that he or she could directly address almost all of the audience. However, it would be tedious if all the action occurred here!

Shakespeare's use of repetition helped to overcome this problem. There are times when the same idea is stated or developed in three ways in order to allow an actor to address each section of the audience. These repetitions were never simply word-for-word repeats but were used to create rhythm, accumulate details and build on an idea through different metaphors and imagery. If you spot significant repetition, it may be a clue that Shakespeare intended the character to move around the stage and engage different parts of the audience.

* **amphitheatre** 竞技场（剧场通常是半圆形的，两个剧场并在一起，就成为一个圆形剧场，即用来举行角斗或斗兽的剧场）

▼ This illustration from 1647 shows the Globe Theatre (the circular building, centre left), built for the second time in 1614 after the first one burnt down. It was mistaken by the artist Wenceslaus Hollar for a bear-baiting pit that was nearby.

The Taming of the Shrew
悍妇降服记

Blocking* is a term used to describe actors' positions on the stage. On Shakespeare's stage, where a character was placed gave the audience clues about their role or authority in the play. Upstage (戏台上部) is furthest away from the audience and downstage (戏台下部) is closer to the audience. Characters absorbed in their own lives, or characters who played out literary or conventional stereotypes, were often placed centre-stage or upstage. Characters who had a comic role, who performed many roles or commented on the action on stage, were often played closer to the audience or at the edge of the stage. In this way they existed on the intersection between stage and audience.

- Choose key points in the play and consider where on the stage you would place Petruchio and Kate. Who would have more movement around the stage? Who would be more likely to talk to the audience with an aside or gestures? Draw a diagram of the stage and plot the movement or position of the characters at different points in the play.

- Choose three different scenes in the play and depict each of these in different diagrams. Remember to use arrows and annotations to show how and when characters move on the stage throughout the scene.

- Discuss with a partner your reasons for where you have placed the characters, how they use the stage space, and why you think this reflects their character and behaviour in this part of the play.

Performance after Shakespeare

Since Shakespeare's day, performances of *The Taming of the Shrew* have inevitably provoked strong reactions and yet have always been popular. The play is often very funny and certainly stimulates discussion concerning marriage and the position of women.

Battle of the sexes

Sometimes, however, the play has been regarded as offensive because it sets men and women in violent opposition. To some extent, the story of the play reflects the confrontation of two mighty opposites: Katherina and Petruchio engaged in a kind of human bullfight. As a consequence, another approach to this play that proved popular in the twentieth century was to cast husband and wife 'teams' such as the 1967 Richard Burton and Elizabeth Taylor movie, directed by Franco Zeffirelli. This vibrant, larger-than-life style of production contained much knockabout physical comedy, apparently reflecting something of the tempestuous real-life relationship of the two film-star leads.

▼ A poster for the 1967 film starring husband and wife Richard Burton and Elizabeth Taylor.

* **blocking**　戏台调度，指导演对演员在戏台上的动作进行的设计和安排，包括演员与演员、演员与戏台景物之间的相对位置及其变化。

The Taming of the Shrew in performance

All-male (below) and all-female (right) productions somehow manage to throw the war between the sexes into even sharper relief and make the conflict seem all the more contentious (引发争议) and challenging. The 1985 all-female version at London's Stratford East, for example, highlighted a vicious brutality in the treatment of Katherina, as did the 2007 all-male production by Propeller, where the two male actors playing Kate and Petruchio engaged in a violently physical kind of conflict which could hardly have been allowed between two members of different sexes. But not all same-sex productions have been like this. An earlier all-female cast presented the violence in an exaggerated style reminiscent of pantomime (哑剧), which encouraged the audience to view the scene critically and ironically.

Class and social status

Michael Bogdanov's 1978 production for the RSC at Stratford-upon-Avon used a combination of male and female actors, yet emphasised the potential violence and cruelty of the play in performance. In addition to its exposure of sexual politics, this production was also strongly political in its focus on the exploitation of the underclass. Financial muscle and social status (class) ruled. This production began with a quarrel in the audience. A drunk argued with an usherette (女引座员), shouting: 'No bloody woman is going to tell me what to do!' The man leapt on to the stage, ripped down the scenery and then collapsed. The lights dimmed and, to the accompaniment of hunting horns, brightened to reveal the Lord and his Huntsmen in hunting pinks. The drunk was Christopher Sly who, as the play proceeded, became Petruchio.

193

The Taming of the Shrew
悍妇降服记

One critic commented that the 1992 RSC production 'nearly convinced me that the play is … about class and that male subjugation (压制) of women is only an example of masters' oppression of servants'. Several productions since have explored the play's concern with class hostility as much as the battle between the sexes.

Productions that focus on class inequalities and violence often use the Induction as a kind of introductory framing device. This encourages the audience to join with Sly in watching a play about the taming of a shrew called Katherina. Shakespeare took his inspiration from popular stories of the beggar who wakes up to find himself a king, which were the subject of many ballads and jigs. He also took inspiration from the folktales and atmosphere of rural Warwickshire where he grew up, where lords hunted, tinkers got drunk and alewives ran the local pubs. Many directors choose to emphasise the fact that we do not experience the story of the 'taming of the shrew' directly, but that we do so indirectly (indeed, ironically) and through the lens of the Induction. The Induction foretells, echoes and offers comments on much that follows in the play itself.

◆ Take each element below and identify examples of it in both the Induction and the main play. How would you want to use the Induction and what elements would you foreground if you were directing a new stage production of the play?

- disguise • hunting • money
- masters and servants • cruelty
- relationship between men and women
- love • dreams and reality • taming
- clothes and costumes • humour
- food and feasts • watching
- classical references

Farce and fun
'Playing for laughs is the key to success', proclaimed the *Lincolnshire Daily Echo* in 1996, advice that has become almost a directorial commonplace. *The Taming of the Shrew* is boldly theatrical and adapts well to colourful settings – especially, it seems, the open air.

Naturally the liberation of women from traditional roles in marriage and society during the twentieth century imposed new pressures on how the more controversial elements in the play should be presented. Since the play is frequently classed as a comedy, a less contentious answer was to concentrate on the play's potential for broad farce. In the first film version of the play, Mary Pickford, playing Katherina, gave an expressive wink at the conclusion of her final speech. What would be the effect of this?

▼ Douglas Fairbanks and Mary Pickford as Petruchio and Katherina in the first movie version of the play, released in 1929.

The Taming of the Shrew in performance

True love

For other directors the play has been seen as neither a misogynistic (歧视女性的) fantasy nor a light-hearted romp (笑剧), but rather a profound love story in which two misfits find true contentment with each other. The 2003 RSC production, directed by Greg Doran, portrayed Katherina as a woman attracted to Petruchio because he listened to her, made her laugh and wanted to get to know her, unlike all the other people in her life. The mutual fascination of two damaged people who desperately needed each other was clear for all to see. This highly praised production was psychologically astute but there was plenty of comedy too, especially in the 'wooing scene', which almost came to a halt when Petruchio discovered Katherina was ticklish (棘手). Their delight was evident – even as they engaged in physical conflict. This Katherina's final speech was warm and sincere, and she and Petruchio celebrated their new-won gold in a shower of coins. However, as they left the stage, it was clear that to him she was more important than all the gold he had just won.

Such a reading ends by celebrating the emotional truth of a woman's heartfelt pledge to maintain something of great constancy – the marriage of true minds. Some actresses interpret Kate's 'surrender' as a gesture of strength. Meryl Streep – Katherina in the 1978 production in New York's Central Park – argued:

> *What I'm saying is, I'll do anything for this man … Why is selflessness wrong here? Service is the only thing that's important about love.*

At Shakespeare's Globe in 2012, Samantha Spiro, who played Katherina, said:

> *I really, really strongly think she does love him and when you are desperately in love with somebody, you'd do anything for them, really. But I also do think there's a slight wink to the audience, in terms of, if we're clever, this is the game that we can play and keep this society happy. But I think what Petruchio and Kate have found is a real equality.*

The Taming of the Shrew
悍妇降服记

Productions that focus on the depth of love between Petruchio and Katherina focus on contemporary ideas of romantic love. Shakespeare himself used many of the conventions of romantic love that were popular in the poetry and ballads of his time and creates a general atmosphere of romance in the sub-plot, by referring to famous lovers from classical literature. However, there is also a sense of parody in the romantic posturing of Lucentio and the presentation of Bianca as the beautiful, demure maid recognisable as a stage stereotype by Shakespeare's audiences. The young lovers who change identities, the servants who are mistaken for their masters, the rich old lover, the stranger who turns out to be the father, and the secret courtship of a young man and woman are all found in popular Italian comedies in Shakespeare's day.

The play invites a satirical perspective on the sub-plot when the audience reconsiders these characters at the end of the play, especially when these characters are compared with the characters in the main plot. The combination of romantic love, comic misunderstanding and disguise in the sub-plot with the down-to-earth and at times violent main plot invites comparison between events and characters. Although the Petruchio–Katherina scenes are often violent, angry and chaotic, in contrast to the wooing of the sweetly demure Bianca, Lucentio and Bianca can be seen to be just as devious, deceitful and manipulative as Petruchio. This prompts a critical or ironic attitude to the sub-plot. By the end of the play Petruchio and Katherina are seen as a straightforward and solid partnership that gains respect and double blessing from her father, whereas Lucentio and Bianca are seen as spoilt, calculating and somewhat shallow.

- ◆ Which of these different interpretations do you think best suits the play and most fits with your understanding of Katherina and Petruchio?
- ◆ Look at the images from recent productions in these pages and discuss with a partner which interpretation of the play you would most like to see at your local theatre if you had a choice.
- ◆ Write a description of what you would expect from a performance if you went to the theatre while you were studying this play. Would you want to see a performance based on one of the interpretations above. Or would you want to see a new production address a combination of them?

International audiences

Most recently, a production of *The Taming of the Shrew* in Pakistan, rewritten in Urdu by three women, added local flavour and concerns to the play. Some of the play's misogynistic elements were airbrushed by portraying both Petruchio and Katherina as strong characters who would never give in to each other. However, despite the irony and humour with which the battle between Petruchio and Katherina was portrayed, there were more sombre undertones. The elements of taming and control in the play were a reminder of the specific religious, moral and social pressures that women in patriarchal (男性主宰的) societies face.

The Taming of the Shrew in performance

Adaptations

Given the level of controversy shown in this brief description of past productions, it is perhaps unsurprising that *The Taming of the Shrew* has long been – and continues to be – one of Shakespeare's most frequently performed plays. It has also inspired many adaptations. In the eighteenth century, David Garrick rewrote the final lines of the play so that Petruchio promised to calm down and looked forward to 'one gentle stream / Of mutual love'. Garrick's version – *Catherine and Petruchio* – was so popular that it held the stage for more than a hundred years. In the second half of the twentieth century, several film adaptations – ranging from the Broadway musical version *Kiss Me Kate* (1953) to the movie *10 Things I Hate About You* (1999), which reworked the play as a high-school comedy romance – further confirmed its enduring popularity.

Any script by Shakespeare should be read as a blueprint (plan) for a live performance, so it is essential that you think about how it can or should be staged. In groups, work together to plan your own production of the play.

- Consider where and when you would set it, and decide whether you would make any changes or cuts to the script. Would you include the Induction? Would you include any additional scenes?

- Design the set – how can it be used for particular scenes? Will it change much through the play? How will the set reflect your chosen setting? Will you attempt to reflect a period or physical place, or will your design be more abstract or unusual?

- Design the costumes (a significant element in this play) – look at past examples, but also invent your own. In particular, consider the importance of hats and uniforms in most productions.

- Create a publicity poster. What elements of your production will you emphasise to persuade people to see your play? Will you include a quotation as a 'slogan'? Whose image or images will you give most prominence to?

- Write the director's notes for the programme. Aim for around 500–1,000 words, justifying your vision of the production to an audience about to watch your masterpiece!

The Taming of the Shrew
悍妇降服记

Writing about Shakespeare 笔论莎士比亚

The play as text

Shakespeare's plays have always been studied as literary works – as words on a page that need clarification, appreciation and discussion. When you write about the plays, you will be asked to compose short pieces and also longer, more reflective pieces like controlled assessments, examination scripts and coursework – often in the form of essays on themes and/or imagery, character studies, analyses of the structure of the play and on stagecraft. Imagery, stagecraft and character are dealt with elsewhere in this edition. Here, we concentrate on themes and structure. You might find it helpful to look at the 'Write about it' boxes on the left-hand pages throughout the play.

Themes

It is often tempting to say that the theme of a play is a single idea, like 'death' in *Hamlet*, or 'the supernatural' in *Macbeth*, or 'love' in *Romeo and Juliet*. The problem with such a simple approach is that you will miss the complexity of the plays. In *Romeo and Juliet*, for example, the play is about the relationship between love, family loyalty and constraint; it is also about the relationship of youth to age and experience; and the relationship between Romeo and Juliet is also played out against a background of enmity between two families. Between each of these ideas or concepts there are tensions. The tensions are the main focus of attention for Shakespeare and the audience; this is also how the best drama operates – by the presentation of and resolution of tension.

Look back at the 'Themes' boxes throughout the play to see if any of the activities there have given rise to information that you could use as a starting point for further writing about the themes of the specific play you are studying.

Structure

Most Shakespeare plays are in five acts, divided into scenes. These acts were not in the original scripts, but have been included in later editions to make the action more manageable, clearer and more like 'classical' structures. One way to get a sense of the structure of the whole play is to take a printed version (not this one!) and cut it up into scenes and acts, then display each scene and act, in sequence, on a wall, like this:

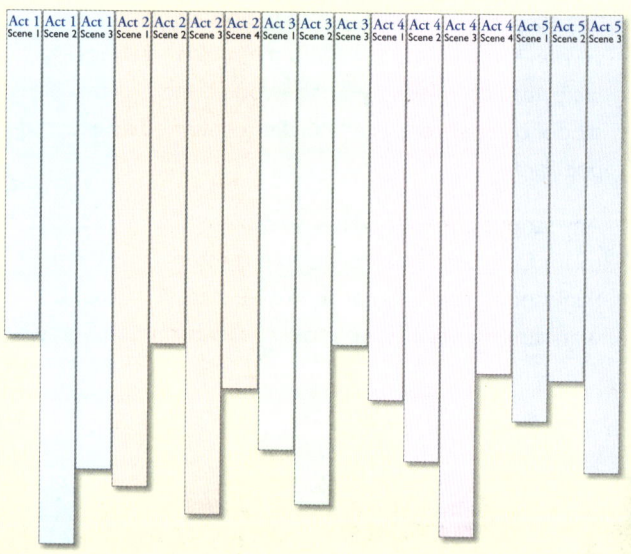

As you set out the whole play, you will be able to see the 'shape' of each act, the relative length of the scenes, and how the acts relate to each other (such as whether one act is shorter, and why that might be). You can annotate the text with comments, observations and questions. You can use a highlighter pen to mark the recurrence of certain words, images or metaphors to see at a glance where and how frequently they appear. You can also follow a particular character's progress through the play.

Writing about Shakespeare

Such an overview of the play gives you critical perspective: you will be able to see how the parts fit together, to stand back from the play and assess its shape, and to focus on particular parts within the context of the whole. Your writing will reflect a greater awareness of the overall context as a result.

The play as script

There are different, but related, categories when we think of the play as a script for performance. These include *stagecraft* (discussed elsewhere in this edition and throughout the left-hand pages), *lighting*, *focus* (who are we looking at? Where is the attention of the audience?), *music and sound*, *props and costumes*, *casting*, *make-up*, *pace and rhythm*, and other *spatial relationships* (e.g. how actors move around the stage in relation to each other). If you are writing about stagecraft or performance, use the notes you have made as a result of the Stagecraft activities throughout this edition of the play, as well as any information you can find about the plays in performance.

What are the key points of dispute?

Shakespeare is brilliant at capturing a number of key points of dispute in each of his plays. These are the dramatic moments where he concentrates the focus of the audience on difficult (sometimes universal) problems that the characters are facing or embodying.

First, identify these key points in the play you are studying. You can do this as a class by discussing what you consider to be the key points in small groups, then debating the long-list as a whole class, and then coming up with a short-list of what the class thinks are the most significant. (This is a good opportunity for speaking and listening work.) They are likely to be places in the play where the action or reflection is at its most intense, and which capture the complexity of themes, character, structure and performance.

Second, drill down at one of the points of contention and tension. In other words, investigate the complexity of the problem that Shakespeare has presented. What is at stake? Why is it important? Is it a problem that can be resolved, or is it an insoluble one?

Key skills in writing about Shakespeare

Here are some suggestions to help you organise your notes and develop advanced writing skills when working on Shakespeare:

- Compose the title of your writing carefully to maximise your opportunities to be creative and critical about the play. Explore the key words in your title carefully. Decide which aspect of the play – or which combination of aspects – you are focusing on.
- Create a mind map of your ideas, making connections between them.
- If appropriate, arrange your ideas into a hierarchy that shows how some themes or features of the play are 'higher' than others and can incorporate other ideas.
- Sequence your ideas so that you have a plan for writing an essay, review, story – whichever genre you are using. You might like to think about whether to put your strongest points first, in the middle, or later.
- Collect key quotations (it might help to compile this list with a partner), which you can use as evidence to support your argument.
- Compose your first draft, embedding quotations in your text as you go along.
- Revise your draft in the light of your own critical reflections and/or those of others.

The following pages focus on writing about *The Taming of the Shrew* in particular.

The Taming of the Shrew
悍妇降服记

Writing about *The Taming of the Shrew*
笔论《悍妇降服记》

Any kind of writing about *The Taming of the Shrew* will be informed by your responses to the play. Your understanding of how characters, plot, themes, language and stagecraft are all inter-related will contribute to your unique perspective. This section will help you locate key points of entry into the play so that your writing will be engaging and original. The best way to capture your reader's attention is to take them with you on a journey – discovering a new pathway into *The Taming of the Shrew*.

But first, how do you find your unique perspective? You may want to start with the title and think about the connotations of the word 'shrew' in Shakespeare's day. Katherina is labelled as an anti-social, violent and uncontrollable woman from the very beginning of the play and treated as such by all the men in her world, especially the men who are suitors to her younger sister Bianca.

As you consider Petruchio and Katherina, their introductory sparring (争论, 拌嘴) match and complicated relationship, you will notice that it is not a simple case of 'love-at-first-sight'. You will be aware of Petruchio's lust for money, his conversations about Katherina's dowry with Baptista, the social pressures for women to marry and behave in certain ways, and the uneven balance of power between men and women. In the light of this, the idea of 'taming' that is central to Petruchio's attitude and actions towards Katherina may prompt a range of responses from you. Is he a cruel, manipulative man who wants total control over the woman he has married and absolute obedience? Or is he interested in developing a healthier relationship between them, aiming to curb Katherina's violence and her mistrust?

While thinking through the range of possible responses to these questions, you might find that reflecting on the performance possibilities offered in the script is helpful.

Whether you act out certain sections of the script, sift through the photographs in this book, or watch a film version of the play, you will notice that some interpretations strike you as truer to your understanding of the characters.

You might want to explore how the use and abuse of language, the witty banter based on puns, and the ability of language to confuse and disorientate reflects the various levels of deception, confusion and confrontation (both physical and psychological) in the play. In particular, the recurring imagery based on the techniques and tools of falconry is striking in its ability to conjure vivid visual images as well as adding depth to Petruchio's idea of 'taming' as a form of training, rather than a form of oppression. You may also find yourself thinking of the way the play links the idea of 'taming' with the correction of unsocial or unruly behaviour through educational or transformative experiences – both at a personal level and in society at large. There are links between the Lord's trick on the drunken Sly in the Induction and the main taming plot that centre on these ideas.

As you can see, your own unique perspective on the play will begin to develop as you think about the aspects you are interested in and allow yourself to make connections between its dramatic, contextual, linguistic and thematic features.

Creative writing

At different times during your study of *The Taming of the Shrew*, and during assessments and examinations, you will be writing about the play and about your personal responses to it. Creative responses to the play, such as those encouraged in the activities on the left-hand pages in this book, can allow you to be as imaginative as you want. This is your chance to develop your own voice and to be adventurous as well as sensitive to the words and images in the play. *The Taming of the Shrew* is a rich, multi-layered text which benefits from many different approaches, both in performance, and in writing. Don't be afraid of larger questions or implications that cannot be reduced to simple resolutions. It is often the problematic and complex issues, which you do not have easy answers for, that can be the most interesting.

- Imagine that you are directing a film version of *The Taming of the Shrew* and the producers want it to have additional scenes for the promotional material. Think about where an extra scene could be used to develop key themes in the play: perhaps a scene showing what life is like for Petruchio and Katherina after the play ends? Or one in which Katherina (now a rich widow) and Bianca have lunch after a year of marriage? Write it yourself in Shakespeare's language (using iambic pentameter if you can).

- For the promotional material, the characters themselves are going to be interviewed so that they explain their actions and their views on the other characters. In pairs, write twenty questions that you would like to ask them. Then in small groups conduct the interviews and film them if you can.

- As part of the Director's Commentary, step into role as the director and prepare either a recording or a written description of how you brought Shakespeare's play to life as a performance. Describe some of the choices you made regarding stagecraft, dramatic impact and engaging your audience in the twenty-first century.

Essay writing

Other responses, such as essays, have a set structure and specific requirements. Writing an essay gives you a chance to explore your own interpretations, to use evidence that appeals to you, and to write with creativity and flair. It allows you to explore *The Taming of the Shrew* from different points of view. You can approach the play from a number of critical perspectives or in relation to different themes. You will also need to explore the play in the social, literary, political and cultural contexts of its production (Shakespeare's day) and reception (today or at any point since Shakespeare's day).

An essay can be seen as an exploration of the play in which you chart a path to illuminate ideas that are significant to you. It is also an argument that uses evidence and structural requirements to persuade your readers that you have an important perspective on the play. You must integrate evidence from the script into your own writing by using embedded quotations and by explaining the significance of each quotation and reference to the play. Some people like to remember the acronym PEA to help them here. P is the POINT you are making. E is the EVIDENCE you are taking from the script, whether it is a direct quotation, a summary of what is happening, or a reference to character, plot and themes. A is the ANALYSIS you give, using this evidence, which will reflect back on the point you are making and contain your own personal response and original ideas.

- Put the following essay questions in order of difficulty (with number one being the most challenging). Choose a few to practise constructing detailed essay plans that reflect the advice given in these two pages.

  1 *The Taming of the Shrew* is one battle between the sexes where the woman loses. Do you agree?

  2 Why is Act 2 Scene 1 so dramatically effective?

  3 How do the themes of disguise, deception and supposing relate to the idea of 'taming' in *The Taming of the Shrew*?

  4 Look at the final scene and comment on how Petruchio and Katherina are presented there compared to elsewhere in the play.

  5 How does Katherina change during the play?

The Taming of the Shrew
悍妇降服记

William Shakespeare 莎翁年表
1564–1616

1564	Born Stratford-upon-Avon, eldest son of John and Mary Shakespeare.
1582	Marries Anne Hathaway of Shottery, near Stratford.
1583	Daughter Susanna born.
1585	Twins, son and daughter Hamnet and Judith, born.
1592	First mention of Shakespeare in London. Robert Greene, another playwright, described Shakespeare as 'an upstart crow beautified with our feathers'. Greene seems to have been jealous of Shakespeare. He mocked Shakespeare's name, calling him 'the only Shake-scene in a country' (presumably because Shakespeare was writing successful plays).
1595	Becomes a shareholder in The Lord Chamberlain's Men, an acting company that became extremely popular.
1596	Son, Hamnet, dies aged eleven.
	Father, John, granted arms (acknowledged as a gentleman).
1597	Buys New Place, the grandest house in Stratford.
1598	Acts in Ben Jonson's *Every Man in His Humour*.
1599	Globe Theatre opens on Bankside. Performances in the open air.
1601	Father, John, dies.
1603	James I grants Shakespeare's company a royal patent: The Lord Chamberlain's Men become The King's Men and play about twelve performances each year at court.
1607	Daughter Susanna marries Dr John Hall.
1608	Mother, Mary, dies.
1609	The King's Men begin performing indoors at Blackfriars Theatre.
1610	Probably returns from London to live in Stratford.
1616	Daughter Judith marries Thomas Quiney.
	Dies. Buried in Holy Trinity Church, Stratford-upon-Avon.

The plays and poems

(no one knows exactly when he wrote each play)

1589–95	*The Two Gentlemen of Verona*, **The Taming of the Shrew**, *First, Second* and *Third Parts* of *King Henry VI*, *Titus Andronicus*, *King Richard III*, *The Comedy of Errors*, *Love's Labour's Lost*, *A Midsummer Night's Dream*, *Romeo and Juliet*, *King Richard II* (and the long poems *Venus and Adonis* and *The Rape of Lucrece*).
1596–99	*King John*, *The Merchant of Venice*, *First* and *Second Parts* of *King Henry IV*, *The Merry Wives of Windsor*, *Much Ado About Nothing*, *King Henry V*, *Julius Caesar* (and probably the Sonnets).
1600–05	*As You Like It*, *Hamlet*, *Twelfth Night*, *Troilus and Cressida*, *Measure for Measure*, *Othello*, *All's Well That Ends Well*, *Timon of Athens*, *King Lear*.
1606–11	*Macbeth*, *Antony and Cleopatra*, *Pericles*, *Coriolanus*, *The Winter's Tale*, *Cymbeline*, *The Tempest*.
1613	*King Henry VIII*, *The Two Noble Kinsmen* (both probably with John Fletcher).
1623	Shakespeare's plays published as a collection (now called the First Folio).

Acknowledgements 鸣谢

Cambridge University Press would like to acknowledge the contributions made to this work by Rex Gibson, Mike Clamp, Michael Fynes-Clinton and Perry Mills.

Picture Credits

p. iii: Shakespeare's Globe 2012, © Geraint Lewis; p. v left: RSC/Royal Shakespeare Theatre 1992, © Donald Cooper/Photostage; p. v right: RSC/Royal Shakespeare Theatre 2003, © Donald Cooper/Photostage; p. vi: left Shakespeare's Globe 2012, © Geraint Lewis; p. vi right: Theatre Wallay/Shakespeare's Globe 2012, © Simon Annand; page vii top: RSC/The Novello Theatre 2008, © Nigel Norrington/ArenaPAL; page vii bottom: Open Air Theatre/Regent's Park 2006, © Donald Cooper/Photostage; p. viii top: Rocco Sisto as Petruchio and Jonathan Croy as Baptista in a Shakespeare & Company production 2005, photo by Kevin Sprague; page viii bottom: RSC/Royal Shakespeare Theatre 1992, © Donald Cooper/Photostage; page ix top: RSC/Royal Shakespeare Theatre 1995, © Donald Cooper/Photostage; page ix bottom: Wilton's Music Hall 2007, © Marilyn Kingwill/ArenaPAL; page x top: RSC/Royal Shakespeare Theatre 1992, © Donald Cooper/Photostage; page x bottom: Stephanie Dodd as Bianca and Matthew Stucky as Lucentio in a Shakespeare & Company production 2005, photo by Kevin Sprague; page xi top: Theatre Royal Haymarket 1986, © Donald Cooper/Photostage; page xi bottom: Shakespeare's Globe 2012, © Geraint Lewis; page xii top RSC/Royal Shakespeare Theatre 2003, © Donald Cooper/Photostage; page xii bottom: RSC/Royal Shakespeare Theatre 1992, © Donald Cooper/Photostage; p. 4: RSC/Royal Shakespeare Theatre 1978, © Donald Cooper/Photostage; p. 12: RSC/Royal Shakespeare Theatre 1995, © Donald Cooper/Photostage; p. 18 RSC/ Regional Tour 1985–86, © Donald Cooper/Photostage; p. 26: RSC/Royal Shakespeare Theatre 2003, © Donald Cooper/Photostage; p. 30: Open Air Theatre/Regent's Park 2006, © Nigel Norrington/ArenaPAL; p. 40: RSC/Courtyard Theatre 2008, © Donald Cooper/Photostage; p. 46: RSC/ Regional Tour 1985–86, © Donald Cooper/Photostage; p. 50: RSC/Royal Shakespeare Theatre 1973, © Donald Cooper/Photostage; p. 55 top: Alex Highsmith as Katherina and Eryn O'Sullivan as Bianca in a National Players production directed by Clay Hopper 2012, © Sonie Mathew/National Players; p. 55 bottom: RSC/The Pit, Barbican Theatre 1999, © Geraint Lewis; p. 56: RSC/The Novello Theatre 2008, © Nigel Norrington/ArenaPAL; p. 60: RSC/Royal Shakespeare Theatre 1973, © Donald Cooper/Photostage; p. 64: RSC/Royal Shakespeare Theatre 1995, © Donald Cooper/Photostage; p. 70: Open Air Theatre/Regent's Park 2006, © Nigel Norrington/ArenaPAL; p. 74: Shakespeare Theatre Company's production of The Taming of the Shrew 2007, directed by Rebecca Bayla Taichman. Charlayne Woodard as Katherina, Nicholas Hormann as Baptista and Christopher Innvar as Petruchio. Photo by Scott Suchman; p. 78: RSC/Royal Shakespeare Theatre 1982, © Donald Cooper/Photostage; p. 83 top left RSC/Courtyard Theatre 2008, © Nigel Norrington/ArenaPAL; p. 83 top right: RSC/Royal Shakespeare Theatre 2003, © Donald Cooper/Photostage; p. 83 bottom: Sacramento Ballet Company 2007, © ZUMA Press, Inc./Alamy; p. 84: Open Air Theatre/Regent's Park 2006, © Donald Cooper/Photostage; p. 88: RSC/Royal Shakespeare Theatre 1982, © Donald Cooper/Photostage; p. 94: RSC/Royal Shakespeare Theatre 1995, © Donald Cooper/Photostage; p. 100: Celia Madeoy as Kate and Rocco Sisto as Petruchio in a Shakespeare & Company production 2005, photo by Kevin Sprague; p. 107 top: RSC/Regional Tour 1985–86, © Donald Cooper/Photostage; p. 107 bottom: Open Air Theatre/Regent's Park 2006, © Donald Cooper/Photostage; p. 112: 'The Taming of the Shrew' by Sir John Gilbert, © Birmingham Museums Trust; p. 120: Shakespeare's Globe 2012, © Geraint Lewis; p. 124: RSC/Royal Shakespeare Theatre 1995, © Donald Cooper/Photostage; p. 134: RSC/Barbican Theatre 1983, © Donald Cooper/Photostage; p. 142: RSC/Regional Tour 1985–86, © Donald Cooper/Photostage; p. 146: RSC/Royal Shakespeare Theatre 1982, © Donald Cooper/Photostage; p. 152: RSC/Royal Shakespeare Theatre 1987, © Donald Cooper/Photostage; p. 153: Lensovet Academic Theater, St Petersburg 1976, © RIA Novosti/Topfoto; p. 154: Open Air Theatre/Regent's Park 2006, © Rex Features; p. 162: RSC/The Pit, Barbican Theatre 1999, © Donald Cooper/

The Taming of the Shrew
悍妇降服记

Photostage; p. 170: Wilton's Music Hall 2007, © Donald Cooper/Photostage; p. 177 top: RSC/Royal Shakespeare Theatre 1987, © Donald Cooper/Photostage; p. 177 bottom: RSC/Royal Shakespeare Theatre 2003, © Donald Cooper/Photostage; p. 178: Bristol Old Vic 2006, © Donald Cooper/Photostage; p. 179: RSC/Courtyard Theatre 2008, © Nigel Norrington/ArenaPAL; p. 180: Rocco Sisto as Petruchio and Celia Madeoy as Kate and in a Shakespeare & Company production 2005, photo by Kevin Sprague; p. 183: Shakespeare's Globe 2012, © Geraint Lewis; p. 184 left: Casey Hoekstra as Lucentio and Eryn O'Sullivan as Bianca in a National Players production directed by Clay Hopper 2012, © Sonie Mathew/National Players; p. 184 right: RSC/Courtyard Theatre 2008, © Nigel Norrington/ArenaPAL; p. 185: Walton Wilson as Christopher Sly, Meg Weider as Biondello, and Mark Saturno as Tranio in a Shakespeare & Company production 2005, photo by Kevin Sprague; p. 187: Lensovet Academic Theater, St Petersburg 1976, © RIA Novosti/Topfoto; p. 190: RSC/The Pit, Barbican Theatre 1999, © Donald Cooper/Photostage; p. 191: 'The Long View of London from Bankside' by Wenceslaus Hollar; p. 192: poster for the movie *The Taming of the Shrew* directed by Franco Zeffirelli 1967, © Photos 12/Alamy; p. 193 left: Propeller/Old Vic Theatre 2007, © Geraint Lewis; p. 193 right: Shakespeare's Globe 2003, © Donald Cooper/Photostage; p. 194: still from the movie *The Taming of the Shrew* directed by Sam Taylor 1929, © The Granger Collection/Topfoto; p. 195 left: RSC/Royal Shakespeare Theatre 2003, © Donald Cooper/Photostage; p. 195 right: Shakespeare's Globe 2012, © Geraint Lewis; p. 196: Theatre Wallay/Shakespeare's Globe 2012, © Simon Annand; p. 197 left: *Kiss Me Kate*, Chichester Theatre Production/Old Vic Theatre 2012, © Geraint Lewis; p. 197 right: poster for *The Taming of the Shrew*, London 1910, © Michael Diamond/ArenaPAL.

Produced for Cambridge University Press by White-Thomson Publishing
+44 (0)843 208 7460
www.wtpub.co.uk

Managing editor: Sonya Newland
Designer: Clare Nicholas
Concept design: Jackie Hill